Book Repair:
A How-To-Do-It Manual®
Second Edition Revised

Kenneth Lavender

Revised by Artemis BonaDea

HOW-TO-DO-IT MANUALS®

NUMBER 178

Neal-Schuman Publishers, Inc.
New York   London

Published by Neal-Schuman Publishers, Inc.
100 William St., Suite 2004
New York, NY 10038
http://www.neal-schuman.com

Library of Congress Cataloging-in-Publication Data

Lavender, Kenneth.
    Book repair : a how-to-do-it manual / Kenneth Lavender. — 2nd ed. rev. / revised by Artemis BonaDea
        p. cm. — (How-to-do-it manuals ; no. 178)
    Includes bibliographical references and index.
    ISBN 978-1-55570-747-7 (alk. paper)
    I. BonaDea, Artemis. II. Title.

Z701.L32 2011
025.8'4—dc23
                                                                        2011022636

To S.R.N

For continued support, for understanding my faults,
and for just "being there."

Contents

List of Figures

Preface

Book Repair: A How-To-Do-It Manual, Second Edition Revised, shows librarians, archivists, and other book collectors how to accomplish an archivally sound repair with a little practice and forethought. This is possible in almost all cases. Even the smallest library or collector can quickly and inexpensively locate archival repair tools and supplies on the Web.

Over the past several decades, those in the book world have become increasingly aware that their general collections need the best care that they are able to give them. This concern has arisen not only because older materials are deteriorating from age and use but also because newer materials are often poorly made and costly to replace. With library usage at all-time highs, books are circulating more (and thus crumbling more quickly) than ever before.

An ever-growing number of out-of-print titles only add to the need for good book repair and care techniques. Treatments are needed that provide the best care for a specific item and are practical for an in-house repair unit. Such repairs should extend the life of a book (and thus the library's investment) and do nothing to hasten its destruction.

This concept applies particularly well to the areas of paper mending and hinge and spine repair, which account for the great majority of preservation problems in general collections. In paper mending, for example, you can easily apply the procedures involving heat-set tissue, and, once you have made the small initial outlay for the heat-set tool, your repair costs are minimal. The same attributes apply to the techniques using Japanese paper and starch paste. In hinge and spine repair, you can use simpler and less intrusive repairs with Japanese paper and other materials that cause less harm to the book while still providing the strength needed for handling.

The breadth of materials to be treated thus ranges from older significant research works to much-used editions of famous authors to newly acquired reference books. Particularly within the confines of a restricted budget, treatments are needed that both provide the best care for a specific item and are practical for an in-house repair unit. The range is broad and is reflected in the book's organization:

- The Introduction discusses basic sound principles to be considered in all repairs (e.g., not making the problem worse).

- Chapter 1 describes how to set up and inexpensively stock a repair station.
- Chapter 2 guides readers through paper cleaning methods.
- Chapter 3 covers treating wet or moldy books.
- Chapter 4 covers paper mending.
- Chapter 5 details procedures for repairing hinges and spines.
- Chapter 6 guides readers in making protective enclosures.

The book ends with four appendixes, including directions for making a disposable box and sources of further information, such as a directory of suppliers and a glossary of basic terms.

Readers familiar with previous editions of this work will notice updates throughout in each chapter, an all-new flowchart for making water-damaged book treatment decisions, many new information sources, a totally updated directory of suppliers, and an all-new glossary.

Throughout the book, the emphasis is on the practical ways to apply archival repairs to all kinds of books. This updated second edition of *Book Repair: A How-To-Do-It Manual* is an important new source to use as you seek to preserve items in your library, archive, or personal book collection.

Introduction to Book Repair

Introduction

Book Repair: A How-To-Do-It Manual is designed so that each treatment chapter can stand alone. That is, Chapter 6, "Protective Enclosures," is not dependent upon Chapter 2, "Paper Cleaning." But before you attempt any of the treatment suggestions you should read thoroughly the Introduction and Chapter 1, "The Basics: Tools and Techniques," for discussions on decision-making, principles of conservation, setting up a workspace, and choosing the right tools, supplies, and equipment. This basic information is necessary for each of the subsequent chapters.

Tools, supplies, and equipment are also listed in Appendix B with their suppliers; the suppliers, their addresses, telephone numbers, and e-mail addresses are listed in Appendix C. Many of the supplies and tools, such as brushes, cloth, bone folders, rulers, and the like, may also be purchased at local art supply and school supply stores.

Organization of the Chapters

The introductory paragraphs of each chapter present the problem and its most common causes, a broad discussion of treatments, general instructions, and specific factors for making appropriate treatment decisions. The next sections present step-by-step repair procedures and a list of tools and supplies. Alternative conservation suggestions are made where appropriate. If you wish to read more about a certain treatment, consult the Resources at the end of each chapter for additional print and electronic sources.

Decisions

Preservation treatment decisions are based, first, on broad factors that govern your expectations for the individual book or other material and, second, on specific factors that affect the repair that you are undertaking. The following broad factors are those that you must consider before beginning any repair work. All else depends upon them. These factors

IN THIS CHAPTER:

✔ Organization of the Chapters

✔ Decisions
  Importance of the Item to the Collection
  Physical Needs of the Item
  Desired Outcome of This Repair
  Resources Available for This Repair

✔ Principles of Conservation
  Harmlessness
  Durability
  Reversibility

✔ Supplies

✔ Procedure

✔ Resources

apply equally to all library materials. (See Figure I.1 for a sample decision flowchart.)

Importance of the Item to the Collections

How essential is this book to my library's collections? Has it been superseded? What is its usage pattern? Is another copy easily available? Do I have other titles to take its place?

Physical Needs of the Item

What condition is the item in? What is the strength of the paper? What can best be done for it?

Desired Outcome of This Repair

How long do I intend to keep this book? Is this repair only temporary until I can do something better? What are the consequences of the treatment I have chosen?

Resources Available for This Repair

Time

How long do I have to spend on this repair? Should I put it aside until I have others like it? Can I work it into my normal routine?

Personnel

Who makes the decision about this repair? Am I the only person who can do this repair? Is there someone who can help me? Are there some steps I can leave to others?

Funds

How much money is this repair going to cost? How can I minimize the expenditures? Are there alternatives? What are the consequences if I have to postpone this repair until funds become available? Are there funds to reformat the item?

Expertise

What techniques do I know that might help me in this repair? Is this treatment beyond my abilities? Should I ask for outside help?

Your answers to these questions will determine how you repair the books in your collection. While you should strive for the best preservation treatment possible, you may need to balance this against the realities of time, money, and expertise. Your choice of repair material, for example, depends upon how long you intend to keep the book in your collections. Your choice of material for page mends, for example, depends on how important the book is to your collections. If you are going to discard the book after a short while and need only a quick repair, then archival tape

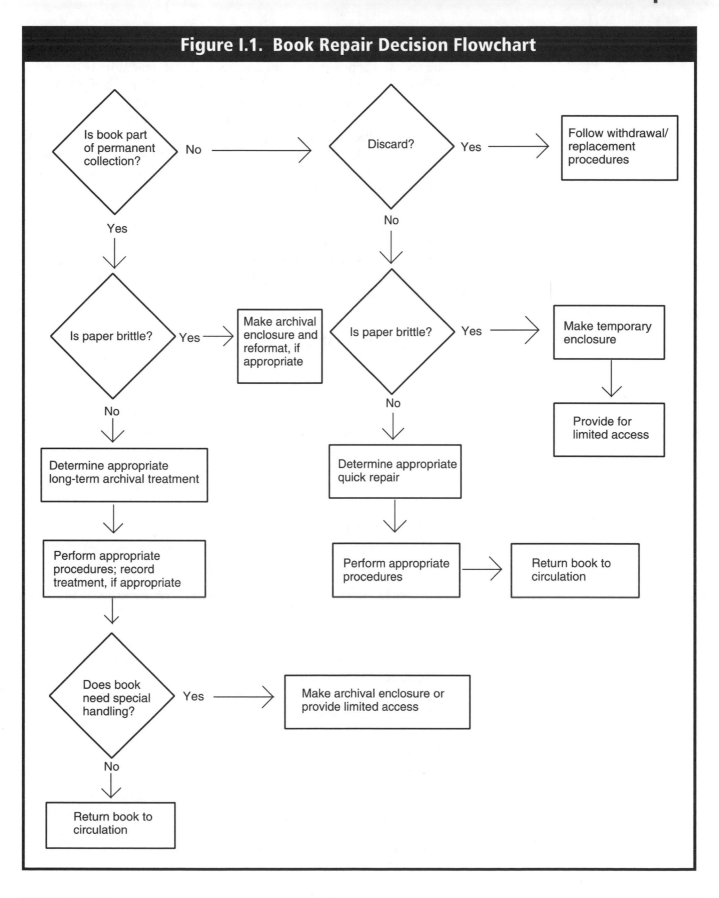

Figure I.1. Book Repair Decision Flowchart

mends may be the most appropriate. If you are planning to retain the book in your collections, then heat-set tissue or Japanese paper mends are the most appropriate. Many libraries find that these latter two mending techniques are both considerably less expensive than archival tape and, with a little training, are as easy to apply. The same type of logic must support your decisions concerning all repair treatments.

The specific factors are dependent upon the nature of the material being repaired, and you must take them into consideration in order to perform a successful treatment. They might include fragility of paper, composition and coating of paper, type of tear to be repaired, size and weight of object to be repaired, and the specific writing medium involved. Equally important, however, is how the specific treatment is going to affect the condition of the object you are repairing. You need to define these factors before beginning the repair procedures. The specific factors listed in each chapter will help guide you in making the right decisions.

Principles of Conservation

Three principles of conservation are basic to all repair decisions. Realistically these are goals that you should strive for with every treatment you choose. Your decisions must balance these goals with the broad factors discussed previously and with the needs of your collections and the book itself. Your decisions should consider the effect of a particular treatment throughout the expected life of the object. These principles should be applied with greater rigor for items of historical or aesthetic significance.

Harmlessness

The repair should do the least harm as possible to the object itself. Many basic book repair materials are eventually harmful, especially those with adhesives. These include hinge and spine tape, paper mending tape (especially non-archival tape), book glue, labels, and covers. A second caution is that the strength of the mend should not be greater than the strength of the material mended. Thus, it is important to consider the probable condition and effect of the materials many years into the future. An obvious disregard of this principle is seen in many hinge repairs where the heavy stiff tape or cloth has caused the pages to break against it because the paper has weakened over time.

Durability

Your mend should be durable enough to provide protection throughout the desired life of the object. Different types of mends have different considerations for durability. Page tear mends, for example, must take into account the flexing of the paper as the page is turned; hinge and spine repairs must take into account the size and weight of the book and the condition of both the cover and the textblock.

Reversibility

The basic principle of conservation is: Do not do anything you cannot undo. This is especially critical in treatment of rare materials and artifacts of historical or research importance. In acknowledgment of this principle, suppliers often stress the reversibility of archival products, particularly those having adhesives. Some adhesives are reversible with water, others with organic solvents. The application of water or chemicals, however, may cause harm to the paper or other materials involved. You should also be aware that tests have shown that these adhesives remain embedded in paper fibers even after many attempts to reverse a treatment.

These three principles should become goals in your treatment decisions. Book tape is harmful, strong, and irreversible. It is also inexpensive and easy to use. How do these qualities apply to the specific book I have to make a decision about? Do I have any alternatives? Are there treatments equally durable but less harmful? The most professional restoration treatment is not accomplished or reversed without some harm to the original book. The materials and techniques used are selected because their durability extends the life of the book while causing the least harm possible. This is why many preservation professionals, when given a book with many problems or conflicting probabilities, follow this sage advice: When in doubt, make a box for it.

These goals for your repair decisions need to be kept in mind as you work with your materials and as you teach others the value of preserving the collections they own or use. You should always follow these ten practical rules when choosing a repair method:

1. Always test before you begin any treatment.
2. Always begin with the least abrasive or complex treatment.
3. Always match the strength of the mend to the strength of the original material.
4. Always seek advice when you need it.
5. When in doubt about a treatment, do not do it.
6. Do not use non-archival pressure-sensitive tape to mend paper.
7. Do not use masking or duct tape to repair hinges.
8. Do not use rubber cement.
9. Do not use paper clips or rubber bands.
10. Do not laminate anything you want to keep.

Supplies

Necessary supplies and tools are listed at the beginning of each repair procedure. Where appropriate, alternative choices will also be listed. For a basic understanding of individual supplies and tools, refer to their entries in Chapter 1.

Procedure

Each repair procedure is presented in specific easy-to-follow steps. These steps take you from the beginning of the repair to the end, detailing each technique required and the materials needed. Please follow the steps exactly in the order they are presented. After you become proficient in these techniques, you will find that many of the steps come naturally and that many of the techniques are used again and again in different procedures.

Resources

Additional sources that offer further information on similar or alternative techniques, supplies and materials, and conservation issues are gathered together in a separate section at the end of each chapter.

The Basics

Tools and Techniques— What You Need and What You Need to Know

Before beginning work on any book repairs, you should set up a suitable workspace. Whether it is small or large, simple or elaborate, the workspace is made up of three basic components: bench area; lighting; tools, supplies, and equipment.

Bench Area

Most professional book repairers prefer to work standing up because of the better leverage and control. A surface of approximately 70 inches wide by 30 inches deep is adequate; the height should be a comfortable working height. Many laboratories use steel-legged tables and place their ends in wooden blocks (see Figure 1.1a). Wooden bar stools or adjustable secretary chairs should be available as seating. The surface should be resistant to scratches and easy to clean, such as a laminate or Formica. If only wood is available, suitable coverings can be purchased or made from materials at your local building supplies dealer.

In addition, adequate storage for supplies is essential. Many book repair stations have a large peg-board at the back to hold tools, as well as built-in shelves for different sizes of paper, book cloth, and the like. However, large and heavy items, such as stacks of binder's board or barrier board, should be stored horizontally to help prevent warpage. A wall- or table-mounted holder (with rods) for rolls of cloth, Melinex, glassine, and spun polyester is also very useful (see Figure 1.2a).

But for many smaller libraries, such a professional workstation is not feasible. Fortunately, any large, flat surface can be adaptable as a book repair station. In fact, this work surface need not be dedicated solely to book repair, although this would be preferable since you would not have to move your materials at inconvenient times. A folding table or a cafeteria table 70 inches wide by 30 inches deep would be suitable to use. Again, the surface should be resistant to scratches and easy to clean.

There are also inexpensive ways to accommodate the storage of tools and supplies. Paper and book cloth may be stored in drawers or on shelves in a closet. A tiered carousel sold for kitchen gadgets is handy for

Figure 1.1. Bench Area and Lighting

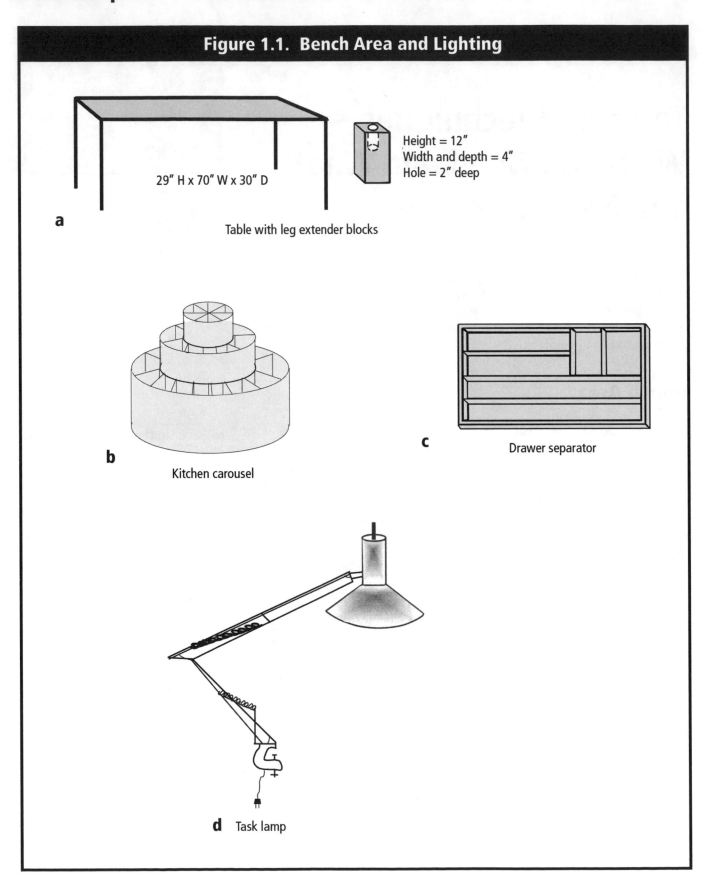

a

29" H x 70" W x 30" D

Height = 12"
Width and depth = 4"
Hole = 2" deep

Table with leg extender blocks

b Kitchen carousel

c Drawer separator

d Task lamp

Figure 1.2. Roll Holder and Book Press

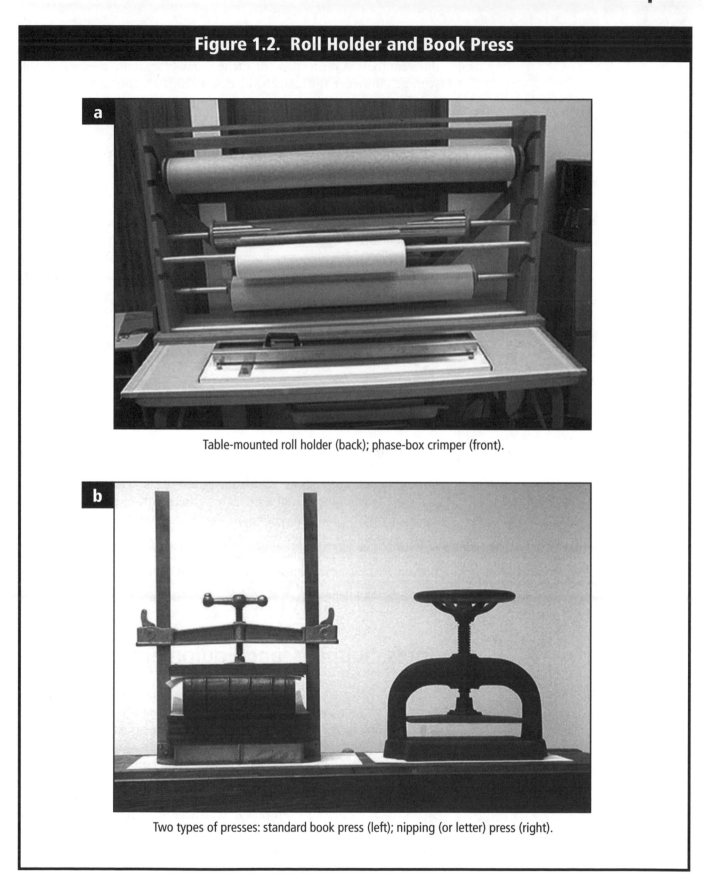

Table-mounted roll holder (back); phase-box crimper (front).

Two types of presses: standard book press (left); nipping (or letter) press (right).

holding tools (see Figure 1.1b). It is high enough for long-handled brushes, and the individual compartments allow quick access to the different tools. A plastic desk- or kitchen-drawer separator makes a suitable storage container for scalpels, blades, knives, and other sharp objects (see Figure 1.1c). Margarine tubs (with lids) are good for holding glue and paste (both raw and made); an empty liquid detergent bottle makes a handy glue container; an empty one-pound coffee can makes an adequate brush holder. (See Appendix A, "A Disposable Box of Paper or Polyester Film.")

You will also need to provide storage for any large equipment you are using. Most commonly this should include a board shear, mat cutter, and book press (see Figure 1.2b). Most libraries will never be able to afford a board shear but can instead use a high-quality, heavy-duty paper cutter; the most commonly used one to cut book board is the Kutrimmer. Access to a sink is a necessity for any book repair station. You will need it for cleaning brushes and containers, for providing water for making paste, and for cleanup. Access to a stove or microwave is also useful. (A hot plate may be used if it is the only thing you have.) These do not need to be located within your workspace, but they do need to be nearby.

Lighting

Natural light is best for any book repair workspace. Besides giving the least distortion, it provides for a good work atmosphere. But in many libraries windows are reserved for the public areas, while the work areas are entirely windowless and artificially lighted. Fluorescent tubes, which are inconsistent and distorting, are the most common source of light. Your workstation should thus also be provided with an incandescent "task lamp," which gives off a concentrated light and can be easily moved to best advantage (see Figure 1.1d). Because the fluorescent lights are often left on for many hours each day, you should provide them with protective UV-filtering tubes.

Tools, Supplies, and Equipment

Your choices for tools, supplies, and equipment are dependent upon the decisions you make concerning treatment. Because library supply dealers have become more aware of and concerned with preservation needs, an increasing number of tools, supplies, and equipment have been made available to satisfy the needs of book repair and conservation personnel. For many basic book repairs, the materials are affordable and easily available from several library supply dealers. They will be used again and again for the same or even different procedures. Be sure to read and understand the descriptions for the products that interest you because they offer helpful advice and will allow you to compare before you buy. For more specialized conservation treatment, however, you may need to search out the offerings of such dealers as art supply stores, bookbinding materials suppliers, paint and chemical suppliers, cloth merchants, and purveyors of fine papers.

The following sections list tools, supplies, and equipment that are needed for a broad range of book repair treatments. Many are used for more than one treatment, and several are basic items used for any repair work. A brief statement is included where we feel that you may need direction in selecting the proper type. Suppliers for most items are listed in Appendix C.

Tools

Bone Folders

Both an 8-inch rounded and 6-inch pointed folders are needed (see Figure 1.3a). Genuine bone is preferred, although some conservators also use Teflon-coated folders.

Brushes

It is best to have an assortment of brushes. The four most useful are the oil painting brush (with a small flat tip), a Japanese watercolor brush (with a pointed tip), a glue brush (with a rounded tip), and a Hake brush (a broad flat tip). All come in various sizes and are readily available from art supply stores. In addition, a long-handled dusting brush is useful for clearing your workspace of eraser particles and dirt. (See Figure 1.3b.)

Dissecting Needle

This is a stiff needle in a wooden or plastic shank used to make small holes or to score Japanese paper (see Figure 1.3c). It is available where laboratory supplies are sold. A good ice pick may also be used.

Glass or Plexiglass

Small pieces (approximately 3 by 3 inches) are used as or with weights. In addition, a large piece of glass (8 by 14 inches) may be used for pasting-out and other repair activities.

Knitting Needles

Metal needles, #1 and #6, can be used in hinge repair.

Knives and Blades

An X-Acto or Olfa knife or scalpel is essential for many repairs (see Figure 1.3d–e). A heavier utility knife is needed for cutting boards. A kitchen paring knife is also useful. Scalpel blades #22, #23, and #25 are the most used for book repair work. A handle #4 will be needed for these blades.

Micro-spatula

This is a thin double-bladed spatula, useful for applications of small amounts of glue and for other repair procedures. The larger one and

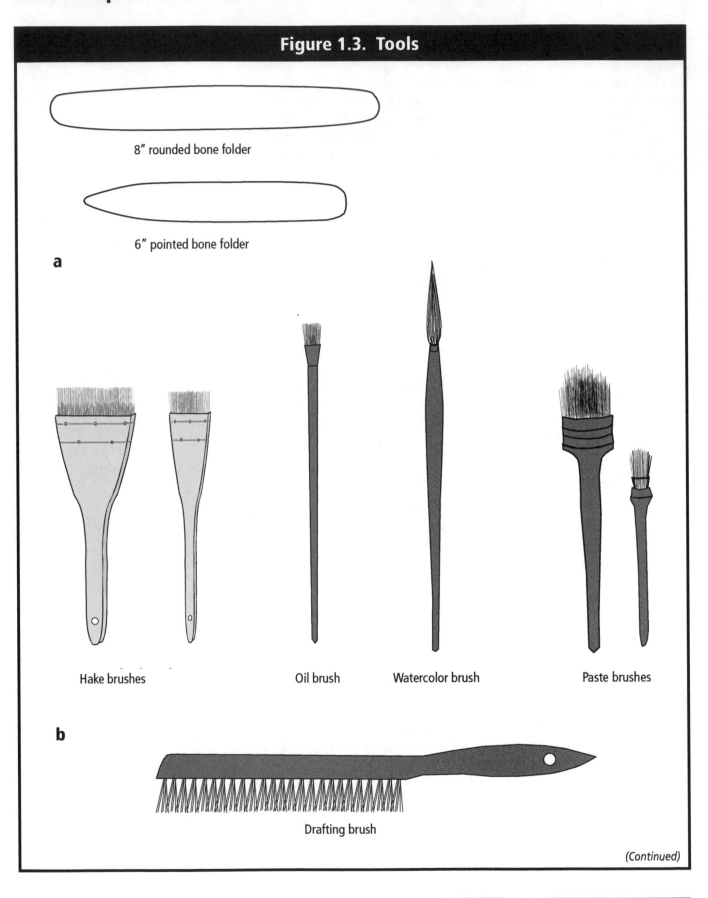

Figure 1.3. Tools

8″ rounded bone folder

6″ pointed bone folder

a

Hake brushes

Oil brush

Watercolor brush

Paste brushes

b

Drafting brush

(Continued)

Figure 1.3. Tools *(Continued)*

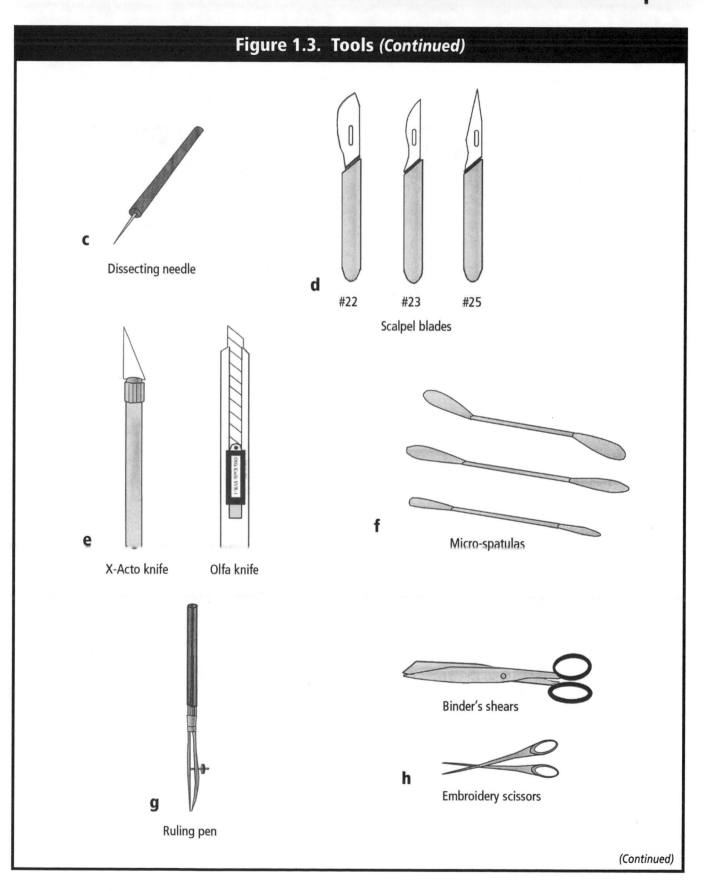

c Dissecting needle

d #22 #23 #25
Scalpel blades

e X-Acto knife   Olfa knife

f Micro-spatulas

g Ruling pen

Binder's shears

h Embroidery scissors

(Continued)

Figure 1.3. Tools *(Continued)*

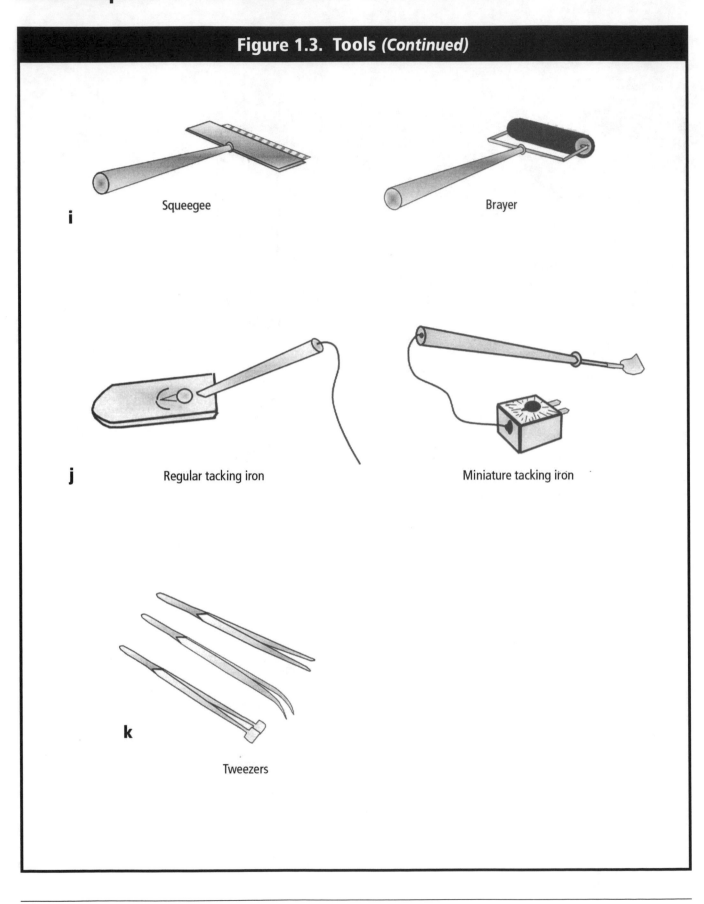

i Squeegee

Brayer

j Regular tacking iron

Miniature tacking iron

k Tweezers

the bent one are useful in various bookbinding procedures (see Figure 1.3f).

Needles

Chenille (or candlewicking) needles are good for sewing with linen book thread.

Rulers

It is good to have an assortment of rulers, from 12 to 36 inches, with at least one that is cork-backed. A heavy metal ruler may also be used as a straightedge.

Ruling Pen

The ruling pen is a good alternative to a brush for laying down a thin line of water, as when tearing Japanese paper for mending strips or for fill-ins (see Figure 1.3g). It is adjustable. It is available from art or drafting supply stores.

Scissors

Two sizes are needed—a pair of blunt-nosed binder's shears and a small pair, such as embroidery scissors (see Figure 1.3h).

Squeegee or Brayer

Either the squeegee or brayer is useful for smoothing out surfaces and for work with encapsulation (see Figure 1.3i).

Tacking Iron

This is a small heating iron used with heat-set tissue and labels. It must have a heat regulator, built-in or attached. A regular-sized iron is good for distributing heat over large areas. The miniature iron is available with a number of different tips, including a flat one for removing tape. (See Figure 1.3j.)

T-square or Triangle

You need some method of making square corners and perpendicular cuts. T-squares are useful for squaring large pieces of paper and board, while triangles are better for smaller applications.

Tweezers

An assortment is best, including one blunt-nosed pair, one straight sharp-nosed pair, and one curved sharp-nosed pair (see Figure 1.3k). Stamp tweezers are useful for handling small pieces of paper.

Weights

Both small and large weights are necessary. They may be beanbags, cloth filled with shot, paperweights, small smooth pieces of glass, or bricks covered with felt.

Supplies

Board

The most common for preservation use are barrier (phase box), binder's (Davey), Bristol, and mat board. Boards come in various thicknesses and weights.

Book Cloth

Many types of book cloth are available, including library buckram, cotlin, and linen. The different properties of each (e.g., weight, flexibility, adhesion), however, are critical in determining which to use for a specific repair. Closely woven cotton and linen are the best choices for the super.

Cleaning Pad

There are several brands available from conservation and art supply stores (Lineco, Opaline, Skum-X).

Erasers

You will need at least four types for your repair work: kneadable rubber, art gum, plastic or white vinyl, and compound. Absorene wallpaper cleaner may be substituted for kneadable rubber erasers.

Glue

Many suppliers are now offering acid-free book glue along with their regular products. Although it is somewhat more expensive, it is preferred for all book repairs. The most widely available type of acceptable book glue is polyvinyl acetate (PVA). Under certain applications and with difficulty, it is reversible with hot water or acetone. Reversible PVA is reversed with water. Many conservators feel, however, that these glues are not ever completely reversible. Avoid using other types of glue, such as rubber cement, since they are harmful to books and are irreversible.

Heat-Set Tissue

This is a finely woven tissue with a heat-activated adhesive. Used with a tacking iron, it is reversible with mineral spirits and is almost invisible. Because of economy and ease of use, it can be considered for all paper mends on a general collection. In addition, it is preferred for mending coated papers where water cannot be used. It is also useful for lining fragile documents.

Nonwoven (Spun) Polyester

Also known generically as release cloth and spunbonded polyester, this is used where you need a nonstick surface. The most widely available are Reemay and Hollitex.

Papers

Several kinds of paper are necessary for book repair. Your assortment should include blotting paper, endpapers, silicon release paper, wax paper, and several weights and shades of Japanese paper.

Endpapers

Endpapers, composed of the pastedown and the flyleaf, may be plain, colored, patterned, or marbled. The plain are what are used most in book repair and conservation. They should be chosen to complement the type of paper used for the text as well as the binding itself. Paper such as Arches, Doves Gray, Ingres Antique, and Rives are good choices to have on hand. When cutting them remember that the grain needs to be parallel to the spine of the book.

Japanese Papers

Japanese papers used for conservation work are made from gampi or mulberry and are available in light, medium, and heavy weights. Many of these papers are handmade, and most are acid-free. For paper mends the light and medium weights are the most commonly used. These come in shades of white, beige, and antique. For hinge and spine repair, all three weights may be used depending on the strength needed and the size and heaviness of the book. Besides the natural shades already mentioned, papers for bookbinding also come in several colors, such as brown, red, and black.

Thin	Tengujo
	Udagami
Medium	Kizukishi
	Kozo-S
	Sekishu
Heavy	Kitakata
	Okawara
	Torinoko
Colored	Moriki

The strength of Japanese paper lies in the length of the fibers, and for this reason papers used for mending tears and replacing corners are *torn* not cut. The fibers bind the mending paper to the rest of the object. This same technique may be used for other types of repairs where the original paper is fragile or where the Japanese paper needs to blend in with the original materials.

Tearing Japanese Paper

Japanese paper must be torn along the grain. If there are chain lines visible, tear the paper parallel to these (see Figure 1.4a). If there are no chain lines, determine the grain direction through one of the methods described in the later section "Grain." Methods of tearing Japanese paper differ with the weight and strength of the particular sheet. In each of the following procedures, your aim is to produce a narrow strip of Japanese paper with the fibers sticking out from both sides (see Figure 1.4b). You will thus separate the strip from the sheet by pulling it apart laterally rather than by tearing it from top to bottom as you would a piece of Western paper. After you have separated the strip, draw out the fibers from the edges with a dry brush.

Figure 1.4. Using the Dry Method to Tear Japanese Paper

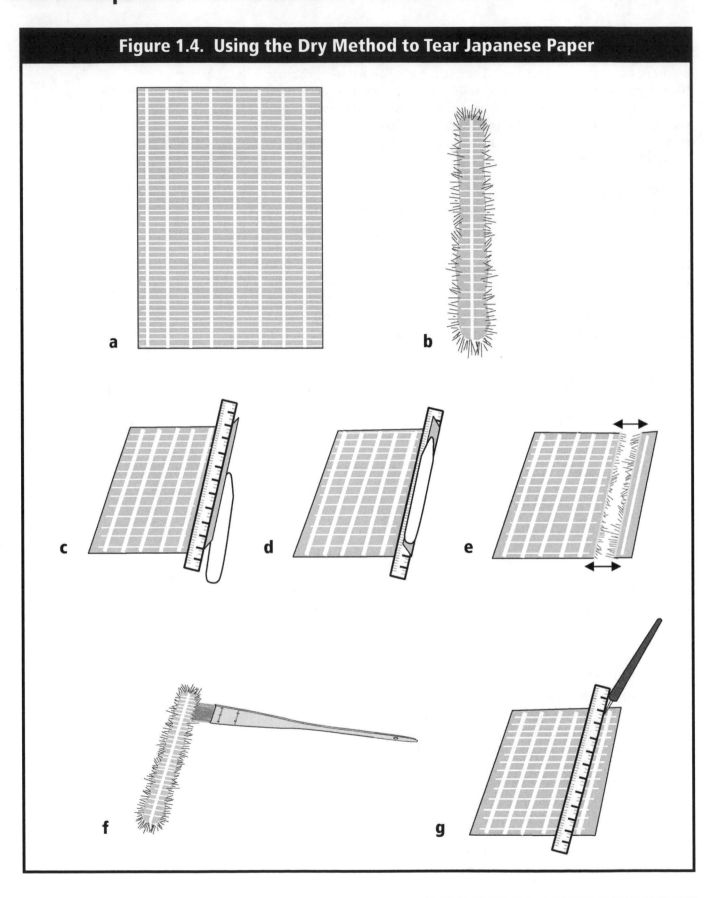

The techniques recommended here are not exclusive; that is, you may use the water method, for example, on medium-weight Japanese paper.

Thin or light-weight paper

1. Lay the piece of Japanese paper on a clean flat surface.
2. Place a straightedge parallel to the grain at the point you want to make the tear (see Figure 1.4c).
3. Place a bone folder under the edge of the paper and fold it up against the straightedge (see Figure 1.4d).
4. Remove the straightedge, and gently separate the fibers along the creased line by pulling them apart laterally (see Figure 1.4e).
5. Brush out the fibers from both sides of the strip (see Figure 1.4f).

Medium-weight paper

1. Lay the piece of Japanese paper on a clean flat surface.
2. Place straightedge parallel to the grain at the point you want to make the tear.
3. Gently draw a dissecting needle or an ice pick along the edge of the ruler, being careful not to cut through the fibers (see Figure 1.4g).
4. Place a bone folder under the edge of the paper and fold it up against the straightedge.
5. Remove the straightedge, and gently separate the fibers along the folded line by pulling them apart laterally.
6. Brush out the fibers from both sides of the strip.

Thick or heavy-weight paper

1. Lay the piece of Japanese paper on a clean flat surface.
2. Place straightedge parallel to the grain at the point you want to make the tear.
3. Dip a small pointed brush, or a drafter's ruling pen, in water and slowly draw it along the edge of the ruler (see Figure 1.5a).
4. Place a bone folder under the edge of the paper and fold it up against the straightedge (see Figure 1.5b).
5. Remove the straightedge, and gently separate the fibers along the wet line (see Figure 1.5c).
6. Brush out the fibers from both sides of the strip (see Figure 1.5d).

Paste

For archival mending use either rice starch or wheat starch (also available in a non-cook variety). The following formula is for medium consistency paste. For a thicker or thinner paste, use less or more water in the formula.

Traditional method

1. Mix one part starch and one part water in the top of a double boiler. Stir well.

Figure 1.5. Using the Water Method to Tear Japanese Paper

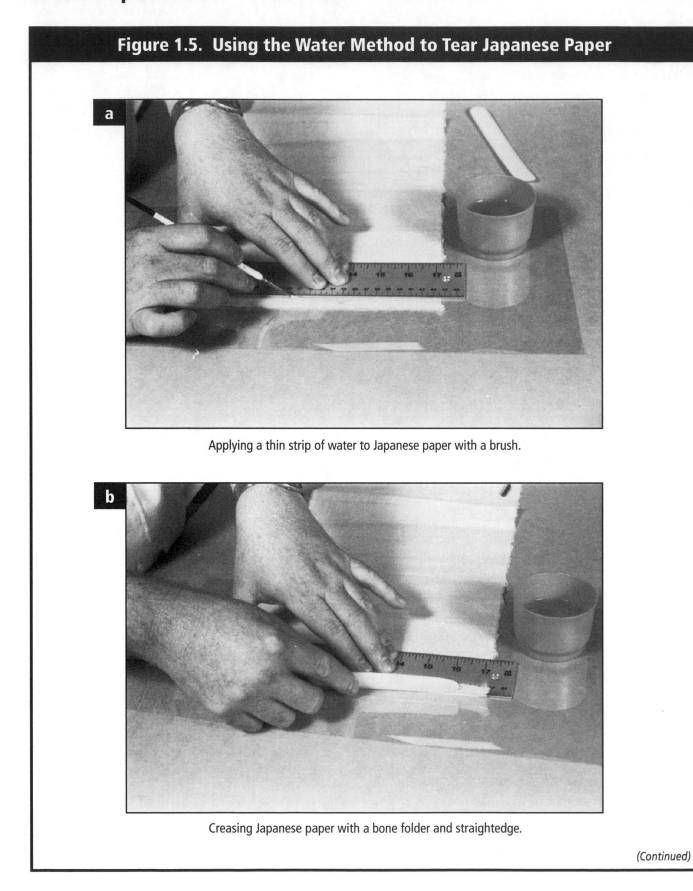

Applying a thin strip of water to Japanese paper with a brush.

Creasing Japanese paper with a bone folder and straightedge.

(Continued)

Figure 1.5. Using the Water Method to Tear Japanese Paper *(Continued)*

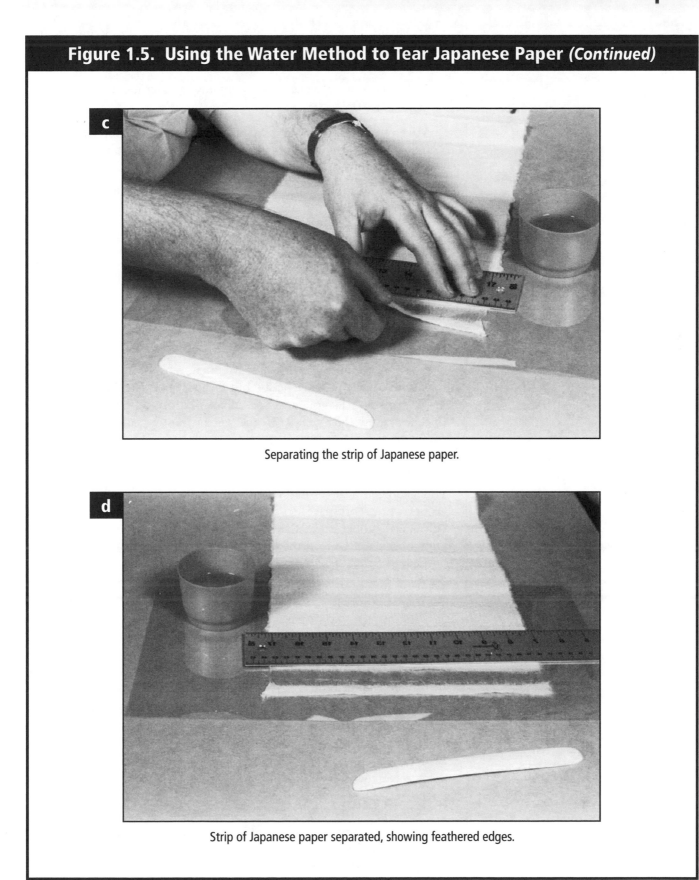

Separating the strip of Japanese paper.

Strip of Japanese paper separated, showing feathered edges.

2. Mix in three more parts water and cook over simmering water until the paste becomes thick and translucent. The longer you cook the paste, the thicker it will become.

3. Remove to a glass or plastic container and let it cool. The paste may be strained, if necessary.

Microwave method: Every microwave cooks differently. Use these instructions as a guideline and adjust cooking times for your individual microwave oven.

1. Mix one part starch and one part water in a microwave-safe bowl. Mix thoroughly.

2. Stir in remaining three parts water and heat on high for 30 seconds.

3. Remove from microwave and stir thoroughly.

4. Repeat steps 2 and 3 for another 3 minutes.

5. Remove and let stand for 3 minutes to cool. Strain, if necessary.

Polyester Film

This film is commonly known as Melinex, a registered product name from DuPont. It is not a plastic but an inert polyester that is used for bookwraps and jackets and for encapsulation. It comes in various thicknesses, but the 3 mil (0.003 inch) is the most versatile. It is important to buy Melinex because it is the most stable form available.

Sponges

You will need a good natural sponge for absorbing any excess water around your workspace. In addition, a dry-cleaning sponge of natural vulcanized rubber is excellent for removing soot and dirt from paper or your workplace. Cut off the dirty parts as you use it.

Book Tape

Book tape comes in a wide variety of styles, colors, and strengths. It is also cut into specific shapes, such as wings. All of these tapes are easy to use and relatively inexpensive. They are, however, irreversible and may be destructive to your books.

Document Repair Tape

Document repair tapes that are archivally safe and yet easy to use are widely available. They include Document Repair Tape by Archival Products and Filmoplast P by Neschen. They are the only mending tapes acceptable for book repair, although many conservators doubt that they are completely reversible.

Double-Sided Tape

For encapsulation and other procedures, you will need to have 3M Scotch Brand 415 double-sided tape. This is the only such tape that is acceptable for these procedures. The quarter-inch-wide tape is recommended.

Thread

Irish linen binder's thread of medium weight (18/3) is needed for sewing sections and pamphlets.

Common Supplies to Have on Hand

Cleaning cloth (e.g., One-Wipe)
Cotton swabs
Double boiler
Glass dishes (various sizes)
Facial tissues
Masking tape
Paper towels (undyed)
Pencils (#2 or harder)
Rags (soft, cotton)
Sandpaper (fine grade)
Waste paper (e.g., old phone books)
Wax paper

Equipment

Board Shear

This is a heavy-duty precision cutter for binder's board, barrier board, and heavy paper. It is an expensive piece of equipment but essential if you are going to create your own hard covers, case bindings, and phase or clamshell boxes. Many libraries that do not have access to or cannot afford a board shear use a Kutrimmer paper cutter. These cutters have a hand clamp to hold the materials tightly, and larger-sized ones can easily cut through binder's board.

Book Press

There are several kinds available, but they are generally suitable only for smaller books. Larger books can be pressed through the use of weights and wooden boards.

Corner Rounder

An expensive item but very helpful if you make many phase boxes or encapsulations. A less expensive hand-held model is useful for paper, polyester film, and thin boards.

Mat Cutter

This is essential for making protective mats for display or storage. Get a good one, with both straight and bevel cutters.

Paper Cutter

Most libraries have a good paper cutter. It is essential for cutting all types of paper but may also be used for polyester film and thin barrier board.

Phase Box Maker

Also called a *crimper*, its sole purpose is to make the creases for phase boxes. These creases may also be made with a bone folder and straight-edge, but if phase boxes are a major part of your storage procedures, this machine can save you a lot of time. The floor model is large and expensive, but the smaller model, about the size of a mat cutter, is more affordable and takes up less room.

Basic Structure of Common Books

It is important to have a basic knowledge of a book's fundamental structure in order to understand how your repairs fit in with and affect the item you are working on. Specific aspects of structure will be discussed with the appropriate repair procedures. You may also, of course, study a book that has come apart, noting its similarities and differences to a whole book. Binding terms that are used in this manual (and in many other repair books) are printed in italics.

The form of our common book is called a *codex* and is essentially a group of leaves hinged at the back and put between two covers (see Figure 1.6a–b). Researchers believe it originated with the hinged wax tablets used by secretaries in Rome, although there is some evidence that the Egyptians employed the same form at a much earlier date. This form was adapted by the early Christians for use in group readings and was refined by monks for copying and preserving texts. The codex form was prevalent by the fifth century and has remained virtually the same since that time. Only the materials have changed, not the form.

Books are printed on large *sheets* of paper, which are then folded into *gatherings* or *sections* (often called *signatures* or *quires*). From this process comes the *format* of the book (e.g., folio, quarto, octavo), which also indicates the number of leaves in each gathering. Thus, a quarto has four leaves. In a regularly sewn book, each gathering is sewn through its middle onto *tapes* or *cords*, or simply looped-stitched to the next section; the *thread* appears between the two middle leaves. Once all the gatherings have been sewn in order, they form the textblock. The endpapers are then added to the texblock. The *spine* is glued and a piece of cloth called the *super* is attached to it to provide strength. Sometimes headbands are sewn or pasted onto the spine. Spines may be flat or rounded; if they are rounded they are said to have *shoulders*. The *joints* of the *cover* fit into the shoulders of the textblock. Also attached across the spine onto the boards is some type of *hinging cloth*; in some instances the super may serve as the hinging cloth. Except for hand-bound books using cords or tapes, the hinging cloth is what attaches the textblock to the cover. The most common type of cover is called a *case* and is made up of two boards and a single piece of material, generally *book cloth*. The hinging cloth is pasted onto the boards, and the outer leaf of the endpapers (called the *pastedown*) is pasted onto each board. The *flyleaves* are left free.

Figure 1.6. Inner and Outer Book Structures

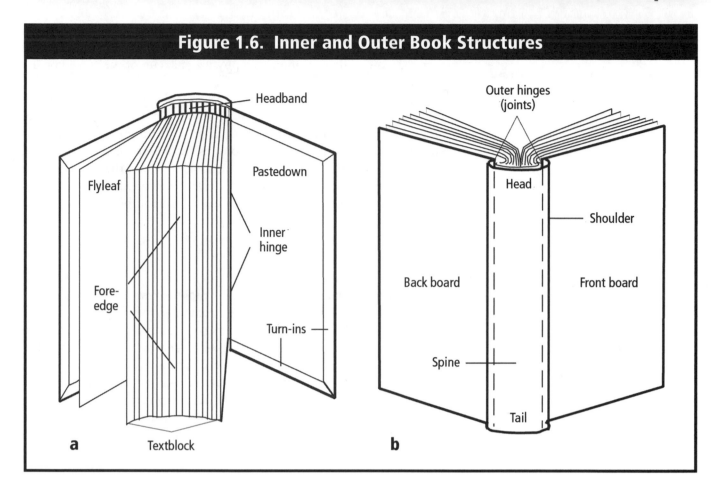

In a *perfect* binding the folds of the gatherings have been sheared off and the individual leaves glued to the spine (as in most paperbacks) or to a piece of super (as in some hard-backed books). This is why the leaves pop out when the spine is cracked. This type of binding is very difficult to repair because there are no tapes or sewing to attach anything to. If the binding margins are wide enough, the textblock may be *oversewn*, which causes problems in opening the book. Bound periodicals in libraries are generally done with this method. Otherwise, it can only be reglued. A better type of perfect binding is the *double-fan adhesive* binding, in which the glue is actually spread on both sides of the leaves, allowing the book to lie open more easily.

Many of the repair techniques in this manual have been developed for the codex form of book. If you take a while to familiarize yourself with the basic elements of this structure, much time and effort will be saved later on.

Grain

Another aspect of binding and repair materials that you will need to become familiar with is *grain*. Grain refers to the direction of the fibers in paper, board, and cloth. Sometimes paper and, particularly, cloth have a grain pattern woven into or embossed on the material. This pattern may or may not be the same as the direction of the actual grain of the material, so you must examine the physical makeup of the piece you are working with.

Paper, board, and cloth are much more flexible *along* the grain; therefore, a book or box opens more easily with the grain, and paper and board crease more easily with the grain. In addition, these materials swell and stretch as atmospheric conditions change. If the grain is running *across* the book, that is, parallel to the head and tail, the hinges of the book will eventually crack. Once you have determined the direction of the grain, mark an arrow lightly in pencil on the board or cloth to remind yourself.

Paper

When paper is handmade in molds, the mold is first shaken side to side and then back and forth. The grain lies parallel to the chain lines, but the dual shaking action makes it much less pronounced than with modern machine-made papers, where the web is shaken only side to side, thus causing all the fibers to line up in one direction. With Japanese paper the grain lies in the direction of the chain lines, if any are present.

There are several ways to determine grain in paper, some more damaging than others. Since the grain of large sheets is easier to determine than that of small pieces, it is always preferable to begin with a large sheet, mark the grain direction, and then cut it into the sizes you need.

1. Lay a sheet of paper on a table, with part of it hanging over the edge. Measure the "droop." Turn the sheet the other way, and again measure the droop. The greater droop will be in the direction of the grain. (See Figure 1.7a.)

2. Lay a sheet of paper on a flat surface. Bend it over one way and measure the height of the curl. Also put your palm on top of the curl, press down, and feel the degree of resistance. Bend it over the other way and try this method again. The shorter curl and less resistance will indicate the direction of the grain. (See Figure 1.7b.)

3. Wet one corner or end of the sheet or piece of paper. Since paper shrinks and stretches along the grain, the direction of the *inside* of the curl will indicate the direction of the grain. (See Figure 1.7c.)

4. Make a crease along one edge of the sheet or piece of paper (see Figure 1.7d). Turn the paper and make another crease on an adjacent side; the crease will be easier to make and much sharper along the grain (see Figure 1.7e). The same results apply to paper that is torn, as in trying to tear an article out of a newspaper. The tear along the grain will be straight, whereas the tear against the grain will be jagged.

Figure 1.7. Methods of Determining the Grain of Paper

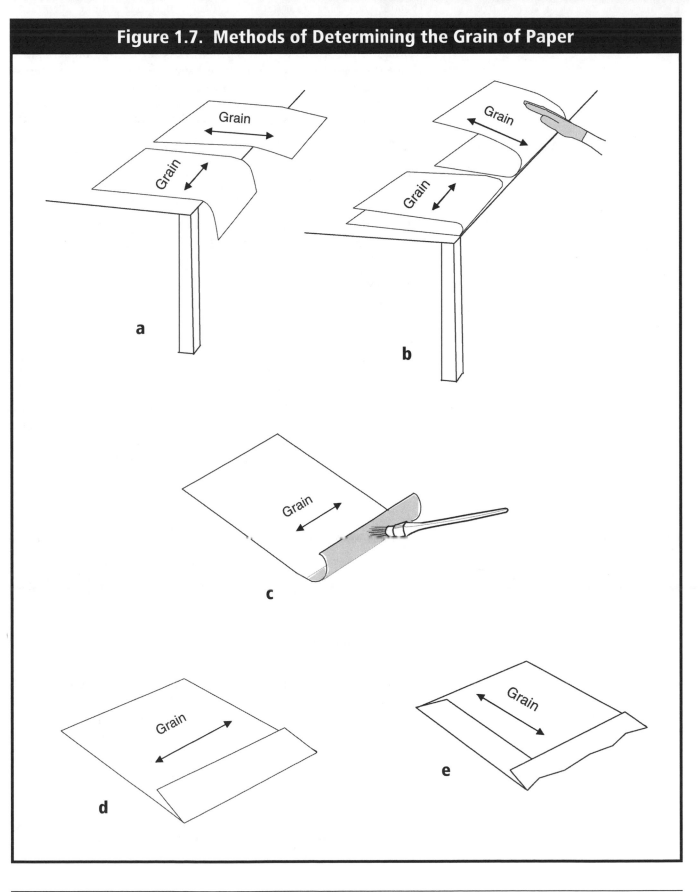

Boards

Although most boards used in repair work (e.g., barrier, binder's, mat) do not show a grain pattern, they all have a grain direction as part of their structure. The differences show up not only in the composition of the boards but also in their weights and thicknesses. Thick boards are harder to bend, but thin boards are more difficult to examine because they bend so easily. The different types of board, however, may all be examined with the following method:

1. Place your hands on opposing sides of a board equidistant from the corners; your thumbs should be touching (see Figure 1.8a).

2. Gently pull the board forward with your fingers, first one side, then the other (see Figure 1.8b). The board will bend more easily and further along the direction of the grain.

3. Very thin boards may also be bent over and measured, or creased, as with paper.

Cloth

Cloth can be deceptive because of its patterns. Many book cloths have patterns that show a definite grain, but the direction is not necessarily the same as that of the actual grain. By far the best way to determine the grain (or warp) of cloth is to find the selvage, the smooth strip running down opposite sides as the bolt of cloth is unrolled. The grain (or warp) will be parallel to the selvage (see Figure 1.9a). Unfortunately, many times the selvage does not exist because the cloth has been cut into pieces. To determine the grain direction, use the following methods:

1. Repeat steps 1 and 2 under "Boards" for determining grain direction in paper.

2. Take hold of two opposite sides of the piece of cloth and pull gently. Repeat for the other two sides. The cloth will stretch more easily and further *across* the grain (see Figure 1.9b–c).

Testing Methods

It is very important that before you begin any treatment you thoroughly test the materials you are working with. Even if you are concerned only with paper objects (as opposed to leather or cloth), you are still dealing with a multitude of possible media and different kinds of fibers and surfaces.

Dry Methods

Some pigments, such as graphite and pastels, rest primarily on the surface of the paper and thus are subject to loss when their images are touched. Other pigments, such as inks and laser toner, may flake off when

Figure 1.8. Bending Board against and with the Grain

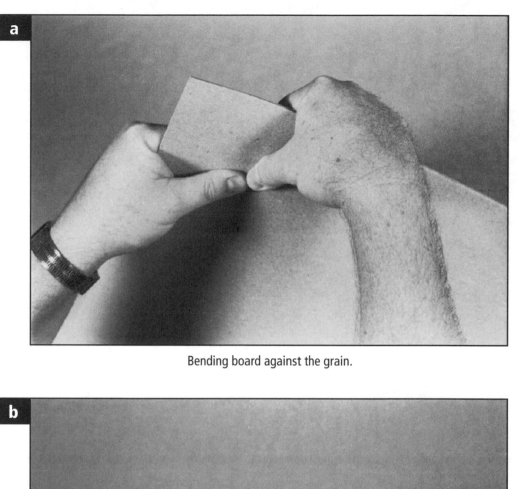

Bending board against the grain.

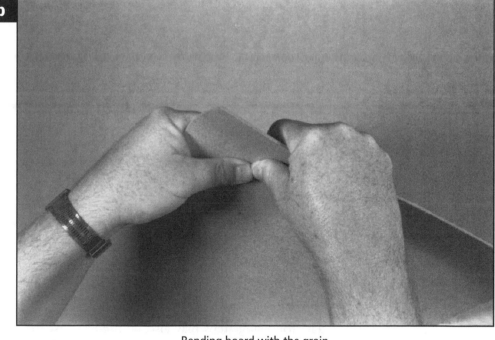

Bending board with the grain.

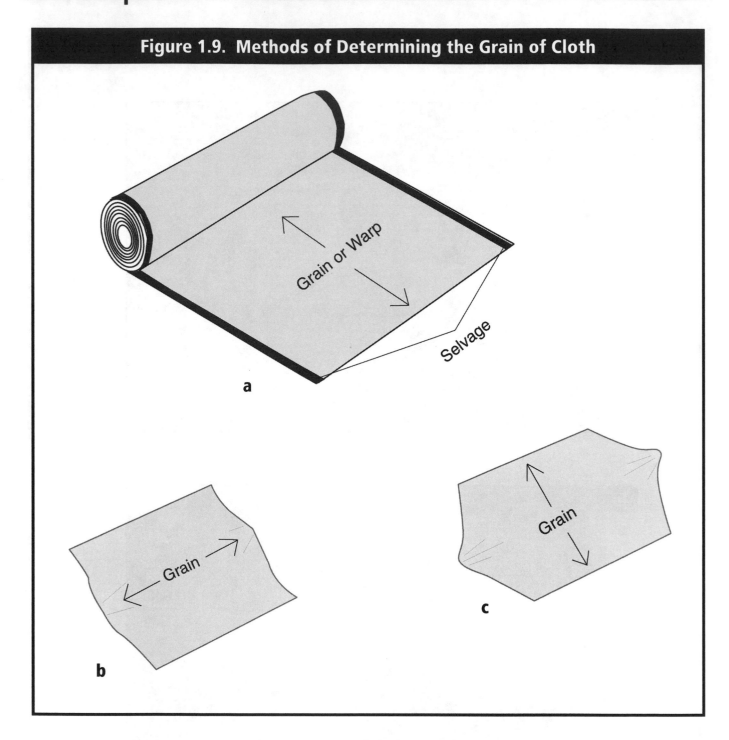

Figure 1.9. Methods of Determining the Grain of Cloth

abraded. In addition, the surface of paper, particularly soft or coated paper, may be scratched by cleaning agents such as document cleaning pads and erasers. It is thus important that both the paper and the media be tested before beginning dry cleaning treatments.

The following steps may also be used to test the properties of the blemish or mark that you are trying to remove. Of course, your conclusions will be different; for example, if a crepe pickup square removes some of the dirt particles, you can continue to use it with good results.

Brushes and Sponges

Procedure

1. Choose a well-pigmented but small area to test, such as the dot of an "i" or the tail of a "y."

2. Roll the tip of a cotton swab over the area (see Figure 1.10a). Examine the tip to see if any pigment has been transferred to the swab. If so, you know that any dry cleaning treatment will damage the image.

3. If no pigment has transferred, gently draw a brush or smoke sponge across the testing area. Examine the area to find if any pigment has been removed by the brush or the sponge. If you are using a sponge, be sure to examine the sponge also to see if pigment has transferred to it.

Crepe Pickup Square, Absorene

Procedure

1. Choose a well-pigmented but small area to test, such as the dot of an "i" or the tail of a "y."

2. Roll the tip of a cotton swab over the area (see Figure 1.10a). Examine the tip to see if any pigment has been transferred to the swab. If so, you know that any dry cleaning treatment will damage the image.

3. If no pigment has transferred, gently dab a clean crepe pickup square over the testing area (see Figure 1.10b). Examine the crepe to determine if it has picked up any pigment off the paper. If so, you know that only a light brushing may be used to clean the area. If not, you may use the crepe to clean the area.

Cleaning Pads and Erasers

Because cleaning pads and erasers are abrasive, it is important that the paper be tested in an inconspicuous place before proceeding with a treatment. The blemish and the image should be tested after this. The results of all three form the basis of your judgment of whether to continue with a treatment.

Procedure

1. Sprinkle a little powder or use the eraser in a corner of your paper (see Figure 1.10c).

2. After a minute of light cleaning action, brush the surface with a light brush and view it under a microscope. Alternatively, gently draw your fingers over the area; you should be able to feel the amount of scratching the abrasion has produced.

3. If you feel it is safe to continue, repeat steps 1 and 2 on the blemish and the medium (such as the printed text). Be very careful in testing any area of the medium. It is alarmingly easy to erase the text along with the dirty smudge.

Figure 1.10. Testing Methods

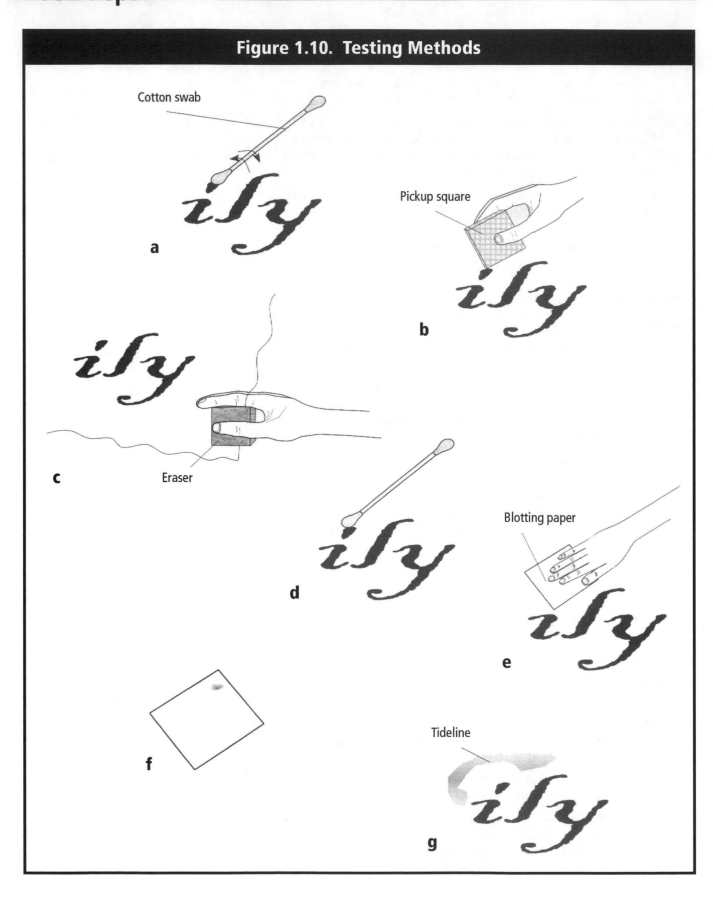

Cotton swab

a

Pickup square

b

Eraser

c

d

Blotting paper

e

f

Tideline

g

Wet Methods

Occasionally it is necessary to apply a liquid to a small area of the paper and the image. Examples are the application of water for a paste mend and the use of solvents to remove adhesives. Again, it is important to test both the image and the paper itself. Because of different rates of absorption by the medium and the paper, it is necessary to test the same area at least three times before continuing with the broader application of the liquid.

Supplies

- Cotton swabs
- Squares of blotting paper (2 by 2 inches)

Procedure

1. Choose a well-pigmented but small area to test, such as the dot of an "i" or the tail of a "y."

2. Dip a cotton swab in a small amount of the liquid you are using. It is important that this testing liquid be of the same concentration as you are planning to use for the treatment. For better testing, all liquids should be at room temperature.

3. Roll the tip of a cotton swab over the area (see Figure 1.10d). Immediately place a corner of the blotting paper square over the dampened area and press with your fingers (see Figure 1.10e). Hold it down for a few seconds; then lift to see if any of the medium has transferred to the blotting square (see Figure 1.10f). If so, you know that any further cleaning treatment using the same liquid will damage the image. If not, repeat two more times.

4. Be sure to examine the reverse side of the page or document for any bleed-through of the medium. If any has occurred, stop immediately. Also, if there seems to be any adverse effect on the paper itself, such as softening of the sizing or coating, stop immediately.

5. Tidelines (generally seen as dirty circles around an area) can be a problem when testing with a liquid, especially water, even though the blotting paper helps contain them (see Figure 1.10g). If they do occur, you will need to use blotting paper frequently during treatment to inhibit their spread.

Resources

Bench Area, Tools, Supplies, and Equipment

Greenfield, Jane. *Books and Their Care.* New York: H.W. Wilson, 1983. See pp. 34–59.

Illinois Cooperative Conservation Program. *A Simple Workstation for the Conservation of Library Materials.* Carbondale, IL: Illinois Cooperative Conservation Program, 1984.

Kyle, Hedi. *Library Materials Preservation Manual*. New York: Nicholas T. Smith, 1983. See pp. 23–29.

Morrow, Carolyn Clark, and Carole Dyal. *Conservation Treatment Procedures: A Manual of Step-by-Step Procedures for the Maintenance and Repair of Library Materials*. 2nd ed. Littleton, CO: Libraries Unlimited, 1986. See Appendix 3.

Young, Laura C. *Bookbinding & Conservation by Hand*. New Castle, DE: Oak Knoll Press, 1995. See Chapter 3 and Chapter 4.

Adhesives and Paste

Kyle, Hedi. *Library Materials Preservation Manual*. New York: Nicholas T. Smith, 1983. See pp. 44–49.

Middleton, Bernard C. *The Restoration of Leather Bindings*. 3rd ed. New Castle, DE: Oak Knoll Press, 1998. See pp. 46–49.

Young, Laura C. *Bookbinding & Conservation by Hand*. New Castle, DE: Oak Knoll Press, 1995. See pp. 35–36.

Basic Structure of the Common Book

Greenfield, Jane. *Books and Their Care*. New York: H.W. Wilson, 1983. See pp. 1–19.

Horton, Carolyn. *Cleaning and Preserving Bindings and Related Materials*. 2nd ed. Chicago: American Library Association, 1969. See pp. 9–20.

Young, Laura C. *Bookbinding & Conservation by Hand*. New Castle, DE: Oak Knoll Press, 1995. See Chapter 1.

Grain

Greenfield, Jane. *Books and Their Care*. New York: H.W. Wilson, 1983. See "Grain," pp. 22–26.

Kyle, Hedi. *Library Materials Preservation Manual*. New York: Nicholas T. Smith, 1983. See pp. 40–43.

Testing

Carrabba, Sheryl. "Guidelines for Testing." In *Conservation of Archival Materials*. Austin, TX: Harry Ransom Humanities Research Center, Conservation Department, 1985. See pp. 73–79.

Paper Cleaning

Paper in books may become soiled through a number of causes: dirty fingers, markings, accidents, and normal air pollution. Each type of soil has its peculiar properties and may take different methods of cleaning for removal. Most common in library books, however, is soil caused by markings and dirt. Unfortunately, certain types of markings are virtually impossible to remove. For example, with ball-point pen and crayon, you may be able to remove the surface components, but the stain will remain. Likewise, for marks that contain grease, such as fingerprints, you may be able to remove the dirt, but the grease will remain. In fact, there is no known cleaning agent, wet or dry, that will completely and safely remove grease or oil from paper.

There are *wet* and *dry* methods of cleaning paper, but for the person engaged in normal book repair only the *dry* methods should be attempted. Even in using these dry cleaning agents it is important to keep in mind that paper is fragile and that its surface is easily scratched or torn. This is particularly true with coated papers, such as those used in art books and encyclopedias. It is thus imperative that you begin with the least abrasive cleaning agent and, only if the dirt or mark still remains, continue with other dry cleaning treatments. As with all things done to paper, test a small unobtrusive place first. Although the printed word is fairly stable and well adhered to the paper, older inks may fade and modern laser inks can flake off during the cleaning process. You also need to test the paper to see if powders or erasers have scratched or roughed up the surface. Cleaning agents should not be used at all on images created by engravings, pastels, charcoal, watercolors, or graphite. This admonition is particularly important when attempting to clean archival materials or works of art on paper. This may result in the image or print area looking even dingier because the surrounding white space has been cleaned.

Many surface cleaning methods, such as document cleaning pads and erasers, can leave behind a residue, which, if not thoroughly removed, can abrade and damage fragile and coated papers. A museum vacuum, with a soft brush and fine-screen filter, is helpful in eliminating this residue. Be sure to pay extra attention to the gutter of a book, since abrasive particles may fall and accumulate there. An air bulb may be used to help dislodge particles so that they can be vacuumed or brushed up.

When performing any surface cleaning treatment, you should keep your workspace clean and free of any dust or other particles. It is very easy for small particles to get underneath paper that you are cleaning and thus become embedded and more abrasive as you rub the paper over them. As a matter of habit, brush or wipe off your workspace after each cleaning attempt. A drafting brush is good for this purpose.

You should also have a means of protecting the paper from your hands, especially if you must use a hand to steady the paper as you work on it. Wear soft cotton gloves or, if you have difficulty working with gloves on, place a piece of blotting paper or polyester film beneath your hand as you steady the document.

Decisions

Specific Factors

Type of mark or stain
Composition and coating of paper
Fragility of paper
Composition of image or print media

Brushes

A soft dusting with a fine brush provides the least abrasive method of surface cleaning of paper. Be sure to wipe up or vacuum up any particles that you have loosened.

Supplies

Soft flat brush, such as a Japanese Hake brush
Cotton gloves
Blotting paper or polyester film
Air bulb
Museum vacuum

Procedure

1. Place the document or book on a clean workspace.

2. With a soft brush, brush from the gutter of the book to the edge of the page, or from the center of the document to its edge (see Figure 2.1a). Repeat until all loose particles have been brushed off.

3. With an air bulb, dislodge any particles that have fallen into the gutter of the book (see Figure 2.1b).

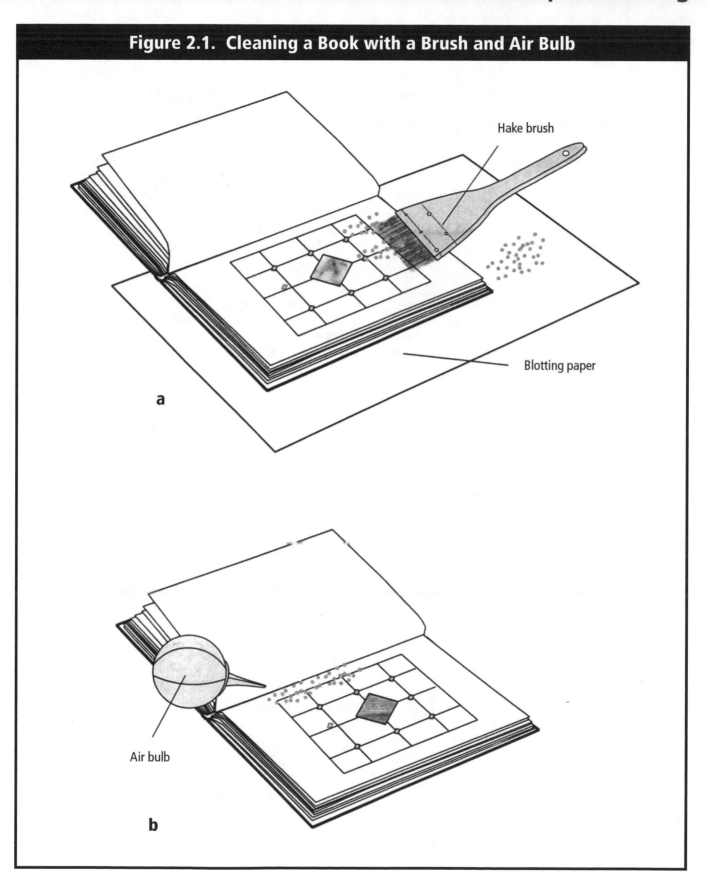

Figure 2.1. Cleaning a Book with a Brush and Air Bulb

Hake brush

Blotting paper

a

Air bulb

b

4. (Optional) Carefully vacuum the page or document to remove small particles. If the book is very small, a mini-vacuum is helpful.

Kneaded Erasers and Wallpaper Cleaner

Use these products to pick up surface dirt and other particles. Both the kneaded rubber eraser and wallpaper cleaner need to be "worked" until they become pliable and tacky. However, if they become too sticky, they leave a residue that is very difficult to remove. The crepe eraser (often called a pickup square) is used by artists to pick up rubber cement and other adhesive substances. Do not try to erase with any of these, as they may mar or damage the paper.

Supplies

Kneaded rubber eraser
Wallpaper cleaner (e.g., Absorene)
Crepe eraser
Cotton gloves
Blotting paper or polyester film

Procedure

1. Place the document or book on a clean workspace.
2. Work a small piece of the kneaded eraser or wallpaper cleaner (e.g., Absorene) until it is pliable and tacky. Dab the small ball onto the paper to pick up dirt and other particles (see Figure 2.2a). If using wallpaper cleaner, pay particularly close attention since it may break apart and leave small bits sticking to the paper. These bits are difficult to remove and may discolor the paper.
3. Make certain that the paper is clean of any bits of eraser or wallpaper cleaner before you continue. The crepe eraser may be used to help pick up these particles (see Figure 2.2b).

Dry Cleaning Sponge

Another product that is very good for removing dirt, soot, and dry mold is a dry cleaning sponge (also called a soot sponge). Made of vulcanized natural rubber, it was originally created to remove soot damage after a fire. It is nonabrasive, leaves no residue, and has no chemical additives. When the sponge becomes dirty, the used portion can be sliced off and thrown away. The sponge needs to be kept in an air-tight container, in a cool, dark place. Do not get it wet, as it takes a long time to dry out.

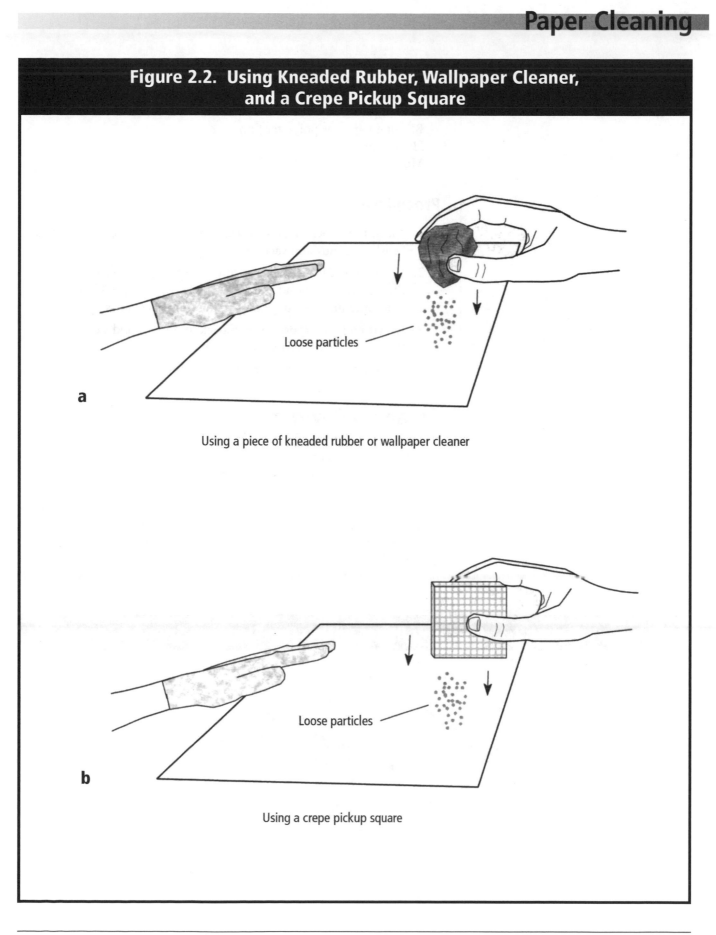

Figure 2.2. Using Kneaded Rubber, Wallpaper Cleaner, and a Crepe Pickup Square

Loose particles

a

Using a piece of kneaded rubber or wallpaper cleaner

Loose particles

b

Using a crepe pickup square

Supplies

Dry cleaning sponge (e.g., Sootmaster)
Cotton gloves
Blotting paper or polyester film
Hake brush
Museum vacuum

Procedure

1. Clean the paper or other surface of loose particles with a hake brush or a museum vacuum.

2. Using gentle long strokes, bring the sponge across a page from the gutter to beyond the edge of the paper (see Figure 2.3). Continue until the page or document is as clean as practicable.

3. As with an eraser, do not rub back and forth and do not bring the sponge back across the edge of the paper.

4. Cut off any soiled portion of the sponge.

Cleaning Powders

Cleaning powders are a low-abrasive form of cleaning agent and are very good for such problems as dingy appearance, smudges, and general dirt marks. They can, however, scratch coated paper and tear very soft or fragile paper. The document cleaning pads also leave a very fine residue that must be removed with thorough brushing or vacuuming. Skum-X has coarser granules than the document cleaning pads; these are easier to brush off but have a greater potential for scratching the surface of the paper.

Figure 2.3. Cleaning Paper with a Dry Cleaning Sponge

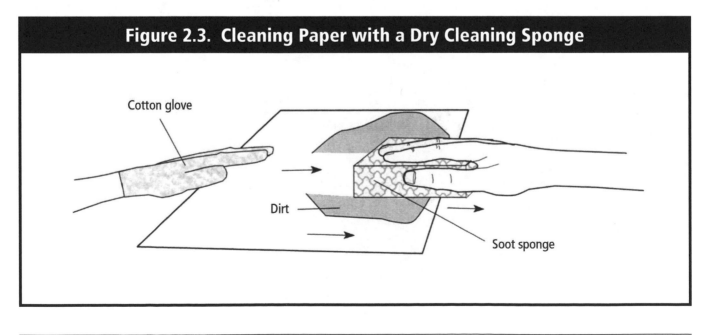

Supplies

Document cleaning pad (Lineco, Opaline)
Skum-X
Cotton gloves
Blotting paper or polyester film
Wiping cloth
Drafting brush
Museum vacuum

Procedure

1. Place your book or document on a clean workspace. Wear cotton gloves, or provide yourself with a piece of blotting paper or polyester film (see Figure 2.4a–b).

2. Sprinkle a small amount of cleaning powder over the dirty area (about three twists of the pad or a good pinch of loose powder) (see Figure 2.4c). If using a document cleaning pad, twist the pad until the proper amount of powder drops out. Do *not* rub the pad itself on the paper. Clean only a small area at one time. Skum-X has coarser granules than the document cleaning pads and is applied directly from its container.

3. Using the flat part of your fingertips, rub gently with a circular motion (see Figure 2.4d). Do not apply force with the ends of your fingers. If you are cleaning near the edge of the paper, rub off the edge of the paper with short strokes rather than with a circular motion (see Figure 2.4e). Rub gently until the powder looks grey or dirty (see Figure 2.4f).

4. Using a soft brush, sweep the dirty powder off the edge of the paper (see Figure 2.4g). Make sure that there is no powder caught under the paper, as this would cause damage to the underside of your document.

5. Continue with clean powder. If the area does not become clean after a few applications, do not try to rub harder. This will only damage the paper. If you have determined not to clean over the image itself, dirtier parts of the soiled area may remain within the image (see Figure 2.4h).

6. Wipe or vacuum the paper to remove the residue of the cleaning powder. Be sure to clean in the gutter of a book.

Erasers

Erasers come in a variety of types and are made from a variety of materials. They range from low abrasive (gum erasers) to high abrasive (typewriter erasers). They are made of gum, rubber, plastic, or a compound. The kind you use depends on the type of dirt or mark you are trying to erase and the importance of the book or paper object you are trying to clean.

Figure 2.4. Cleaning Paper with a Cleaning Powder

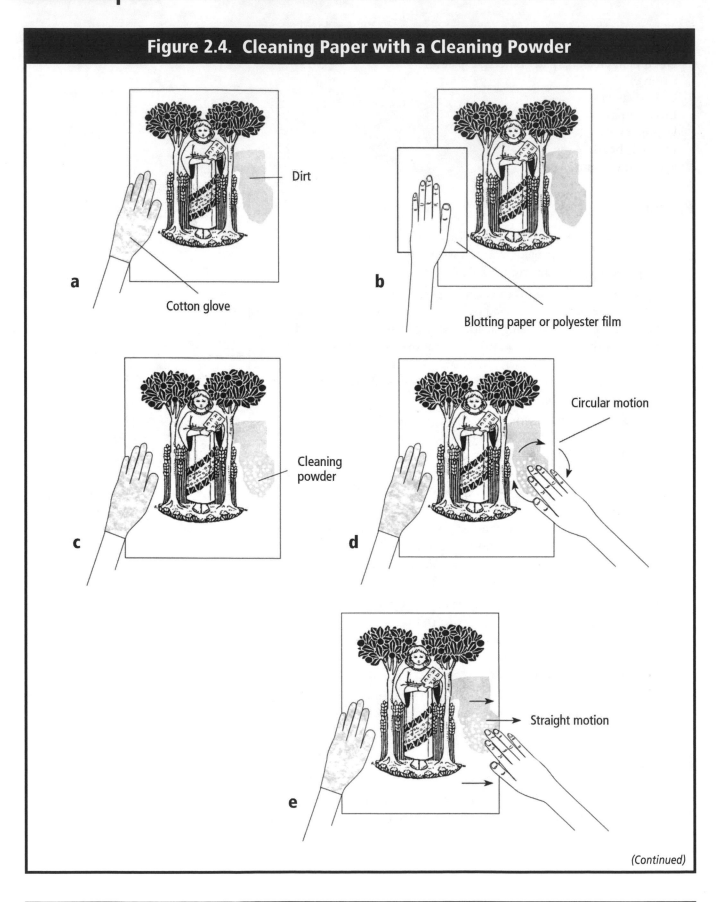

a — Dirt · Cotton glove

b — Blotting paper or polyester film

c — Cleaning powder

d — Circular motion

e — Straight motion

(Continued)

Figure 2.4. Cleaning Paper with a Cleaning Powder *(Continued)*

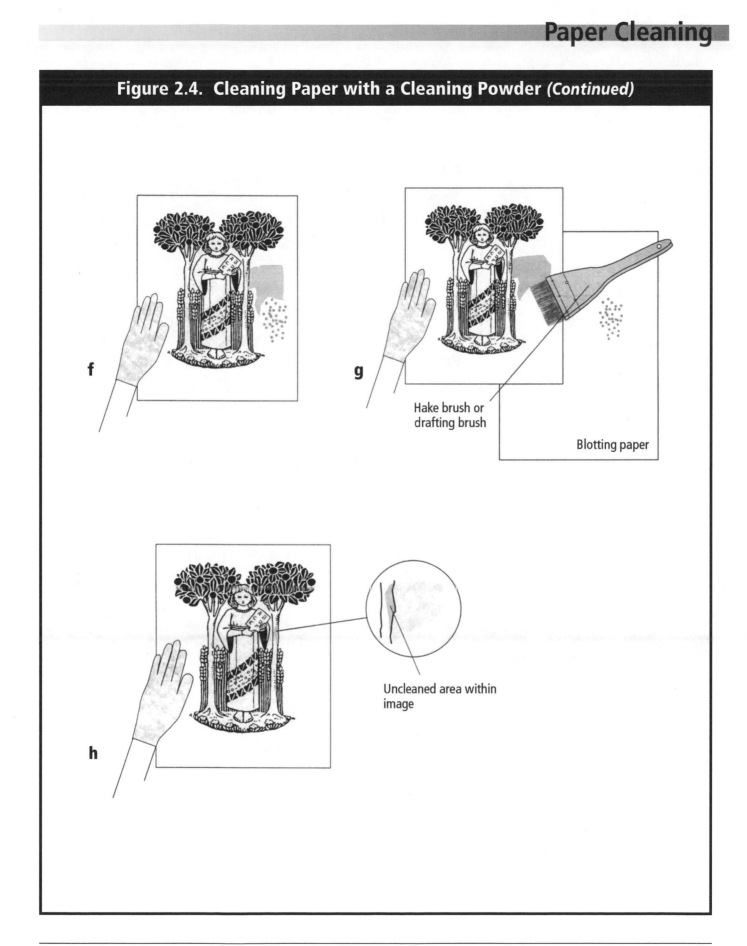

f

g

Hake brush or
drafting brush

Blotting paper

h

Uncleaned area within
image

It is good to remember, however, that all erasers will damage the surface of paper to one degree or another. As with all cleaning agents, use the least-abrasive eraser first and clean only a small area at one time. Avoid using a high-abrasive eraser on delicate or coated paper.

Supplies

These are listed from least to most abrasive:

Gum eraser (ArtGum, Star): for pencil marks on delicate paper

Plastic and vinyl erasers (Magic Rub, Staedtler): for pencil and graphite marks on paper and film

Compound erasers:
Pink (Pink Pearl): for use on pencil
White (White Pearl): for use on ball point ink

Procedure

1. Rub slowly in one direction with small, gentle strokes, being careful to hold the edge of the paper down with your fingers. Work toward the edge of the paper. (See Figure 2.5.) Do not rub back and forth. This only damages the paper.

2. After several strokes, gently brush any residue off the edge of the paper, making certain that the particles do not remain on your workspace.

3. Feel the paper. If it has become rough, this means that you are removing the paper's surface along with the mark. Although it is often impossible to avoid this, the paper is being weakened and is in danger of being torn. It is always better to leave dirt or a mark rather than damage the paper.

Figure 2.5. Cleaning Paper with an Eraser

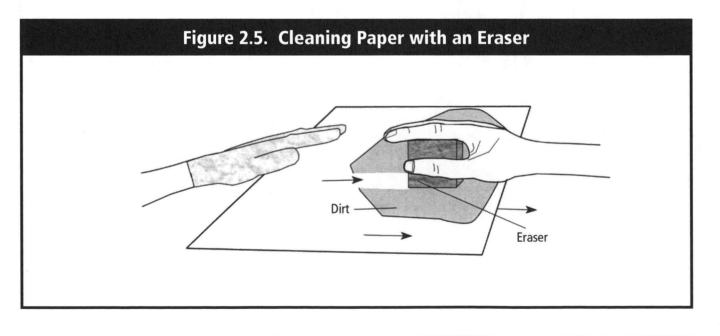

Alternative Conservation Suggestions

Paper objects whose value and condition merit extensive cleaning treatment may be candidates for advanced cleaning techniques. Because of the extreme danger these techniques present to paper of all kinds, they must be attempted only by trained conservators. In general, they may include the application of water and, sometimes, chemicals; dipping in a tray or placing on a suction table; the possible application of deacidification and buffering agents. The decision to consider such a treatment rests on the importance and value of the object, the condition of the paper, the possible harm to the paper or image, and the cost of restoration.

Resources

Clapp, Anne F. *Curatorial Care of Works of Art on Paper.* 2nd ed. rev. Oberlin, OH: The Intermuseum Laboratory. 1974. See pp. 48–50.

Dartmouth College. "Book Cleaning." In *A Simple Book Repair Manual.* Hanover, NH: Dartmouth College, 2000. http://www.dartmouth.edu/~preserve/repair/html.

Greenfield, Jane. *Books and Their Care.* New York: H.W. Wilson, 1983. See pp. 62–64.

Horton, Carolyn. *Cleaning and Preserving Bindings and Related Materials.* 2nd ed. Chicago: American Library Association, 1969. See pp. 32–34.

Ogden, Sherelyn. "Surface Cleaning of Paper." In *Preservation of Library and Archival Materials: A Manual.* 3rd rev. ed. Andover, MA: Northeast Document Conservation Center, 1999.

Ritzenthaler, Mary Lynn. *Archives & Manuscripts: Conservation.* SAA Basic Manual Series. 2nd ed. Chicago: Society of American Archivists, 1993. See pp. 178–184.

Treatment of Water-Damaged Books and Papers and Removal of Mold and Mildew

Books and papers receive water damage in many ways. A book is dropped in a puddle; letters taken outside are forgotten in a rainstorm; a water heater breaks, soaking boxes of books in the garage. All of these occurrences are unanticipated, and all have serious consequences for the materials damaged by them. But these disasters are small and usually do not threaten your health or safety, unless those soaked boxes also house a mold invasion in your garage. The treatments recommended in this chapter for cleaning and drying of books and papers should help you restore your damaged books and papers to at least a usable state. They will never be as nice as they once were, and the signs of damage will always remain.

Larger disasters, however, are serious occurrences that should be anticipated long in advance. Regrettably, few libraries have written disasters plans and thus must respond with little time for careful and logical thinking. If disaster strikes, you *must* do the following:

- Call civil authorities *immediately*.
- Evacuate the building, if occupied.
- Do not enter the building until it is declared safe to do so.
- If at all possible, contact a company that specializes in disaster recovery (see "Disaster Recovery Specialists," pp. 62–63).

If a serious mold outbreak is discovered:

- Evacuate the affected areas.
- Close off the areas from further use.
- Alert your civil authorities to the outbreak and the possible dangers. Remember that some molds are very toxic to humans.
- If at all possible, contact a company that specializes in disaster recovery or mold eradication (see "Disaster Recovery Specialists," pp. 62–63). It is crucial that the types of mold involved in the outbreak be identified, for reasons of both safety and treatment.

The following recommendations for treatment of water-damaged materials and removal of mold and mildew are to be undertaken only after it is safe to do so and if there are sufficient staff, space, expertise, and time to carry them out. These procedures are therefore most applicable to small numbers of affected materials that may be accommodated in a timely manner.

Treatment of Water-Damaged Books

The procedures for treating water-damaged materials depend upon how many and what kinds of materials are involved, how wet the items are, and how much time has elapsed. It is tempting to treat these materials in-house, since the procedures are low cost and, with a little training, easily accomplished. In reality, however, air-drying wet books takes a lot of time, effort, and space—often more than can be allotted from your resources. Thus, for most library and other large collections, it is almost always most cost-effective to employ a disaster recovery company that can provide freeze-dry chambers and other services. These specialists will contract to transport, pack, clean, freeze, dry, rebind, relabel, and return the materials to your shelves. If the number of items you are concerned with can be easily accommodated, however, relatively simple procedures may be followed that will give satisfactory results. But you should realize that even with the most sophisticated treatment, rarely can a water-damaged item be returned to its original condition.

Decisions

Perhaps the most important step to take first is to decide what materials are to be saved. Factors to consider include importance of an item to your collections, its ability to be replaced, its intrinsic worth, and the difficulty of treatment. For example, because modern encyclopedias and popular magazines are easy to replace and difficult to treat, they are obvious candidates for discard. Modern fiction and dictionaries may also fall into this category. On the other hand, many art books, though difficult to treat, are costly or impossible to replace and thus may be candidates for treatment. It must be remembered, however, that almost no book will return to your shelves after treatment looking the same as it did before it got wet. In almost all cases, a book must be rebound, unless intensive and costly treatment is deemed justified to save the original binding. Your decisions will save time and costs for the recovery specialists to handle your books and will direct your own in-house time and efforts to those items most needed for your collections. (See also the Water-Damaged Book Treatment Decision Flowchart at the end of this chapter.)

Timing

Timing is critical in treatment decisions for water-damaged books. As a general rule of thumb, you have 48 hours before mold starts to grow, even if the book is merely damp or if only the edges are wet. Thus, freezing is often an important interim step if you decide on in-house treatment. Once a book is thawed, however, it must be dried within 48 hours, or mold will start to grow.

Coated Paper

Coated paper has been filled and coated with materials such as clay and starch to provide a heavier stock and slick surface for printing. These materials are water-soluble and, when wet, mix to form an adhesive. Thus, coated papers need to be removed from water much more quickly than other materials. The recommended time-lapse period is 6–8 hours. In a process called "blocking," the coated pages bond together *permanently* as they dry out. Almost all magazines, most art books, and many reference books (particularly encyclopedias) are printed on this type of paper. It is thus critical that these items be considered early on in your decisions about what to salvage. If you decide to retain them and cannot treat them immediately, place them in a freezer until you have time and personnel to expend on them. Be aware, however, that even the vacuum freeze-drying method offers only minimal assurance that these items will be usable again.

Freezing

Disaster recovery companies have facilities for vacuum freeze-drying, which employs a process called "sublimation" that takes a liquid directly from a solid to a gaseous state. This greatly reduces the swelling and distortion caused by water damage. If you wish to undertake in-house treatment, however, putting books in a frost-free freezer allows you time to make decisions on how to treat these materials, but swelling will occur because they will be subjected to the freezing-warming-refreezing cycle. At the very least, however, the freezing will inhibit the growth of mold. Each book should be loosely wrapped in freezer paper or layers of unprinted newsprint. This helps absorb moisture accumulated from the defrosting cycle. Books that are already opened should be left open when they are wrapped.

CAUTION: Do *not* microwave a book. Experience has shown that adhesives may lose their holding power, pages may fall out, plasticized covers may shrivel, and the metal elements inherent in many varieties of bookboard may cause damaging arcing in your oven.

Cleaning Books

Books that have evidence of mud or silt may be cleaned before drying procedures are considered. Because of the possibility of damage to the wet materials, however, cleaning procedures should be carefully supervised. The important cautions here are not to abrade the paper or the covering material and not to wash books that have any evidence of bleeding from the print. Books with leather or vellum bindings are difficult to treat and should be left to professional care. Do not attempt these cleaning procedures with single sheets, manuscripts, photographs, works of art on paper, books with coated papers, or books that are already open.

Cleaning procedures should be undertaken away from any drying area you have set up. The running water would add significantly to the level of humidity, and air-borne particles of dirt may adhere to the books you are drying.

1. Hold the book tightly closed, with its spine facing towards you.

2. Use a gentle flow of cold water, such as a hose with a fine spray attachment, to dislodge particles of dirt. You may use a soft sponge with a light dabbing motion or a soft brush to help, but do not rub the book or the particles will be further ground in. Alternatively, the tightly closed book may be submerged in a series of tubs with clean water to dislodge the dirt. Mud or other particles that remain are best removed after the book has dried.

Drying Books

Follow procedures for air-drying books after you have performed any cleaning treatments or have removed the items from a freezer. Be sure to remove only as many items as you are able to work on immediately. After the drying period, the books may need to be repaired or rebound. Once they have been returned to your shelves, you will need to check them periodically for the next few months to ensure that no evidence of mold has appeared. Especially important in this regard are the spine area and the boards, which retain moisture much longer than the leaves do.

Environment

These recommendations for environmental conditions pertain to all air-drying procedures. Have a dry room (preferably about 45 percent humidity) with circulating air. Portable fans should direct the current of air *over* the books; air-conditioning and dehumidifying units should be kept on around the clock; windows should be open. Heat should *not* be turned on, as it will not significantly help the drying process and will certainly support the growth of mold. If it is a warm and dry day, the books may be placed outside. Be aware, however, that sun may damage paper and fade covering materials.

Wetness

Three degrees of wetness are generally used to determine which air-drying procedures to follow: *saturated books*, where the cover and pages have been soaked; *damp books*, where the pages are damp and cool to the touch; and *edge wetness*, where only the edges of the textblock are wet or damp. Particularly important areas of concern are the spine and the boards, since they may retain water after the pages themselves are dry to the touch.

Saturated Books

Saturated books are soaked throughout, including the pages, the spine area, and the covers. They need to be drained before they can be air-dried. If they are dripping, they may be gently squeezed between the hands to eliminate some of the water.

1. Place a sheet of absorbent material (blotting paper, mat board, layers of white paper toweling) on a flat surface that is large enough to accommodate an individual book. Be sure to change frequently.

2. Stand book on its head (or on its driest edge).

3. Open just enough to stand up. Paperback books and books with loose covers may need support, such as covered bricks or bookends.

4. Tilt book back by placing a thin piece of doweling (a chopstick, wooden skewer, or pencil will also do) about a quarter of the way back under both boards. Alternatively, a piece of styrofoam (¼ inch high by 1 inch wide by 2 inches longer than the width of the opened book) may be used. Round toothpicks may be placed on the inside and outside of each board to keep the book stable. (See Figure 3.1a–b.)

5. Place a set of barrier material between boards and flyleaves: a sheet of polyethylene, polyester film, or aluminum foil next to the flyleaves, then blotting paper between this sheet and the boards.

6. Once books have drained and feel *damp* to the touch, proceed with recommended techniques for drying damp books.

7. *Do not* hang saturated books up on lines to drain. Distortion of the spine, tearing of the folds of paper, and weakening of the hinges are likely to result.

Damp Books

Have a dry room with circulating air (portable fan directed *over* the book). If it is warm and dry outside, the books may be placed outside. Be aware, however, that sun may damage paper and fade covering materials.

1. Place a sheet of absorbent material (blotting paper, mat board, layers of white paper toweling) on a flat surface that is large enough to accommodate the book. Change when sheet becomes wet.

2. Stand book on its head (or on its driest edge). Paperback books and books with loose covers may need support, such as covered bricks or bookends.

3. Open book to no more than 30 degrees and fan pages gently.

4. Place a set of barrier material between boards and flyleaves: a sheet of polyethylene, polyester film, or aluminum foil next to the flyleaves, then blotting paper between this sheet and the boards.

Figure 3.1. Draining Saturated Books

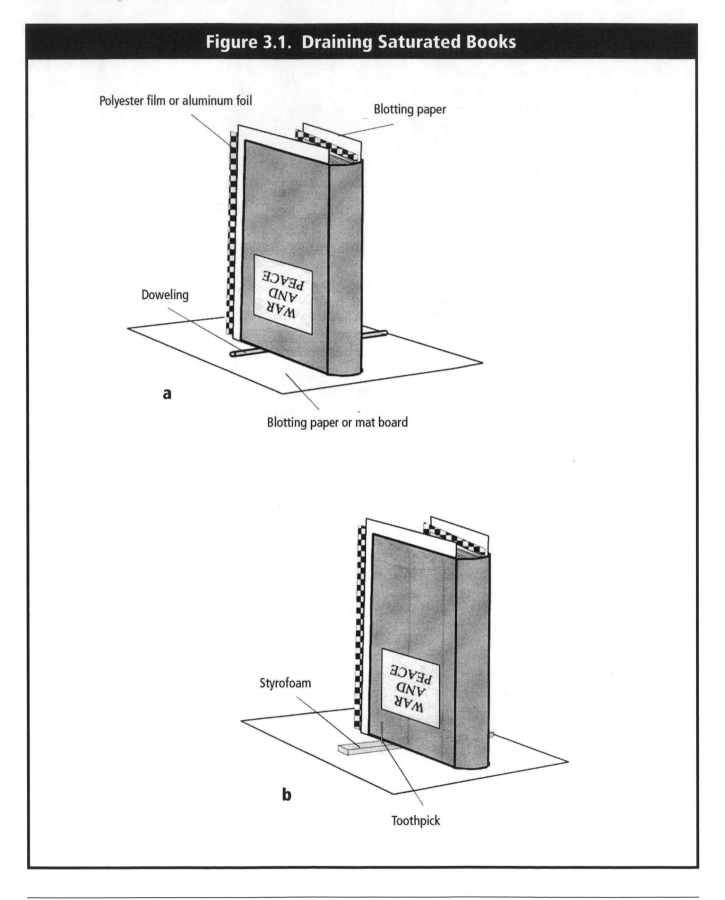

Polyester film or aluminum foil

Blotting paper

Doweling

WAR AND PEACE

a

Blotting paper or mat board

Styrofoam

WAR AND PEACE

b

Toothpick

5. Separate pages gently, but do not force apart those which are stuck together.

6. Place interleaving material every 50 pages or so (see Figure 3.2). Unprinted newsprint and plain white paper toweling are the best for this purpose. But if you cannot get these materials in a short period of time, you may use the white sections of old phonebooks. Make certain, however, that there is no color printing on them. Also be on guard for any smearing or transfer of ink.

7. The paper should extend beyond the top edge and fore-edge of the book so that the moisture can be wicked out.

8. The paper should be changed frequently, particularly during the early stages of drying. As leaves of the book become dry, shift the interleaving places forward to accommodate still-wet pages.

9. With each shift, turn the book on its opposite edge.

10. In conditions of high humidity, interleaving of every 20 pages may be necessary. Except with books printed on coated paper, interleaving should never expand the textblock more than 30

Figure 3.2. Air-Drying a Damp Book

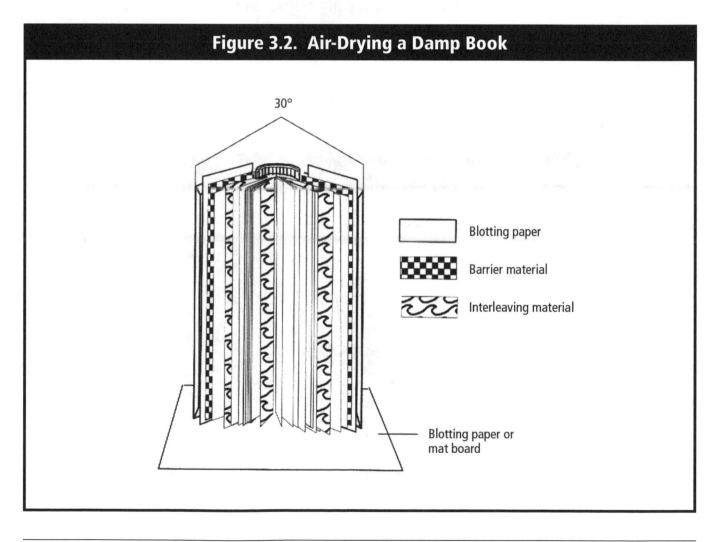

30°

Blotting paper

Barrier material

Interleaving material

Blotting paper or mat board

percent of its original size. Frequent replacing of interleaving materials is much more effective than allowing large numbers of them to remain for longer periods of time.

Coated Papers

Books with coated papers must be treated immediately, before they start to dry out. Even with early attention, however, the results are often unsatisfactory and disappointing, particularly in consideration of the amount of time and effort put into the treatment.

1. Carefully separate pages and place a sheet of wax paper between each. This amount of interleaving will cause irreparable damage to the binding structure, but it is the only way that there is a chance of keeping the pages from becoming a solid block.

2. In replacing the interleaving paper, do *not* pull it out; rather, gently lift each adjoining leaf away from the wax paper before removing it. The ink on the surface of damp or wet coated paper is very unstable and will smear with any abrasion.

Books with Only Edges Wet

A book that is wet only at the edges may be interleaved and placed flat on an absorbent surface (see Figure 3.3).

1. Close the book, but do not put a weight on it.
2. As the edges become damp to the touch, remove the interleaving material.

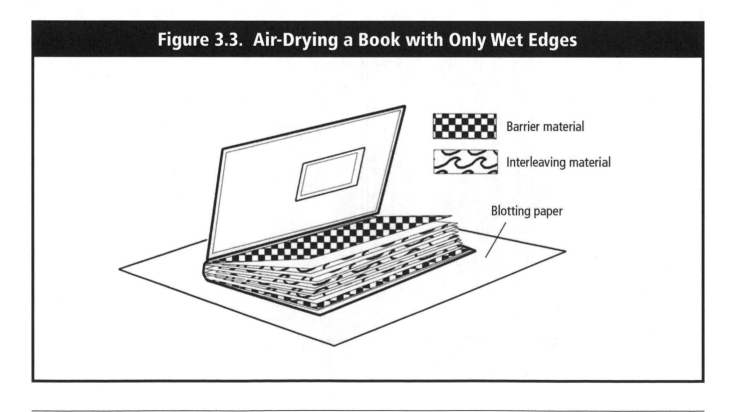

Figure 3.3. Air-Drying a Book with Only Wet Edges

Barrier material

Interleaving material

Blotting paper

3. Stand the book on its head end and fan the pages, gently separating those that adhere to each other. Do not force the leaves apart, or they are likely to tear. Fan the leaves every 2 hours to allow for maximum air penetration.

4. When the book is dry but still cool to the touch, gently re-form the book to its original shape (i.e., convex spine and concave fore-edge).

5. Close it, put a weight (such as a cloth-covered brick) on it, and let it remain for several days. Do not stack books on top of each other.

Hanging

Pamphlets and books that are damp may also be hung up to dry.

1. The lines should be of a monofilament material (such as fishing line) and not more than 1/32-inch thick.

2. They should be strung 1/2-inch apart and not more than 6 feet in length (see Figure 3.4a). Three lines will accommodate books 1 1/2 inches wide (the most common width), but in no case should a book weigh more than 6 pounds.

3. Care must be taken not to tear the paper or the inner folds of the signatures (see Figure 3.4b–c).

4. This method of drying will help a distorted spine regain its normal convex shape.

5. Once the pamphlet or book has dried, lay it on a flat surface and put a light weight on it. A book may also be gently re-formed to its original shape before the weight is placed on it.

Treatment of Water-Damaged Papers

Single-sheet items may be air-dried according to the following procedures. If at all possible, however, archival or rare documents, works of art on paper, and large items (maps, posters, playbills) should be carefully removed from their enclosures and frozen immediately, and a conservator consulted for later treatment. There is the real probability of irreversible damage to inks, colored pencil, charcoal and pastel, watercolor images, and other fragile surfaces if the materials are handled incorrectly. If there is any indication of feathering of inks, the item should be frozen immediately.

For air-drying single-sheet items, the considerations of decisions, timing, coated paper, freezing, environment, and wetness apply as they do for books. Coated papers should be separated immediately or frozen until they can be treated. Items that are matted should be carefully removed from their enclosures. It is best, however, not to attempt to clean single-sheet items because of damage the water may do to the paper and surface media. There will inevitably be some cockling, even after the papers have been thoroughly dried.

Figure 3.4. Hanging a Damp Book or Pamphlet

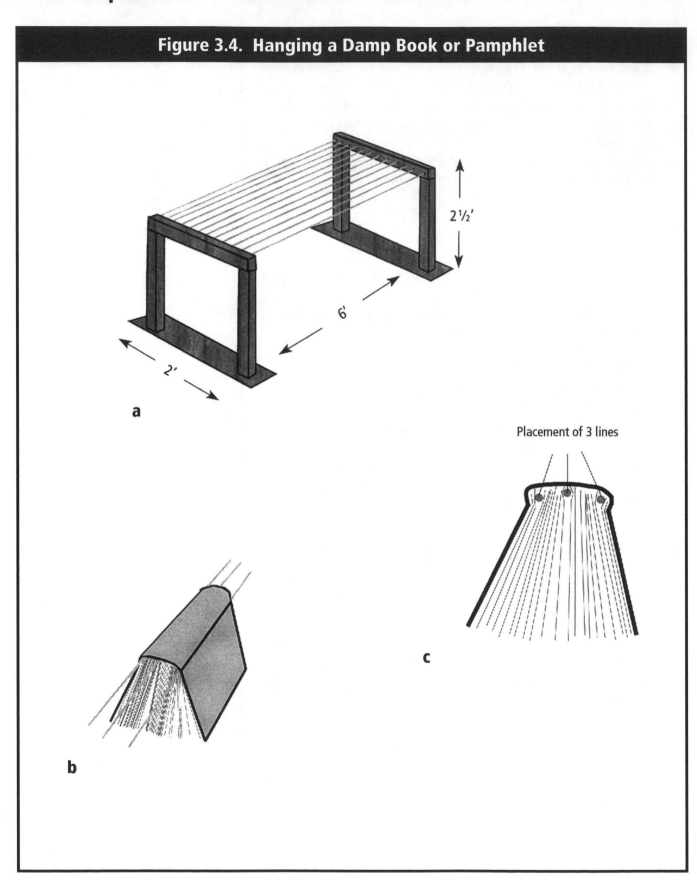

Separating Papers

Saturated Papers

If a stack of documents is saturated, do not attempt to remove single sheets from it. Separate the stack into piles ¼-inch high and leave them until they have become damp. When the sheets have started to separate, use the following procedures.

Damp Papers

Before attempting to separate damp papers, place them in stacks ¼-inch high.

1. Dampen a piece of polyester film such as Melinex and place it on top of the stack (see Figure 3.5a–c).

2. Alternatively, place a piece of kitchen plastic wrap on top of the stack, lightly rub it, and then continue with the following procedures (see Figure 3.5d–e).

3. Carefully peel the film or cling wrap back, with the top sheet from the stack adhering to it (see Figure 3.5f).

4. If more than one sheet comes up with the film or wrap, place this new stack on a flat surface with the film or wrap on the bottom (see Figure 3.5g).

5. Repeat with a new piece of film until you have separated each of the items in the stack.

Drying Papers

Single-sheet items need air circulation to dry. Construct a drying rack of nonmetallic screening and brick or boards, or string lengths of fishing line about ½-inch apart. The number of lines depends on how large your documents are. If only a flat surface is available to you, lay down absorbent paper or mat board before you spread out the items. In all cases, it is important to handle the items carefully and to provide support for lifting them. A good means of support is a "sandwich" of spun polyester, which is known generically as "release cloth" and is available from preservation suppliers as Reemay or Hollitex. If time or funds do not permit, you may also use dress facing purchased from a fabric store. Since spun polyester also keeps papers from sticking together, it is particularly important if you are using a flat surface covered with absorbent paper.

1. Lay the piece of polyester film or kitchen wrap with the document adhered to it onto a surface with the film or wrap on the bottom (see Figure 3.6a).

2. Place a piece of spun polyester on top and lightly rub it (see Figure 3.6b).

3. Turn the package over, and gently peel the film or wrap back from the document, diagonally from one corner to its opposite (see Figure 3.6c).

Figure 3.5. Separating Damp Papers

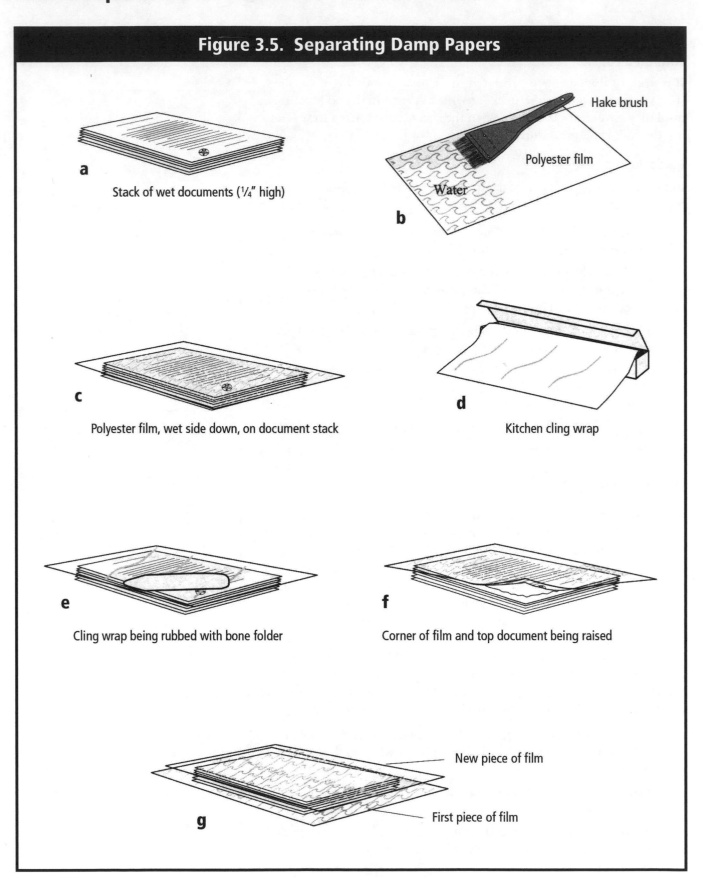

a Stack of wet documents (¼" high)

b Hake brush / Polyester film / Water

c Polyester film, wet side down, on document stack

d Kitchen cling wrap

e Cling wrap being rubbed with bone folder

f Corner of film and top document being raised

g New piece of film / First piece of film

4. Replace with another piece of spun polyester (see Figure 3.6d).

5. If you move this "sandwich," be sure to lift it by opposite corners (see Figure 3.6e). This will help to keep it from buckling.

6. Place the "sandwich" on clean blotting paper and remove the top piece of spun polyester. Alternatively, place the "sandwich" on a drying rack and remove the top piece of spun polyester.

7. When the single sheets are nearly dry, they may be interleaved and placed in stacks ½-inch high (see Figure 3.6f).

8. Place a board larger than the documents on top and a weight on top of that. Leave until thoroughly dried out, checking every few hours for evidence of mold.

Removing Mold and Mildew

Mold and mildew are two types of fungi that attack paper objects housed in a warm and humid environment. Mold spores are always with us in the air and on surfaces. In the right conditions (temperature above 70°F and relative humidity above 65 percent), they may become active and start to form colonies. Active mold appears fuzzy and slimy and may smear when brushed. Dormant spores appear dry and powdery. It is very difficult to kill mold spores and almost impossible to keep them from recurring; thus, it is essential to treat the environment as well as the books or papers. If treated books are placed back in a warm and humid atmosphere, the mold spores will grow once again.

It is important to remember that mold can be allergenic or toxic to humans. In some cases, the reactions may be severe and require extended treatment. In addition, many chemicals, such as thymol, which in the past were used to treat mold are no longer recommended because of their adverse effects on the environment and on humans. If the mold outbreak is larger than you can manage or if you suspect that the building is also infected, you must call in an expert, who will determine what kinds of mold are involved and when it is safe to remove books for treatment.

Removal Procedures

If the books affected are few in number and can be easily handled, the following procedures should give satisfactory results. Water-damaged books and papers are particularly susceptible to mold growth because of their moisture content. They should be treated within 48 hours. Be aware, however, that stains caused by mildew cannot be removed without chemical bleaching and irreversible damage to the paper.

CAUTION: When working with mold and mildew take these precautions:

1. Use a respirator with a HEPA (high efficiency particulate air) filter. Normal dust masks will not filter out the mold spores.

Figure 3.6. Air-Drying Damp Papers

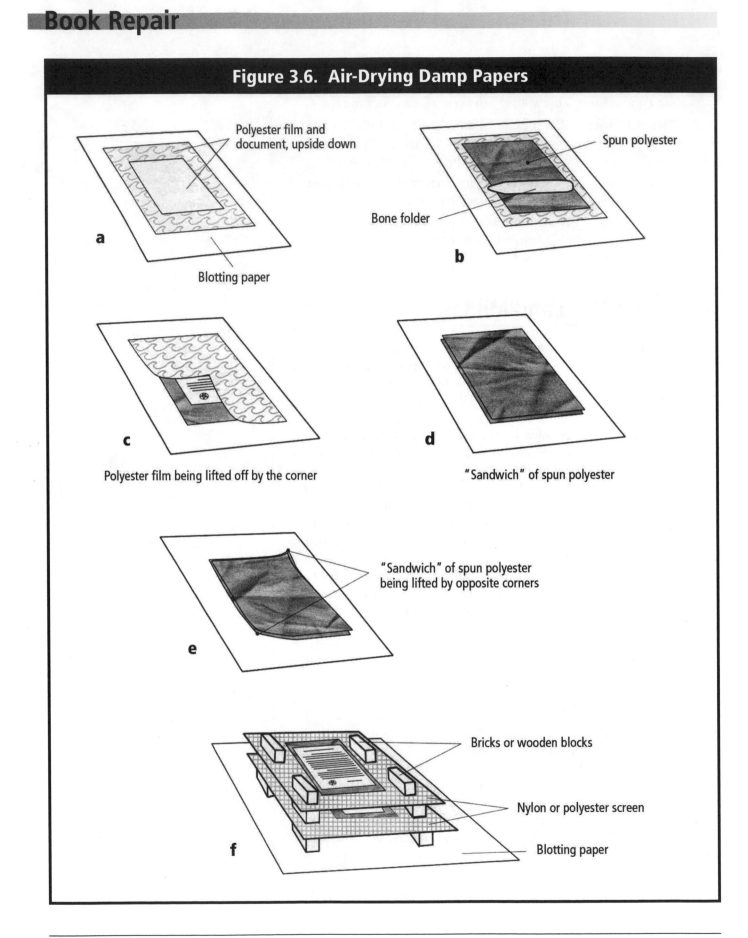

a — Polyester film and document, upside down / Blotting paper

b — Spun polyester / Bone folder

c — Polyester film being lifted off by the corner

d — "Sandwich" of spun polyester

e — "Sandwich" of spun polyester being lifted by opposite corners

f — Bricks or wooden blocks / Nylon or polyester screen / Blotting paper

People with allergies, asthma, and facial hair may not be able to wear a respirator at all.

2. Use disposable gloves and dispose of them in a sealed plastic bag.

3. Wear protective clothing and wash it out with hot water and bleach.

Freezing

If it is not possible to treat moldy books within 48 hours, they should be frozen, loosely wrapped in freezer paper. Freezing is a fungistatic process; that is, it will cause the mold to become dormant but it will not kill it.

Packaging

Books and papers that are to be treated within 48 hours must be removed as soon as possible to prevent further contamination of unaffected areas. Two methods of packaging moldy or mildewed material are recommended:

1. If the mold is obviously active, place items in a paper box with a tight-fitting lid. A desiccant such as silica gel will help reduce the moisture level. Remove box to a clean treatment area.

2. If the mold is dry and powdery and the paper feels dry, place each item in an air-tight plastic bag and remove to a clean treatment area.

Drying

Mold and mildew cannot be removed effectively until they are dormant. Follow the procedures outlined earlier for drying damp books, being careful not to smear the active mold. If you take the books outside on a dry sunny day, fan them open so that the sun may penetrate to the moldy areas. Do not leave the books outside for more than 1 hour or the pages may become yellowed and brittle.

Removing Dormant Mold and Mildew

1. Vacuum the mold and mildew with a HEPA-filtered vacuum. Use a soft brush attachment, and for fragile papers use also a fine-mesh screen or cheesecloth inserted in the mouth of the hose. Empty the contents of the vacuum into sealed bags and dispose of them off-site.

2. If you have taken the books outside, you may use a white soft-bristled brush to remove the mold. Brush lightly away from you and downwind. When the bristles become dirty, wash them in hot water and bleach and dry thoroughly.

Monitoring

After the treated books have been returned to their shelves, they need to be monitored carefully for any recurrence of mold or any infection of adjacent areas. The temperature and humidity levels likewise need to be monitored. For the first few months, once a week is recommended.

Disaster Recovery Specialists

American Freeze-Dry, Inc.
http://americanfreezedry.com/
1722 Hurffville Road, Bldg. 2A
Five Points Business Center
Sewell, NJ 08080
Telephone: 856-939-8160
Toll free: 866-939-8160

Amigos Library Services—Preservation Services
http://amigos.org/
14400 Midway Road
Dallas, TX 75244-3509
Toll Free: 800-843-8482
Fax: 972-991-6061
Assistance by phones M–F 8:30–5:00 Central Time
Also offers referrals to resources in a particular area

Belfor USA Headquarters
http://www.belforusa.com/
185 Oakland Avenue, Suite 300
Birmingham, MI 48009-3433
Telephone: 800-856-3333
Fax: 248-594-1133
Multiple locations throughout the United States

Blackmon-Mooring Steamatic Catastrophe, Inc.
http://www.bmscat.com/
International Headquarters
303 Arthur Street
Fort Worth, TX 76107
Toll Free: 800-433-2940
Telephone: 817-332-2770 (24-hour hotline)
Fax: 817-332-6728

Document Reprocessors
http://www.documentreprocessors.com/
West Coast:
1384 Rollins Road
Burlingame, CA 94010
Toll Free: 800-437-9264 (24-hour hotline)
Telephone: 650-401-7111
East Coast:
40 Railroad Avenue
Rushville, NY 14544
Toll Free: 888-437-9264 (24-hour hotline)

Telephone: 585-554-4500
24 Hour Disaster Line: 800-437-9464

Midwest Freeze-Dry, Ltd.
http://www.midwestfreezedryltd.com/
Midwest Center for Stabilization and Conservation
7326 North Central Park
Skokie, IL 60076
Telephone: 847-679-4756
Fax: 847-679-4191

Munters Corporation—Moisture Control Services
http://www.munters.us/en/us/
79 Monroe Street
Amesbury, MA 01913
Toll Free: 800-959-7901 (24-hour hotline)
Telephone: 978-241-1100
Multiple locations throughout the United States

Northeast Document Conservation Center
http://www.nedcc.org/
100 Brickstone Square
Andover, MA 01810-1494
Telephone: 978-470-1010
Fax: 978-475-6021

Solex Environmental Systems
http://solexrobotics.com/
PO Box 55045
Houston, TX 77055
Telephone: 713-963-8600

Resources

Treatment of Water-Damaged Books and Papers

Bishop Museum, Honolulu. "Disaster Preparedness and Recovery for Works of Art on Paper." Bishop Museum Art Conservation Handout. http://www.bishopmuseum.org/research/pdfs/cnsv-disaster.pdf.

Buchanan, Sally. "Emergency Salvage of Wet Books and Records." *NEDCC Technical Leaflet*, Section 3, Leaflet 7. Andover, MA: Northeast Document Conservation Center, 1999. http://www.nedcc.org/tleaf37.html.

Dion, Kathleen B. "These Leaves Were Not Made to Be Wet Or...Help, My Books Have Water on Them!" *The New Library Scene*, September 1997: 24–26.

Fortson, Judith. *Disaster Planning and Recovery: A How-To-Do-It Manual for Librarians and Archivists*. New York: Neal-Schuman, 1992.

Frellsen, Ann V. "Thawing Frozen Books." *Conservation DistList*, January 26, 1995.

Kahn, Miriam. *Disaster Response and Planning for Libraries*. Chicago: American Library Association, 1998.

Ketchum, John. "Guidelines for Dealing with Water-Damaged Property." *Conservation DistList*, January 11, 1995.

Library of Congress. "Emergency Drying Procedures for Water Damaged Collections—Collections Care." Preservation, Library of Congress. http://www.loc.gov/preservation/care/dry.html.

Waters, Peter. *Procedures for Salvage of Water-Damaged Materials*. Washington, DC: Library of Congress, 1993. http://cool.conservation-us.org/bytopic/disasters/primer/waters.html.

Removal of Mold and Mildew

Mold (General)

McCrady, Ellen. "Mold: The Whole Picture, Parts 1–4." *The Abbey Newsletter*, 23 (1999). http://cool.conservation-us.org/bytopic/mold/.

Removal of Mold and Mildew

Kaplan, Hilary A. "Mold: A Follow-Up." February 1998. http://cool.conservation-us.org/byauth/kaplan/moldfu.html.

Nyberg, Sandra. "Invasion of the Giant Spore." *SOLINET Preservation Program Leaflet* No. 5. Atlanta, GA: SOLINET, 1987. http://www-sul.stanford.edu/tools/tutorials/html2.0/spore.html. Updated version: http://cool.conservation-us.org/byauth/nyberg/spore.html.

Patkus, Beth Lindblom. "Emergency Salvage of Moldy Books and Paper." *NEDCC Technical Leaflet*, Section 3, Leaflet 9. Andover, MA: Northeast Document Conservation Center, 1999. http://www.nedcc.org/resources/leaflets/3Emergency_Management/08SalvageMoldyBooks.php.

Price, Lois Olcott. *Managing a Mold Invasion: Guidelines for Disaster Response.* CCAHA Technical Series No. 1. Philadelphia: Conservation Center for Art and Historic Artifacts, 1996.

Figure 3.7. Water-Damaged Book Treatment Decision Flowchart

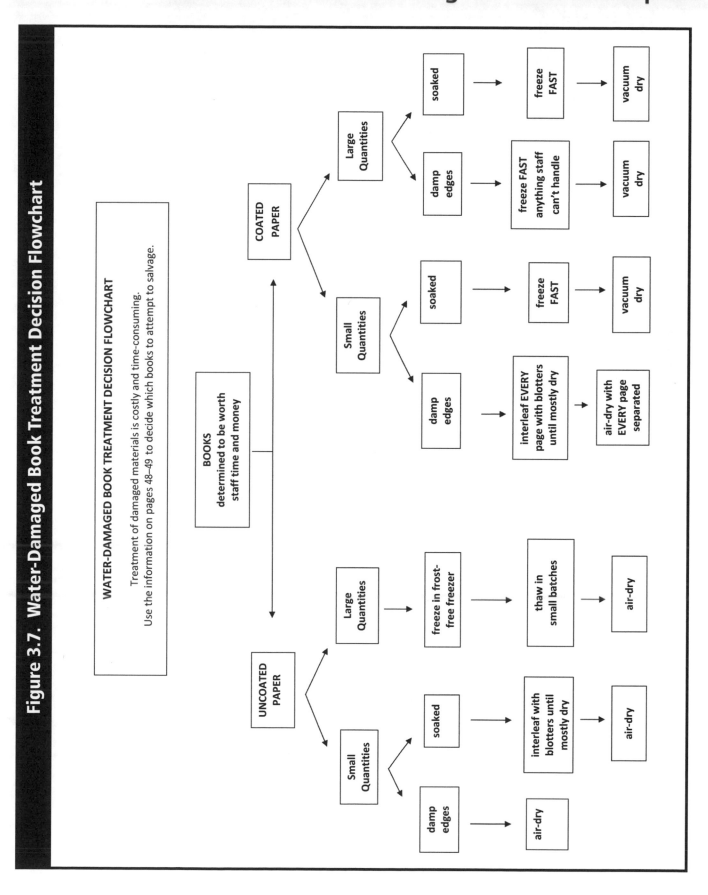

WATER-DAMAGED BOOK TREATMENT DECISION FLOWCHART

Treatment of damaged materials is costly and time-consuming.
Use the information on pages 48–49 to decide which books to attempt to salvage.

BOOKS
determined to be worth
staff time and money

COATED PAPER

Large Quantities

soaked → freeze FAST → vacuum dry

damp edges → freeze FAST anything staff can't handle → vacuum dry

Small Quantities

soaked → freeze FAST → vacuum dry

damp edges → interleaf EVERY page with blotters until mostly dry → air-dry with EVERY page separated

UNCOATED PAPER

Large Quantities

freeze in frost-free freezer → thaw in small batches → air-dry

Small Quantities

soaked → interleaf with blotters until mostly dry → air-dry

damp edges → air-dry

Paper Mending

All paper objects are susceptible to wear along folds, tears along the edges, and losses, both intentional and accidental. While some tears seem minor, it is important to repair these tears in order to stop further damage when the item is used again. Losses, too, must be repaired in order to prevent further loss. Tears in paper objects can be mended with simple adhesive, repair tape, heat-set tissue, or with Japanese paper and starch paste. Losses can be mended with heat-set tissue or Japanese paper and starch paste. Variations of these methods provide solutions to a wide range of paper mending problems.

It is important to prepare the document to be mended before the repair is begun. If the repair is in a map or flat document, it is best to flatten the object before repairing it. This can be done by placing the item between clean sheets of blotting or other paper, and then pressing this package under boards and weights. If the repair is in a book, it is a good idea to place a clean piece of wax paper under the page to be repaired. Large gaps in a tear may require a tape mend on both sides, or an insert mend, using the same techniques employed to repair losses.

If the paper object is going to be cleaned or deacidified, these steps should be taken prior to mending. It is necessary to be very cautious when cleaning a torn piece of paper in order that it not be torn further.

Decisions

The following factors will influence your decision regarding the most appropriate mending repair treatment:

Type of tear to be repaired

Size of object to be repaired

Number of printed sides on the paper to be repaired

Further treatment for the object to be repaired

Repairing Simple Tears

Each of the following methods of repair depends on the type of tear (e.g., whether it has bevels, how wide the bevels are), the size of the object (large objects may require a stronger repair), whether both sides of the paper have text or image, and whether you intend to encapsulate or mat the object. The type of paper also helps determine the type of repair you undertake. Coated paper, for example, is difficult to repair with a treatment that uses water.

Glue and Paste Mends

The simplest way to repair a tear in a piece of paper is by gluing or pasting the torn edges back together. This can be done only when the torn edges of the paper are beveled to some extent. Torn edges are said to be beveled when one edge overlaps another; conversely, a cut has no bevels and therefore there is nothing to overlap (see Figure 4.1a–b). It is this overlap that may be glued or pasted, and thus this type of mend is not possible if the paper has been cut rather than torn. It is not even possible on every tear, as some tears in papers simply do not have a substantial enough bevel.

The PVA or paste that you use for this type of repair should be rather thin. If you are using PVA, dilute it with approximately 3 parts PVA to 1 part water. PVA is difficult to reverse, however, and thus should not be used on archival or valuable objects. If you are using rice or wheat paste, dilute the resulting paste (such as from the formula in Chapter 1) with water until it is the consistency of smooth cream (about 2 parts paste to 1 part water).

Supplies

> PVA or paste (rice or wheat)
> Small glue brush
> Blotting paper
> Spun polyester
> Bone folder
> Weight

Procedure

1. If you are mending a page in a book or a flat item, place a piece of wax paper under the tear. Be sure to line up the bevels of the tear before you begin this procedure. The edges of some tears will fluctuate along the length of the tear, with first one edge on top, then the other.

2. Gently lift one torn edge and spread the thinned glue or paste on the bevel of the bottom, brushing across the bevel onto the wax paper (see Figure 4.2a).

3. If the tear is in a book, replace the piece of wax paper under the page with a clean piece; then place another piece on top of the tear. Smooth down with a bone folder, close the book, place a weight on top, and let the mend dry. (See Figure 4.2b–c.) It is

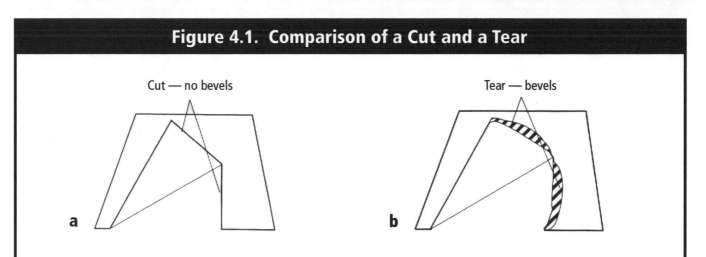

Figure 4.1. Comparison of a Cut and a Tear

Cut — no bevels

a

Tear — bevels

b

generally a good idea to replace the pieces of wax paper after an hour of drying time.

4. If the tear is in a flat object, lay the bevel of the raised edge down on the glued bevel and carefully tap the tear to tack the bevels together (see Figure 4.2d).

5 Place the repaired object on top of a piece of spun polyester, on top of a piece of blotting paper. Place another piece of spun polyester on top of the mended paper and gently smooth down the repair with a bone folder (see Figure 4.2e).

6. Place another piece of blotting paper on top, and put the repaired object, with the blotting paper and spun polyester "sandwich" under weights and allow the glue or paste to dry (see Figure 4.2f). For small PVA and paste mends, the drying time is 1–2 hours. Check the repair after 30 minutes, and replace the wax paper or blotting paper if they seem to be getting too wet.

Tape

Archival mending tape can be used on virtually any type of cut or tear, although it is not recommended for items of artistic or historical value because it is very difficult to remove. Such items should be repaired with heat-set tissue or Japanese paper and starch paste.

Document repair tape is not only versatile, but its initial expense is often offset by the personnel time saved because of its ease of use. It has the added advantage of being virtually transparent so that it may be used over text portions of a page.

Supplies

Archival mending tape
Bone folder
Small piece of polyester film
Metal ruler
X-Acto or Olfa knife or scalpel

Figure 4.2. Mending a Simple Tear with Glue or Paste

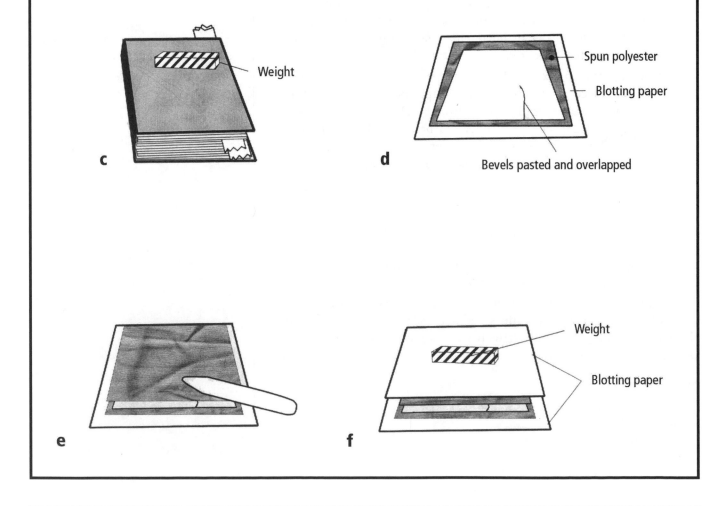

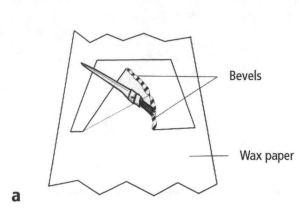

Bevels

Wax paper

a

Tear underneath wax paper

b

Weight

c

Spun polyester

Blotting paper

Bevels pasted and overlapped

d

e

Weight

Blotting paper

f

Procedure

With the exception of step 8, this procedure may be used either for books or for flat objects.

1. Because archival tape may stick to any paper product, place a piece of spun polyester under the tear. Line up the torn edges to be repaired. Be careful to follow the bevels of the edges of the tear.

2. Tear off a piece of tape as long as the tear. If repairing an edge tear, you can use a piece twice as long as the tear, folding it around the edge of the paper to strengthen the tear on both sides.

3. Gently place the piece of tape on the tear. Carefully tack the tape in place, starting at one end of the repair and working to the other end (see Figure 4.3a).

4. Lay a piece of spun polyester on top of the tear and smooth down with a bone folder (see Figure 4.3b).

5. Turn the page or the object over and place a piece of spun polyester underneath (see Figure 4.3c).

6. If you are repairing an edge tear and have extended the tape beyond the edge of the paper, follow one of these two steps before continuing:
   a. Lift up the end of the tape and pull it gently until it rests on the edge of the paper. Tack it down with a bone folder, and then continue to bring the tape down over the tear. (See Figure 4.3d.) The initial tacking keeps the edge from being damaged as you pull the tape over.
   b. Fold the tape just past the edge of the paper and continue putting the tape down over the tear (see Figure 4.3e).

7. When the tape is in place, lay another piece of spun polyester on the repair and use the bone folder to gently rub down the tape (see Figure 4.3f).

8. When tape is firmly affixed to the paper, use a piece of board or a metal ruler and trim any overhang off with an X-Acto or Olfa knife or scalpel (see Figure 4.3g). If the edge tear is in a book, follow the steps for Trimming an Endsheet (see Figure 5.9a–b, p. 119) to remove the tape overhang. Not all repairs will require this step.

Heat-Set Tissue

Items that require a more archival repair should be repaired with heat-set tissue or Japanese paper and starch paste. For objects that may be adversely affected by water, such as coated paper stock or water-colored maps, heat-set tissue is the best archival repair method. Mending with heat-set tissue is a simple process that is also economical once you have made the initial purchase of tools and supplies. The tissue is removable with mineral spirits, although it is often messy and difficult to do so.

Figure 4.3. Mending a Tear with Archival Tape

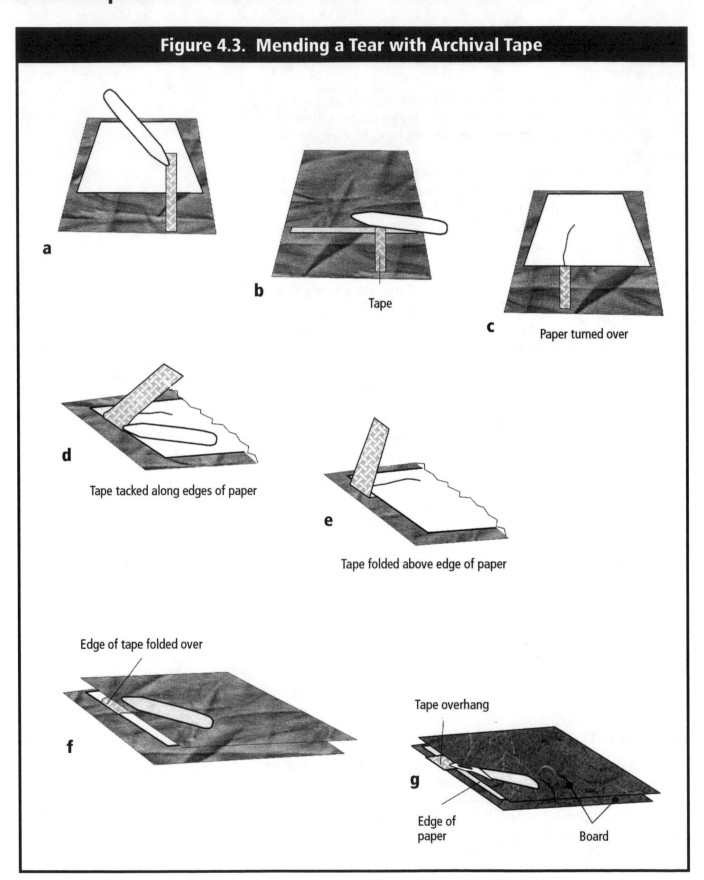

a

b

Tape

c

Paper turned over

d

Tape tacked along edges of paper

e

Tape folded above edge of paper

Edge of tape folded over

f

g

Tape overhang

Edge of paper

Board

Supplies

Heat-set tissue
Tacking iron
Spun polyester
Metal ruler and X-Acto or Olfa knife or scalpel

Procedure

With the exception of step 9, this procedure may be used either for books or for flat objects.

1. Preheat the tacking iron to medium heat.

2. Place a piece of spun polyester under the tear to be repaired. Line up the torn edges to be repaired, being careful to follow the bevels of the edges of the tear. (See Figure 4.4a.)

3. Cut a strip of heat-set tissue that is large enough to cover the tear. For an edge tear, you may wish to make the strip long enough to be folded over and adhered to the reverse side. The strip may also be cut into more precise measurements with embroidery scissors.

4. Place the heat-set tissue on the tear; the shiny side should be down. Cover the tissue with spun polyester.

5. Lightly rub the tissue with the heated tacking iron, gently moving the iron over the repair (see Figure 4.4b). If there is difficulty with the tissue adhering to the paper, either turn up the temperature on the tacking iron or remove the spun polyester and iron directly on the tissue. Be careful, however, not to touch the paper itself with the iron. When the heat-set tissue is almost invisible, it should be firmly adhered to the paper.

6. Turn the page or the object over and place a piece of spun polyester underneath (see Figure 4.4c).

7. If you are repairing an edge tear and have extended the strip of tissue beyond the edge of the paper, follow one of these two steps before continuing:
    a. Lift up the end of the tissue and pull it gently until it rests on the edge of the paper. Tack it down with the iron, and then continue to bring the strip down over the tear. (See Figure 4.4d.) The initial tacking keeps the edge from being damaged as you pull the strip over.
    b. Fold the strip of tissue just past the edge of the paper and continue putting it down over the tear (see Figure 4.4e).

8. When the strip of tissue is in place, lay another piece of spun polyester on the repair and use the tacking iron to adhere the tissue to the paper (see Figure 4.4f). If you have difficulty in getting the tissue to stick, follow the suggestions in step 5.

9. When tissue is firmly affixed to the paper, use a board or metal ruler and trim off any overhang with an X-Acto or Olfa knife or scalpel (see Figure 4.4g). If the edge tear is in a book, follow

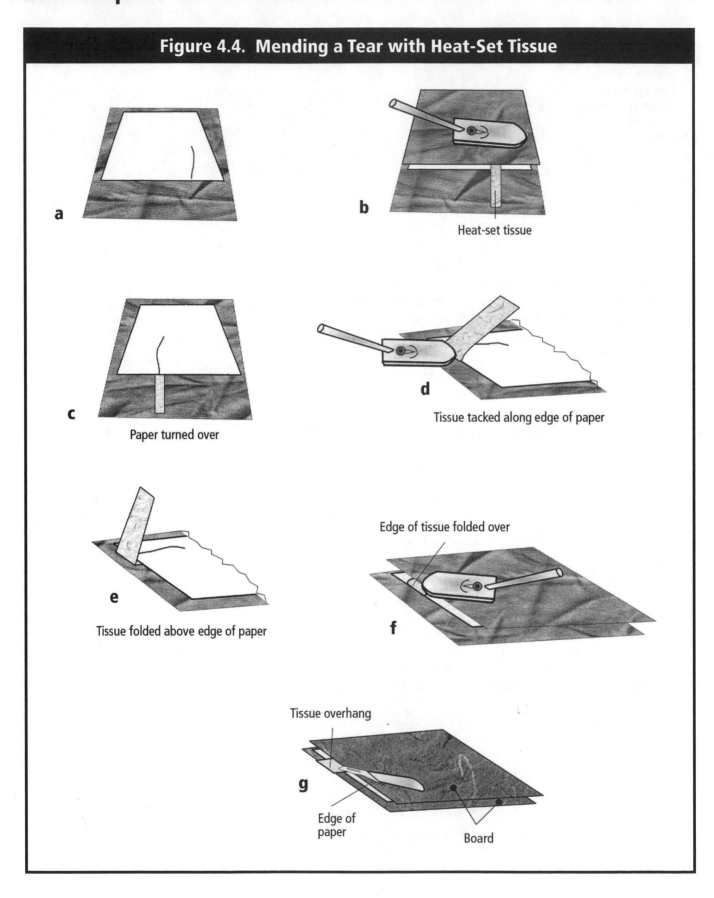

Figure 4.4. Mending a Tear with Heat-Set Tissue

a

b

Heat-set tissue

c

Paper turned over

d

Tissue tacked along edge of paper

e

Tissue folded above edge of paper

Edge of tissue folded over

f

Tissue overhang

g

Edge of paper

Board

the steps for Trimming an Endsheet (see Figure 5.9a–b, p. 119) to remove the tape overhang. Not all repairs will require this step.

10. If you wish the tape to be more transparent, brush a light coating of ethanol over it with a cotton swab or tip.

Japanese Paper and Starch Paste

For items that are not adversely affected by moisture, Japanese paper and starch paste provide the strongest, most archival repair. It is also the only method for making an "over-and-under" repair; that is, it may be placed *between* the edges of the cut or tear, thus making a very strong bond. This is particularly useful in places where you want the minimum amount of repair material showing.

Japanese paper comes in many weights and generally in shades of white, neutral, and beige. For specialty work, it is also available in colors such as brown, red, green, and blue. You may also dye your own paper to match your needs. If you intend to use a lot of Japanese paper, it is best to keep an assortment of weights and colors best suited to the types of items you repair. If you intend to use it only occasionally, it is more economical to purchase the paper you need for each repair. For the majority of simple tears, a medium-weight Japanese paper, such as Sekishu, is recommended. For methods of tearing Japanese paper, see Chapter 1.

Japanese paper and starch paste mends are considered the most archival mending treatment because they are reversible with water. Even though this may be true, there is still the harm caused to paper by the application of even a small amount of water. In addition, when the paste mend is old, often a thin film of fresh paste needs to be applied before the old paste will soften up or dissolve.

Supplies

Japanese paper, such as Sekishu or Kizukishi
Rice or wheat starch paste
Metal ruler
X-Acto or Olfa knife or scalpel
Blotting paper
Spun polyester
Paste brush
Micro-spatula
Small tweezers
Bone folder
Small weights
Waste paper or wax paper

Procedure

1. Select a mending paper that is appropriate for the paper to be repaired. If possible, the mending paper should be just a bit lighter in weight than the paper to be repaired.

2. Using one of the methods described in Chapter 1, make a mending strip about ¼-inch longer than the tear and wide enough to extend approximately ⅛-inch on either side of the tear. The long sides of this strip should be parallel to the grain of the Japanese paper.

3. Place the object to be repaired on a piece of spun polyester on top of a piece of blotting paper. Line up the torn edges to be repaired, being careful to follow the bevels of the edges of the tear. If the tear is in a book, place a piece of wax paper under the page (see Figure 4.2b–c).

4. Spread paste evenly over a piece of wax paper or polyester film. Lay the mending strip in the paste on the waste paper and tamp down with a paste brush. Brush the fibers outward from the edges of the strip. (See Figure 4.5a.) Allow a few minutes for the Japanese paper to absorb the paste (you will see it change color). If it seems too dry, brush on a very light coating of paste. If less moisture is desired on the mending strip, place a piece of spun polyester over the paste, then a piece of blotting paper, and rub lightly with a bone folder.

5. Gently lift the mending strip out of the paste using the micro-spatula or tweezers. Do not lift too quickly or the strip will stretch, which will cause the mend to wrinkle as it dries.

6. While holding up the top bevel of the tear, place the end of the strip as far as possible into the tear (see Figure 4.5b).

7. Bring the top bevel down onto the mending strip, lay a piece of spun polyester on top, and lightly rub with a bone folder to tap down the mend (see Figure 4.5c). If the tear is in a book, place another piece of wax paper over the mend and rub with bone folder. Close the book, put a weight on top, and let dry for 1 hour. Change the pieces of wax paper and let dry for another hour.

8. Place another piece of blotting paper on top and rub more firmly with a bone folder to adhere the mend to the paper and to absorb extra moisture. Place a weight on top and allow to dry for 1–2 hours (see Figure 4.5d). Change the blotting paper if it seems too wet after 30 minutes or so.

9. Remove the weight, the nonwoven polyester, and the blotting papers, and, using a metal ruler and scalpel, trim the mending strip to the edge of the page or object if necessary (see Figure 4.5e–f). If a softer edge seems more appropriate, fine sandpaper may be used to remove the excess mending paper.

Repairing Losses

Losses in the pages of a book or other pieces of paper take three basic forms. Some losses occur along the edge of a piece of paper; others occur at the corner; still others occur in the center of the page, often the

Figure 4.5. Mending a Tear with Japanese Paper and Starch Paste

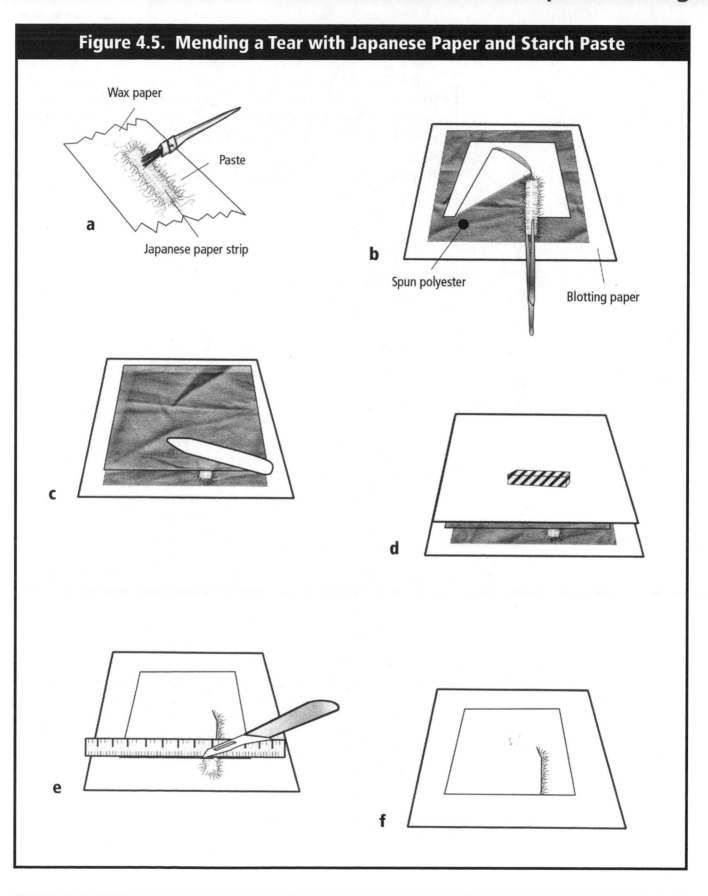

a — Wax paper, Paste, Japanese paper strip

b — Spun polyester, Blotting paper

result of vandalism. While each of these types of losses requires slightly different treatments, many of the same techniques can be applied to their repair; therefore, all of these treatments will be described as one.

Both heat-set tissue and Japanese paper and starch paste may be used to create a fill-in. The basic procedure utilizes three layers of repair material. A filler piece is cut to fit in the loss, and two thinner outer pieces are applied to hold the filler piece in place.

Repairing Losses with Heat-Set Tissue

Supplies

Heat-set tissue
Tacking iron
Spun polyester
Embroidery scissors
Pencil
Gum eraser
Metal ruler
X-Acto or Olfa knife or scalpel

Procedure

1. Preheat the tacking iron to medium heat.

2. Cut one piece of filler paper and two pieces of heat-set tissue, all the same size and shape. These pieces should be large enough to cover the loss as well as to extend ¼ inch beyond it in all directions. (See Figure 4.6a–b.)

3. Place a piece of filler paper under the loss in the page or sheet of paper to be repaired. This filler paper should be approximately the same thickness as the torn page. If possible, it should be close to the same color as well.

4. Holding the torn page firmly down on the filler paper, lightly trace the outline of the loss on the filler paper. Remove the filler paper and cut out the insert piece with the small scissors or scalpel. (See Figure 4.6c–d.) Cut along the outside edge of your line to get the best fit. Gently erase the pencil mark with the gum eraser.

5. (Optional) Use the fill-in piece as a template to mark and cut the two outer pieces. There should be about ¼-inch overlap of the outer pieces over the edge(s) of the loss. This allows space for the tissues to be adhered to the page or paper.

6. If you are repairing an edge loss, allow the insert to extend beyond the edge of the paper. If you are repairing a corner loss, allow the insert to extend beyond both edges of the paper. (See Figure 4.6e.)

7. Place a piece of spun polyester down on your worktable. Place the paper and the fill-in in position on top. The fill-in must fit snugly into the outline of the loss. (See Figure 4.6e.)

Figure 4.6. Repairing a Loss with Heat-Set Tissue

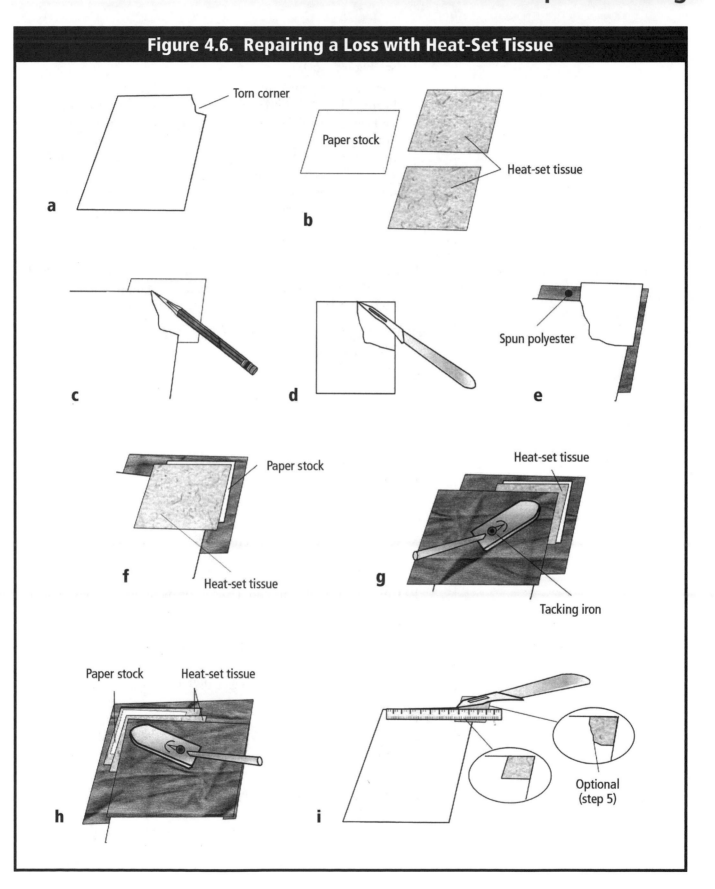

8. Place a piece of heat-set tissue shiny side down over the loss, with its edges matching up closely with those of the fill-in piece (see Figure 4.6f).

9. Iron the tissue with the heated tacking iron, moving the iron thoroughly over all areas of the repair to adhere the tissue to the fill-in and to the paper itself (see Figure 4.6g). If there is difficulty with the tissue adhering to the paper, either turn up the temperature on the tacking iron or remove the spun polyester and iron directly on the tissue. Be careful, however, not to touch the paper itself with the iron. When the heat-set tissue is almost invisible, it should be firmly adhered to the paper.

10. Turn the page or paper over, and repeat steps 8 and 9 for the second outer piece (see Figure 4.6h).

11. Place the mended page on a board, and with a straightedge and scalpel, trim the edges, if appropriate (see Figure 4.6i).

Repairing Losses with Japanese Paper and Starch Paste

Supplies

Japanese paper (thin: Gampi, Kozo; medium: Kizukishi, Sekishu)
Rice or wheat starch paste
Paste brush
Spun polyester
Embroidery scissors
Pencil
Gum eraser
Metal ruler
X-Acto or Olfa knife or scalpel

Procedure

1. Cut 2 pieces of thin and 1 piece of medium Japanese paper large enough to cover the loss you are mending with ¼ inch extra extending in every direction. Make sure that the grain direction is the same on all pieces and is parallel to that of the paper being mended. (See Figure 4.7a–b.) For a discussion of grain in Japanese paper, see Chapter 1.

2. Place the middle piece (i.e., the medium-weight piece) under the loss you are repairing. On corner and edge losses, make sure that the Japanese paper extends beyond the edges of the page or paper item. With a light pencil draw the outline of the loss onto the Japanese paper. (See Figure 4.7c.)

3. Cut along the line you have drawn with a pair of embroidery scissors or with a scalpel (see Figure 4.7d). Erase any pencil marks that remain.

4. Use the cut-out middle piece as a template to draw the outline for the two outer pieces (i.e., the thin-weight pieces). Place one

outer piece on a portion of wax paper, and, with a ruling pen or a fine thin brush, draw a line of water just *outside* the pencil outline you have drawn (see Figure 4.7e). Allow this piece to dry, gently erase the pencil mark, and brush the edge fibers out with a dry brush. Repeat for the second outer piece.

5. Paste out some rice or wheat starch paste on a strip of waste paper. Lay the middle Japanese paper piece in the paste and brush over it with a paste brush. Allow the paper to absorb the paste (it will change color as it does). Meanwhile, paste out *only* the edge fibers of the outer pieces. (See Figure 4.7f.)

6. Place a piece of blotting paper on your worktable, then a piece of spun polyester on top of it. Place the paper with the loss to be mended on it. With a pair of tweezers or a micro-spatula, lay one of the outer pieces of Japanese paper onto the area of the loss, with the pasted-out fibers extending beyond the cut-out outline. Brush the fibers down onto the paper with a paste brush. (See Figure 4.7g.)

7. Put a piece of spun polyester and a piece of blotting paper over the mend and rub down with a bone folder (see Figure 4.7h).

8. Turn the page or paper over onto another piece of spun polyester and blotting paper (see Figure 4.7i). With a pair of tweezers or a micro-spatula, lift the middle piece out of the paste on the wax paper strip, being very careful not to stretch it. Place it into the loss area on top of the first outer piece, fitting its cut outline snugly up against that of the paper (see Figure 4.7j).

9. With a pair of tweezers or a micro-spatula, lay the second outer piece of Japanese paper onto the middle piece, being careful to align its edges up properly. Its fibers should extend beyond the cut-out outline. (See Figure 4.7k.)

10. Place a piece of spun polyester over the mend and rub down with a bone folder (see Figure 4.7l).

11. Place another piece of blotting paper on top and a weight (see Figure 4.7m). Let dry for 2 hours, replacing the blotting papers after 1 hour if they seem to be very wet.

12. Trim off the Japanese paper mend at the edge(s) of the page or paper, if appropriate (see Figure 4.7n).

Tipping-In and Hinging-In

One particularly useful type of paper mending technique is the tipping-in of leaves that have come loose or have been torn out. If a leaf has come loose from the binding, the simplest method of reattachment is to paint a thin strip of glue on the gutter edge and "tip" the leaf back into the book. A better but more difficult method is to create a hinge for the loose leaf and secure that into the gutter of the book. A combination of these methods may be used to reattach several consecutive leaves that

Figure 4.7. Repairing a Loss with Japanese Paper and Starch Paste

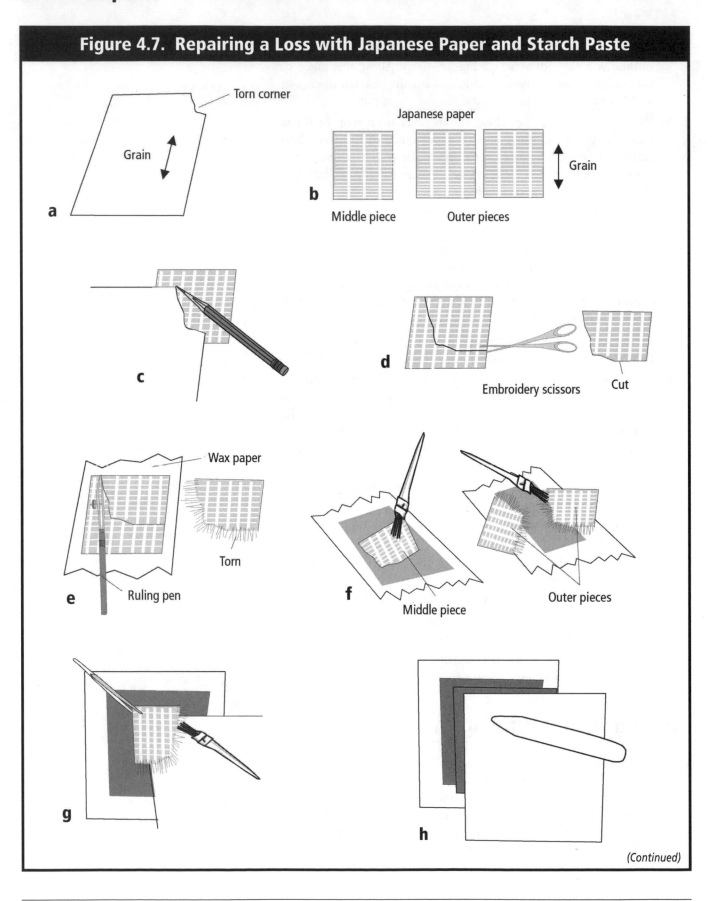

(Continued)

Figure 4.7. Repairing a Loss with Japanese Paper and Starch Paste (Continued)

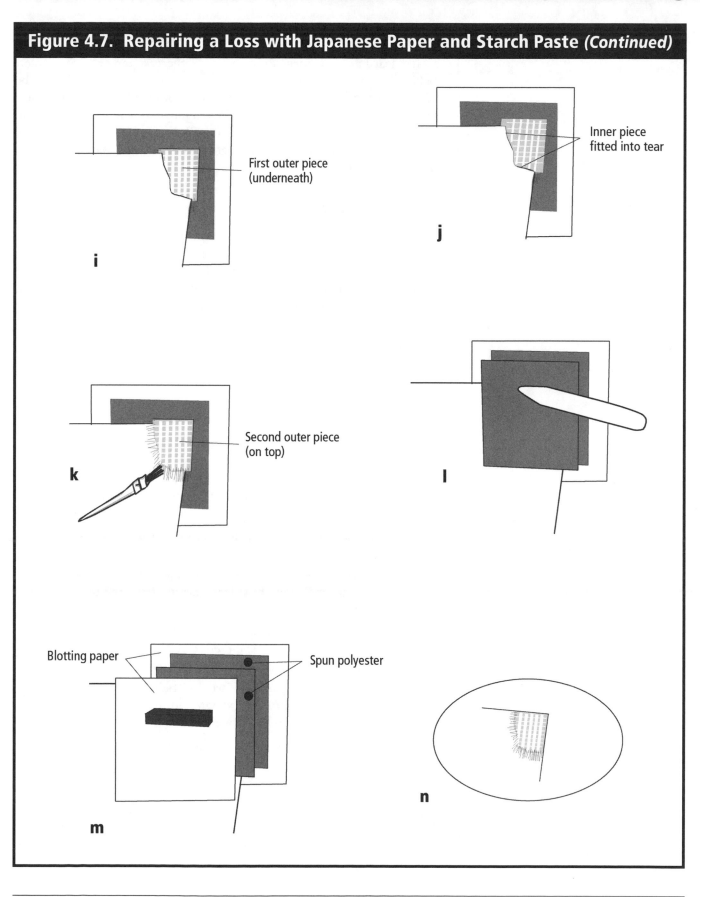

i — First outer piece (underneath)

j — Inner piece fitted into tear

k — Second outer piece (on top)

l

m — Blotting paper / Spun polyester

n

have fallen out. A hinge may also be created to reattach loose sections of a book.

If a leaf has been torn out of a book, there is generally a stub left behind in the gutter. If the stub is as wide as ½ inch, then the leaf may be reattached according to one of the methods for mending tears. If it is less than that, it is best to disregard it and use a hinge to reattach the torn leaf.

Single leaves may be reattached using PVA, starch paste, or a mixture of these two. If you are using a Japanese paper hinge, starch paste or a mixture is the best to use.

Tipping in Single Leaves

This simple method of reattaching a loose leaf has two potential problems. First, if the paper or binding is weak, the leaf to which the tipped-in one is attached will probably come loose also. Second, if the book receives heavy use, the thin strip of adhesive may soon lose its holding power. Nevertheless, this method does have the advantages of being easy to apply and inexpensive.

Supplies

Adhesive (PVA, starch paste, or a mixture)
Waste paper sheets
Wax paper
Glue brush
Bone folder

Procedure

1. Lay the leaf face-down on a clean sheet of waste paper.

2. Place another piece of waste paper on top, allowing ⅛ inch of the gutter edge of the leaf to extend beyond the edge of this waste paper.

3. While firmly holding the top piece of waste paper in place, paste out the exposed edge of the leaf, starting from the top piece of waste paper (see Figure 4.8a–b).

4. Carefully line up the edges of the leaf with the edges of the textblock, and press the spine edge of the leaf against the leaf behind it. Smooth down with a bone folder. (See Figure 4.8c.)

5. Place strips of wax paper before and behind the inserted leaf, close the book, and place a weight on it (see Figure 4.8d–e). Let dry for several hours or overnight.

6. (Optional) If the tipped-in page extends beyond the fore-edge of the textblock, follow the steps for Trimming an Endsheet (see Figure 5.9a–b, p. 119).

Hinging in Single Leaves

A Japanese paper hinge may be used to attach a leaf that has been torn out of a book or one that has simply come loose. It may be used also for

Figure 4.8. Tipping in a Single Leaf

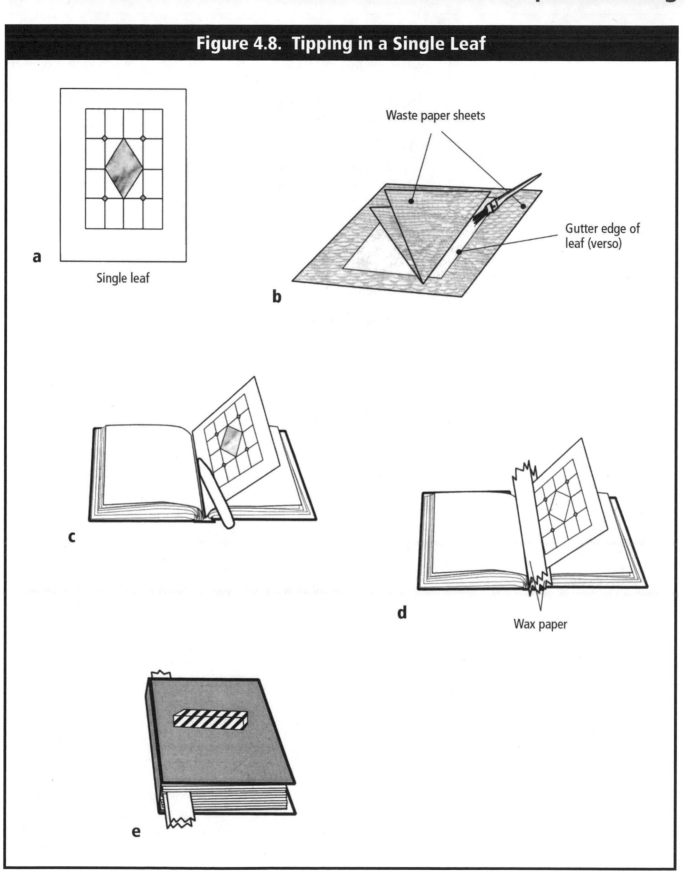

a — Single leaf

b — Waste paper sheets / Gutter edge of leaf (verso)

c

d — Wax paper

e

reattaching a single folded sheet or for reattaching a gathering of several folios, once they have been sewn together as a pamphlet. For most reattachments, the hinge may be cut. If the paper is fragile, however, tear the Japanese paper to make the hinge, using one of the methods discussed in Chapter 1 (see Figure 4.5a–d). The grain of the hinge must be parallel to the spine of the book.

Supplies

Rice or wheat starch paste, or a 50/50 mixture of paste and PVA
Medium-weight Japanese paper
Blotting paper
Spun polyester
Wax paper
Straightedge
Paste brush
Bone folder

Hinging in a Torn Leaf

Procedure

1. Trim the torn edge of the leaf into a straight line (see Figure 4.9a).

2. Cut a strip of Japanese paper that is ½-inch higher than the height of the textblock and as wide as the loss area + ⅛ inch. Measure the width of your trimmed leaf; measure the width of a normal leaf in the book; take the difference and add ⅛ inch. The hinge must fit all the way down into the gutter of the book and overlap the trimmed leaf by ⅛ inch. (See Figure 4.9b.)

3. Place the trimmed leaf face-up on a sheet of waste paper. Place another sheet of waste paper on top, leaving a ⅛ inch margin exposed. Paste out this area. (See Figure 4.9c.)

4. Place a piece of blotting paper on your worktable, then a piece of spun polyester on top. Situate the trimmed leaf so that its pasted-out edge is on the spun polyester. Carefully put down the strip of Japanese paper so that it is ⅛ inch over the trimmed edge. (See Figure 4.9d.)

5. Place a piece of spun polyester on top of the Japanese paper and rub down the pasted-out portion with a bone folder (see Figure 4.9e).

6. Place another piece of blotting paper on top and then a weight (see Figure 4.9f). Let dry for 1 hour.

7. Remove the blotting paper and the pieces of spun polyester. Trim the strip of Japanese paper to the height of the textblock with a pair of embroidery scissors or a scalpel (see Figure 4.9g).

8. Place a piece of blotting paper on your worktable, then a piece of spun polyester on top. Situate the leaf and its attached hinge face-up so that hinge is on top of the spun polyester. Place sheet of waste paper on top, leaving the unpasted-out portion of the hinge exposed. Paste out this area. (See Figure 4.9h.)

Figure 4.9. Hinging in a Torn Leaf

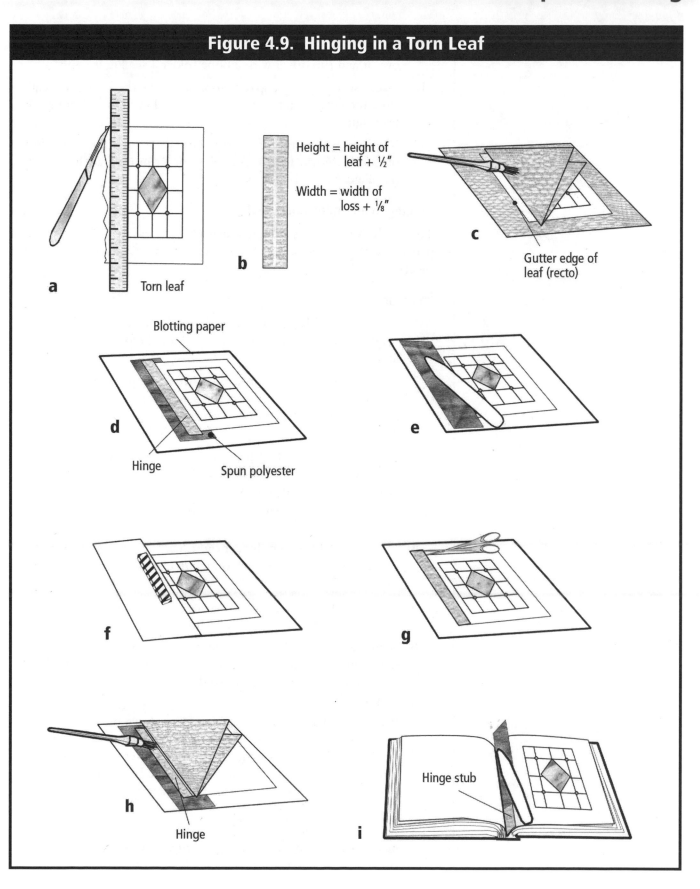

a Torn leaf

b Height = height of leaf + ½"

Width = width of loss + ⅛"

c Gutter edge of leaf (recto)

d Blotting paper / Hinge / Spun polyester

e

f

g

h Hinge

i Hinge stub

9. With the book held open to the right place, insert the hinge as far into the gutter as possible. Place a piece of spun polyester over it and rub down with a bone folder. (See Figure 4.9i.)

10. Places strips of wax paper before and after the tipped-in leaf, close the book, and place a weight on it. Let dry for 2 hours or overnight.

11. (Optional) If the tipped-in page extends beyond the fore-edge of the textblock, follow the steps for Trimming an Endsheet (see Figure 5.9a–b, p. 119).

Hinging in an Undamaged Leaf

This method may be used to reattach a single leaf or a folded sheet of paper into the textblock. It is also a simple way of attaching new end-sheets.

Procedure

1. Cut a strip of Japanese paper that is ½ inch higher than the height of the textblock and ¾ inch wide. Fold this strip in half lengthwise. (See Figure 4.10b.)

2. Place the leaf face-up on a sheet of waste paper (see Figure 4.10a). Place another sheet of waste paper on top, leaving a 3/8 inch margin exposed. Paste out this area. (See Figure 4.10c.)

3. Place a piece of blotting paper on your worktable, then a piece of spun polyester on top. Situate the leaf so that its pasted-out edge is on the spun polyester. Carefully put down the strip of Japanese paper so that it is 3/8 inch over the pasted-out edge. (See Figure 4.10d.)

4. Place a piece of spun polyester on top of the Japanese paper and rub down the pasted-out portion with a bone folder (see Figure 4.10e).

5. Place another piece of blotting paper on top and then a weight (see Figure 4.10f). Let dry for 1 hour.

6. Remove the blotting paper, the pieces of spun polyester, and the weight. Trim the strip of Japanese paper to the height of the textblock with a pair of embroidery scissors or a scalpel (see Figure 4.10g).

7. Place the leaf and its attached hinge face-down on a clean sheet of waste paper. Place a strip of wax paper up against the hinge edge of the leaf and a strip of spun polyester on top of that. Bend the free part of the hinge onto the top spun polyester. Crease the hinge with a bone folder. Paste out the hinge. (See Figure 4.10h.)

8. Remove the spun polyester but leave the wax paper. Insert a piece of barrier board (or a metal ruler) between the leaf and the wax paper. With the book held open to the right place,

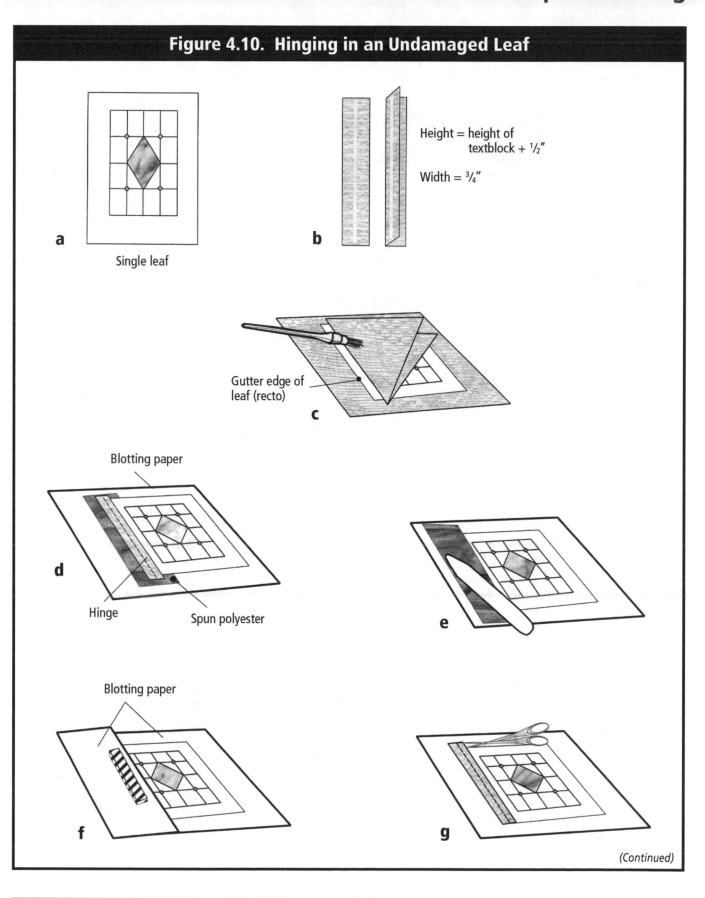

Figure 4.10. Hinging in an Undamaged Leaf

a — Single leaf

b — Height = height of textblock + ½″

Width = ¾″

c — Gutter edge of leaf (recto)

d — Blotting paper, Hinge, Spun polyester

e

f — Blotting paper

g

(Continued)

Figure 4.10. Hinging in an Undamaged Leaf (Continued)

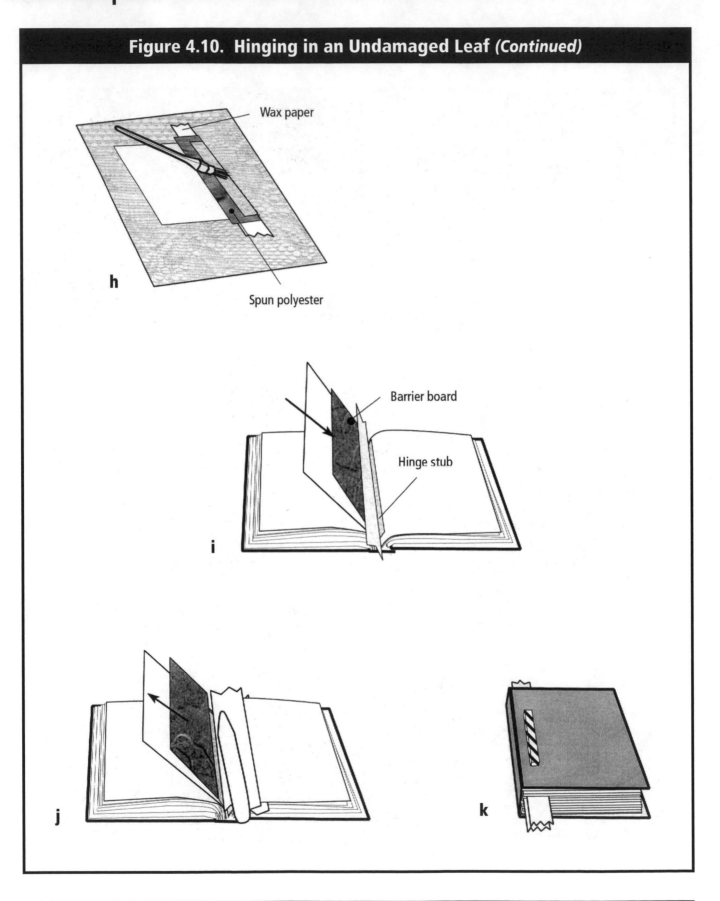

h — Wax paper / Spun polyester

i — Barrier board / Hinge stub

j

k

insert the hinge as far into the gutter as possible, using the board or ruler to help guide you and give you added "push." (See Figure 4.10i.)

9. Place a strip of wax paper behind the leaf the hinge is attached to and turn the other wax paper strip over onto the hinge. Smooth down the hinge with a bone folder. Remove the board or ruler. (See Figure 4.10j.)

10. Close the book, and place a weight on it (see Figure 4.10k). Let dry for 2 hours or overnight.

11. (Optional) If the tipped-in leaf extends beyond the fore-edge of the textblock, follow the steps for Trimming an Endsheet (see Figure 5.9a–b, p. 119).

Hinging in a Group of Consecutive Leaves

This technique is a combination of the simple tipping-in of single leaves and the hinging-in of single leaves.

Procedure

1. Cut a strip of medium-weight Japanese paper ½ inch higher than the textblock and 1 inch wide (see Figure 4.11b).

2. On a clean sheet of waste paper, put down the first leaf you want to attach, face-down, and then put the second on top of that, leaving a ⅛-inch margin exposed. Continue until all the leaves are thus laid down. Paste out these margins. (See Figure 4.11a and c.)

3. Stack them immediately to form a block of leaves. Put another piece of waste paper on top and rub down with a bone folder. (See Figure 4.11d.)

4. Place a board on top and then weights on top of that (see Figure 4.11e). Let dry for 1 hour.

5. Turn the stack of leaves over onto a clean waste sheet with a strip of spun polyester beneath the gutter edge. Paste out a ¼-inch strip along the gutter edge. Carefully place the strip of Japanese paper so that a ¼ inch rests on the pasted-out edge. Place a piece of spun polyester over this and smooth down with a bone folder. (See Figure 4.11f.) Place a board and weight on top and let dry for several minutes. Trim off the hinge to the height of the textblock with embroidery scissors or a scalpel.

6. Turn the stack of leaves over again onto a clean waste sheet and strip of spun polyester. Place a strip of wax paper on top at the gutter edge. Paste out the Japanese paper hinge. (See Figure 4.11g.)

7. Put another strip of spun polyester on top of the wax paper and another strip of wax paper on top of that. Place your bone folder underneath the bottom strip of spun polyester and bring

Figure 4.11. Hinging in Consecutive Leaves

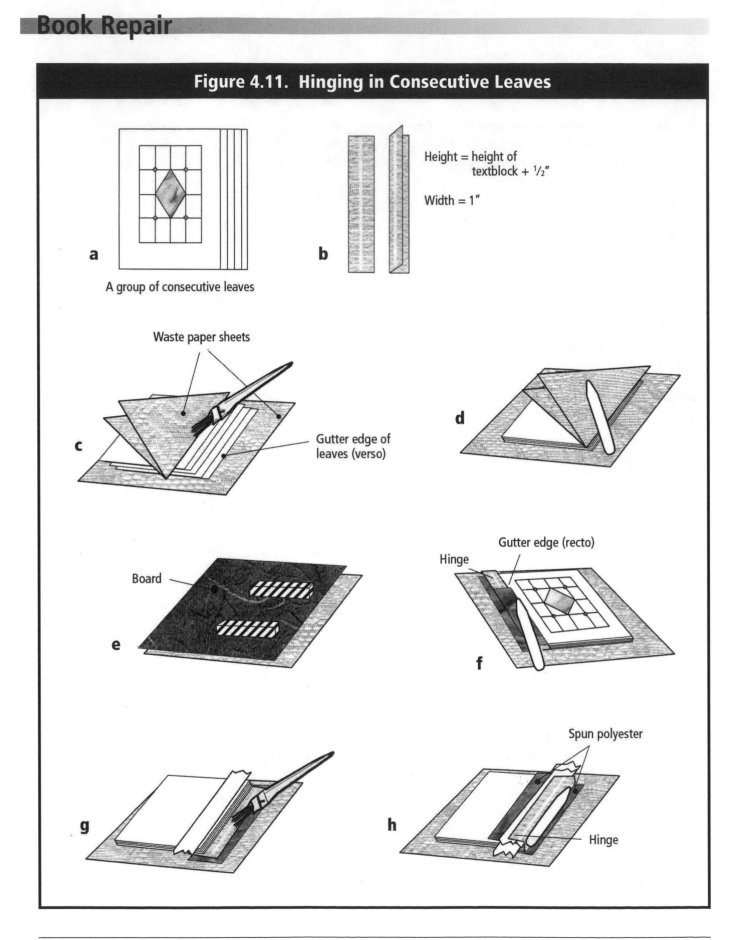

a — A group of consecutive leaves

b — Height = height of textblock + ½"
Width = 1"

c — Waste paper sheets / Gutter edge of leaves (verso)

d

e — Board

f — Hinge / Gutter edge (recto)

g

h — Spun polyester / Hinge

the hinge up to the edge of the stack of leaves. Rub with a bone folder to adhere the hinge to the edges of the stack. Fold the hinge over onto the top strip of wax paper with a bone folder. (See Figure 4.11h.)

8. Remove the top strips of wax paper and spun polyester.

9. To insert the leaves into the book, follow steps 8–11 of Hinging in an Undamaged Leaf.

Hinging in Individual Sections

Frequently the sections or gatherings at the front and back of a book come loose and need to be reattached. If the section is a simple folio (i.e., a sheet folded once), it may be reattached with the technique for hinging in single leaves. If the section is made up of several leaves, however, they must be sewn together first and then hinged into the book.

Supplies

Linen binder's thread (18/3)
Needle (e.g., candlewicking)
Rice or wheat starch paste, or a 50/50 mixture of paste and PVA
Medium-weight Japanese paper
Blotting paper
Spun polyester
Wax paper
Barrier board or a straightedge
Paste brush
Bone folder

Procedure

1. Cut strip of Japanese paper as long as the height of the textblock and 2 inches wide. Fold this in half. (See Figure 4.12a.)

2. Place the folded sheets of the section inside each other in their proper order.

3. Place the outside fold of the section into the crease of the Japanese paper strip. This must be held in place while the section is sewn.

4. Sew the section as you would a pamphlet, making sure that the sewing goes through the Japanese paper hinge (see Figure 4.12b).

5. It is important that the sewing be as taut as possible and that the tie-off knot be close to the center hole.

6. The finished section will have the sewing on the inside fold of the inner folio and on the outside of the hinge (see Figure 4.12c).

7. Place a strip of wax paper and a strip of spun polyester between the hinge and the paper. This needs to be done on both sides. Paste out the hinges onto the spun polyester. (See Figure 4.12d.)

Figure 4.12. Hinging in an Individual Section

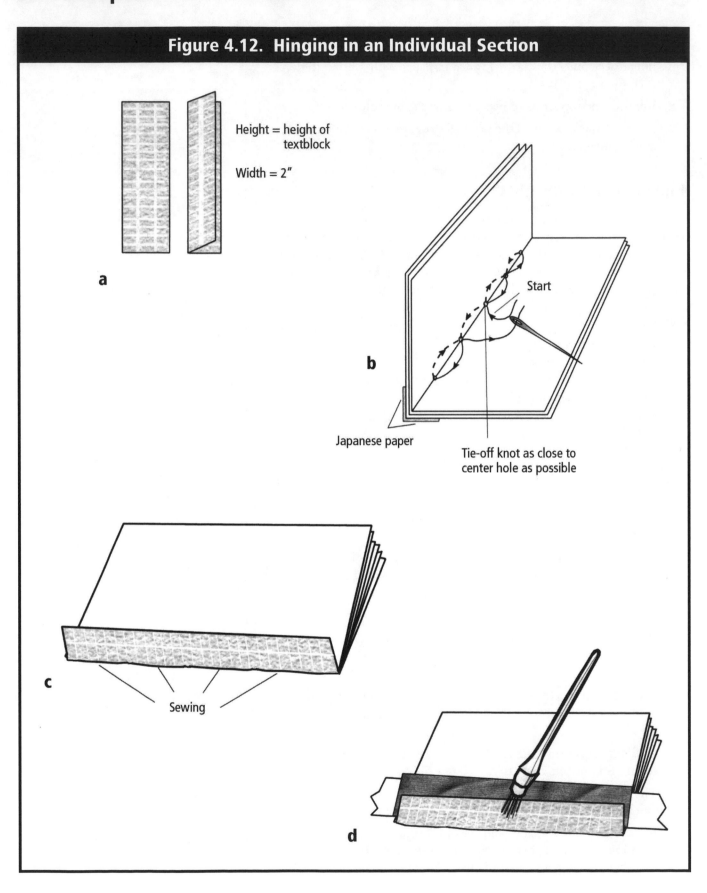

Height = height of textblock

Width = 2″

a

Start

Japanese paper

Tie-off knot as close to center hole as possible

b

Sewing

c

d

8. To insert the section into the book, follow steps 8–11 of Hinging in an Undamaged Leaf.

Lining or Backing

Lining or backing refers to the attachment of a support piece to the back of a single sheet. This technique is best used on single-sheet objects, such as documents and maps, or on single leaves that have become detached from books. Lining may be done as a prelude to encapsulation or as an end in itself. If lining is done on both sides of a sheet, it is called "lamination."

Methods of lining or backing are generally divided into two broad categories. The *dry* method includes heat-set tissue and, perhaps confusingly, Japanese paper and starch paste. The *wet* method involves the submersion of the object in a water bath prior to the application of a backing. The latter is a delicate and potentially damaging process and is best left in the hands of a trained conservator.

The two types of lining material most useful for paper objects are heat-set tissue and Japanese paper. The first is particularly important for backing objects that would be adversely affected by the application of water. This would include prints on clay-coated paper or water-colored works such as maps. It has the added advantage that, unlike a Japanese paper lining, it can be made transparent enough to be read through. Its greatest disadvantage is that it is difficult to reverse, although it is possible to do so with mineral spirits. Japanese paper and starch paste are the preferred method of backing paper objects because of their archival quality and the ease of reversing the process with water. However, the effects of water on the particular paper or image are of foremost concern when considering this type of lining. Thorough testing of the paper and all other media must be done before attempting a lining method that uses water. (See "Testing Methods," Chapter 1.)

Decisions

Type of media and paper
Condition of paper
Number of sides with image or print
Size of object

Lining with Heat-Set Tissue

Supplies

Heat-set tissue
Tacking iron
Polyester film
Spun polyester
Barrier board
Straightedge
X-Acto or Olfa knife or scalpel

Lining a Document

1. Clean, mend, and deacidify the document if appropriate.

2. Heat the tacking iron to medium.

3. Cut a piece of heat-set tissue 1 inch taller and 1 inch wider than your document (see Figure 4.13a–b).

4. Cut a piece of spun polyester 2 inches taller and 2 inches wider than your document (see Figure 4.13c).

5. Turn your document face-down in the middle of the spun polyester (see Figure 4.13d).

6. Center the piece of heat-set tissue (shiny side down) over the document and place a weight on top of it. Cut a strip of spun polyester as long as the document and about 4 inches wide. Rub the tacking iron across the strip to adhere the tissue to the back of the object. Continue down the object, repositioning the weight when needed. (See Figure 4.13e.) If there is difficulty with the tissue adhering to the paper, either turn up the temperature on the tacking iron or remove the spun polyester and iron directly on the tissue. When the heat-set tissue is almost invisible, it should be firmly adhered to the paper.

7. (Optional) If the document is too large to be effectively handled with a single piece of tissue, cut the tissue into wide strips and proceed as above, remembering to reposition the weight each time to keep the tissue in place.

8. Remove the lined document from the spun polyester. If the tissue sticks to the polyester along its exposed sides, gently separate it with a bone folder (see Figure 4.13f).

9. Turn the lined document over onto a board. Place a ruler at the very top of one of the edges, being sure to include any protruding bits of paper, such as those found on deckled edges. Cut away the excess tissue with a scalpel. (See Figure 4.13g.) Repeat for each edge of the document.

10. The finished document may be stored in a folder or may be encapsulated for further protection (see Figure 4.13h).

11. (Optional) If the heat-set tissue covers up any image or text, spread a thin layer of ethanol over the tissue with a cotton swab. After it dries, the tissue should be transparent enough to read through.

Lining a Badly Torn Object

Sometimes an object, such as a map, has broken or been torn into several pieces. The best treatment for such an object is encapsulation, but lining the object beforehand enables it to be handled more easily and safely. With the following method, static electricity is used to hold the pieces of the object in place. Thus, it is important that the object has no surface media, such as graphite, charcoal, or pastels.

Figure 4.13. Lining a Document with Heat-Set Tissue

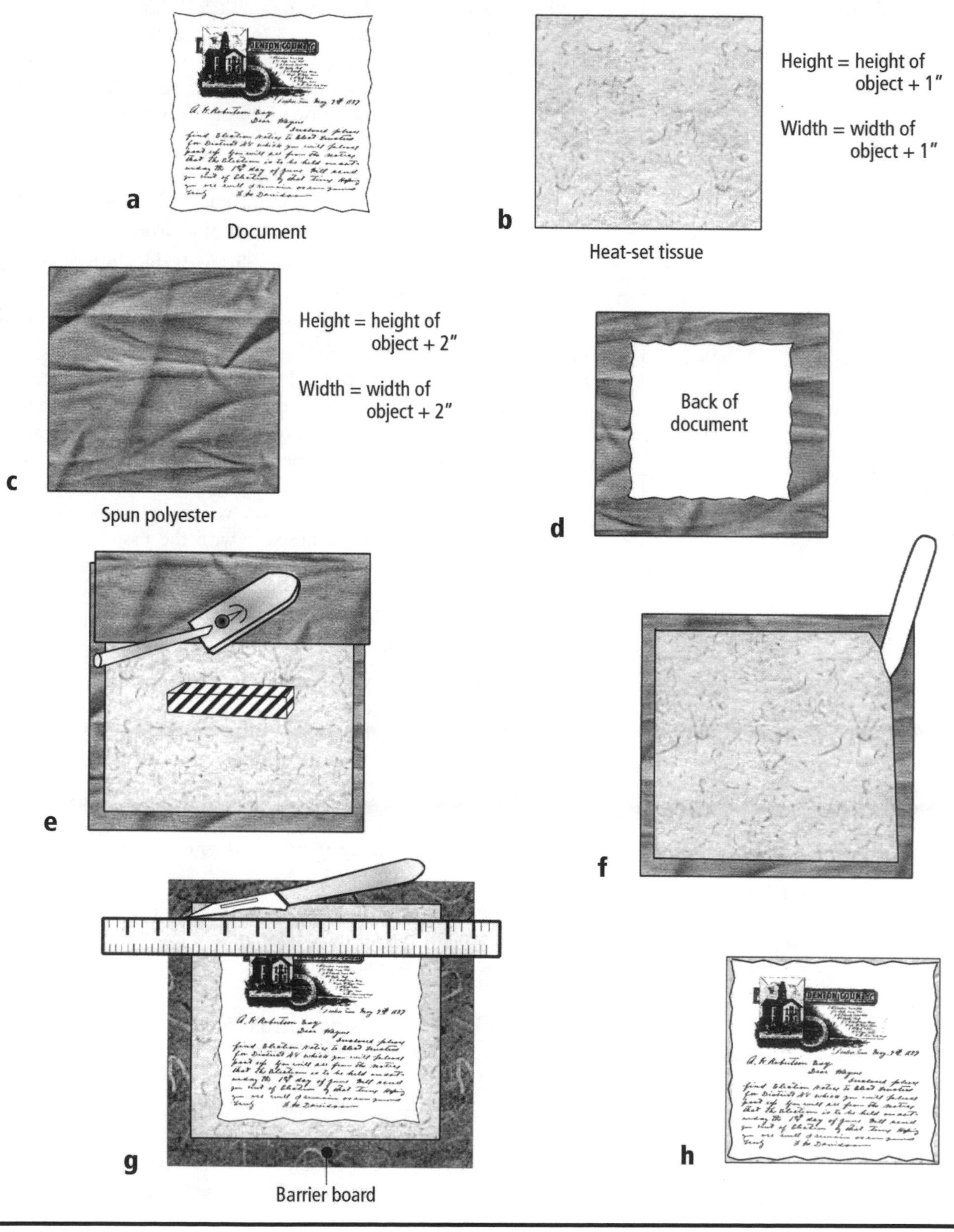

a

Document

b

Heat-set tissue

Height = height of object + 1"

Width = width of object + 1"

c

Spun polyester

Height = height of object + 2"

Width = width of object + 2"

d

Back of document

e

f

g

Barrier board

h

Procedure

1. Clean and deacidify the object if appropriate. Turn it upside down on your worktable. (See Figure 4.14a.)

2. Cut a piece of polyester film (3 mil or heavier) that is 2 inches taller and wider than your object will be when it is assembled. Rub the top left section with a dust-free cloth. This will generate static electricity on the polyester film. (See Figure 4.14b.)

3. Place the upper left-hand piece onto the polyester film 2 inches away from the top and left-hand edge (see Figure 4.14c). Remember that the pieces must be upside down.

4. Rub a contiguous section of the film with the cloth, and place the appropriate piece on it. Continue rubbing with the cloth and placing the pieces until the entire object has been correctly situated. (See Figure 4.14d.)

5. Cut a piece of heat-set tissue 1 inch wider and 1 inch taller than the completed object. Center the tissue on the object and place weights on top. Cut a strip of spun polyester as long as the object and about 4 inches wide. Rub the tacking iron across the strip to adhere the tissue to the back of the object. Continue down the object, repositioning the weight when needed. (See Figure 4.14e.) If there is difficulty with the tissue adhering to the paper, either turn up the temperature on the tacking iron or remove the spun polyester and iron directly on the tissue. When the heat-set tissue is almost invisible, it should be firmly adhered to the paper.

6. (Optional) If the document is too large to be effectively handled with a single piece of tissue, cut the tissue into wide strips and proceed as above, remembering to reposition the weight each time to keep the tissue in place.

7. Turn the lined object over and gently pull the polyester film off. If the film sticks to the heat-set tissue along its exposed sides, gently separate it with a bone folder (see Figure 4.14f).

8. Turn the lined object back over onto a board. Place a ruler at the very top of one of the edges and cut away the excess tissue with a scalpel (see Figure 4.14g). Repeat for each edge of the object.

9. The finished object may be stored in a folder or may be encapsulated for further protection. This treatment may be particularly needed if there are large gaps remaining after the object has been pieced together (see Figure 4.14h).

10. (Optional) If the heat-set tissue covers up any image or text, spread a thin layer of ethanol over the tissue with a cotton swab. After it dries, the tissue should be transparent enough to read through.

Figure 4.14. Lining a Badly Torn Document with Heat-Set Tissue

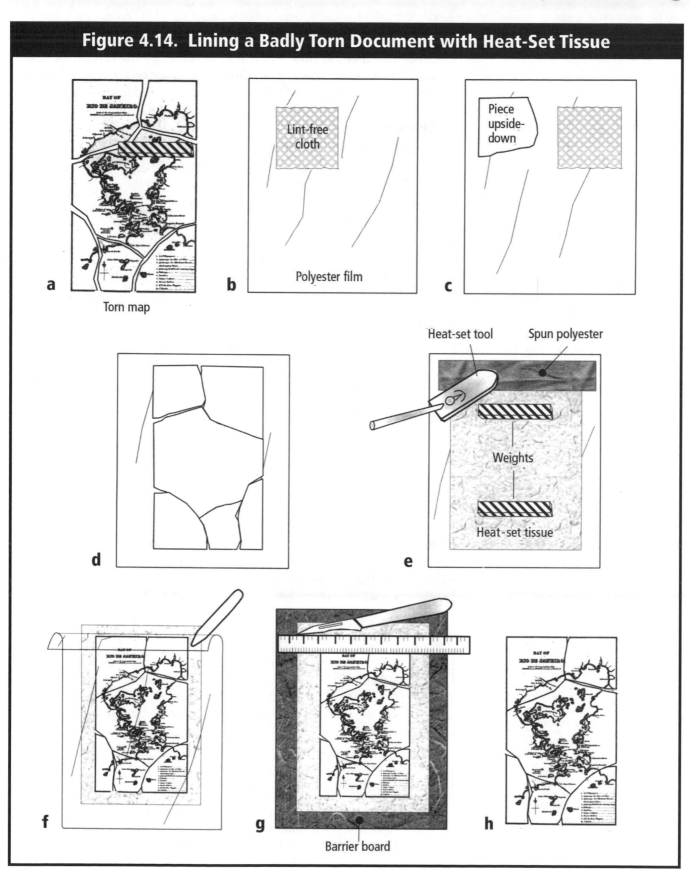

a — Torn map

b — Lint-free cloth / Polyester film

c — Piece upside-down

d

e — Heat-set tool / Spun polyester / Weights / Heat-set tissue

f

g — Barrier board

h

Lining with Japanese Paper

Since this method uses water, the object to be lined must be tested beforehand (see "Testing Methods" in Chapter 1.) If you have any doubts after testing, use the heat-set tissue method instead.

Supplies

Rice or wheat starch paste
Medium-weight Japanese paper (e.g., Sekishu)
Polyester film (3 mil or heavier)
Spun polyester
Blotting paper
Barrier board
Paste brush
Straightedge
X-Acto or Olfa knife or scalpel

Procedure

1. Clean, mend, or deacidify the object if appropriate (see Figure 4.15a).

2. Make a thin smooth paste from rice or wheat starch. It must be able to be spread easily and evenly.

3. Cut two pieces of polyester film 2 inches wider and 2 inches taller than the object to be lined (see Figure 4.15b).

4. Cut a piece of Japanese paper 1 inch wider and 1 inch taller than the object to be lined (see Figure 4.15c). The grain of the Japanese paper must run the same direction as that of the object (see "Grain" in Chapter 1 for determining the grain of Japanese paper).

5. Turn the object face-down on the piece of polyester film. Paste out the back of the object starting from the center and radiating outward over the edges. (See Figure 4.15d.)

6. Place the piece of Japanese paper on the other piece of polyester film. Paste out as in step 5. (See Figure 4.15e.)

7. Lift the polyester film under the Japanese paper liner (it should adhere to the film) and turn the package over onto the pasted-out back of the object, carefully positioning it so that the liner covers the entire object. There should be a 1-inch border around the object.

8. Carefully peel the top piece of polyester film off of the liner. If the liner should start to lift up with the film, hold it down with a bone folder. (See Figure 4.15f.)

9. Place a piece of spun polyester on top of the Japanese paper liner and put a weight on it. With a bone folder, smooth down the polyester over the liner, repositioning the weight as necessary. Be as smooth and even as possible, since this action helps

Figure 4.15. Lining a Document with Japanese Paper and Starch Paste

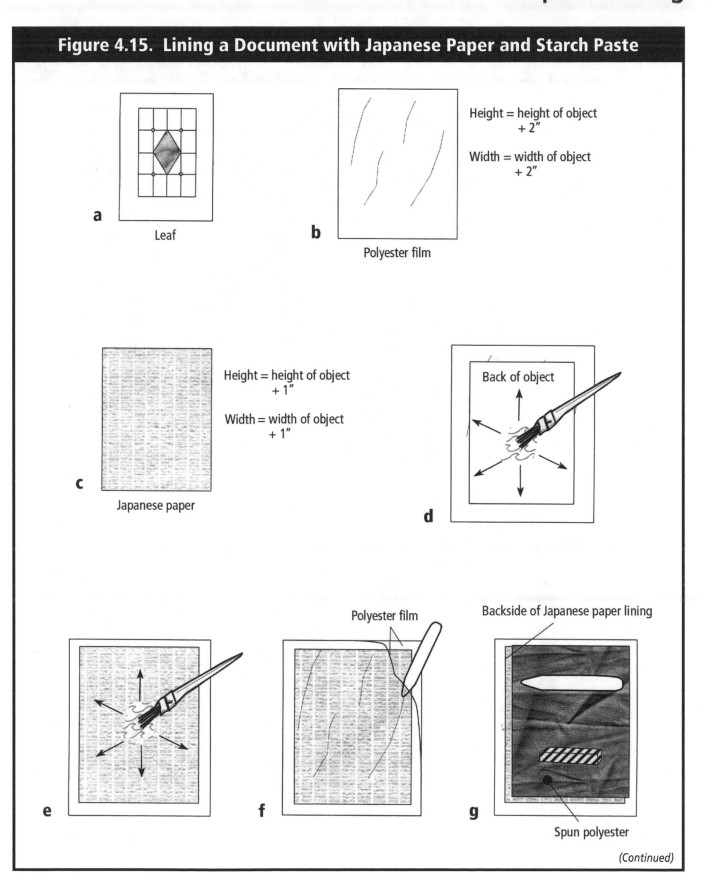

a Leaf

b Polyester film

Height = height of object
+ 2″

Width = width of object
+ 2″

c Japanese paper

Height = height of object
+ 1″

Width = width of object
+ 1″

d Back of object

e

f Polyester film

g Backside of Japanese paper lining

Spun polyester

(Continued)

Figure 4.15. Lining a Document with Japanese Paper and Starch Paste *(Continued)*

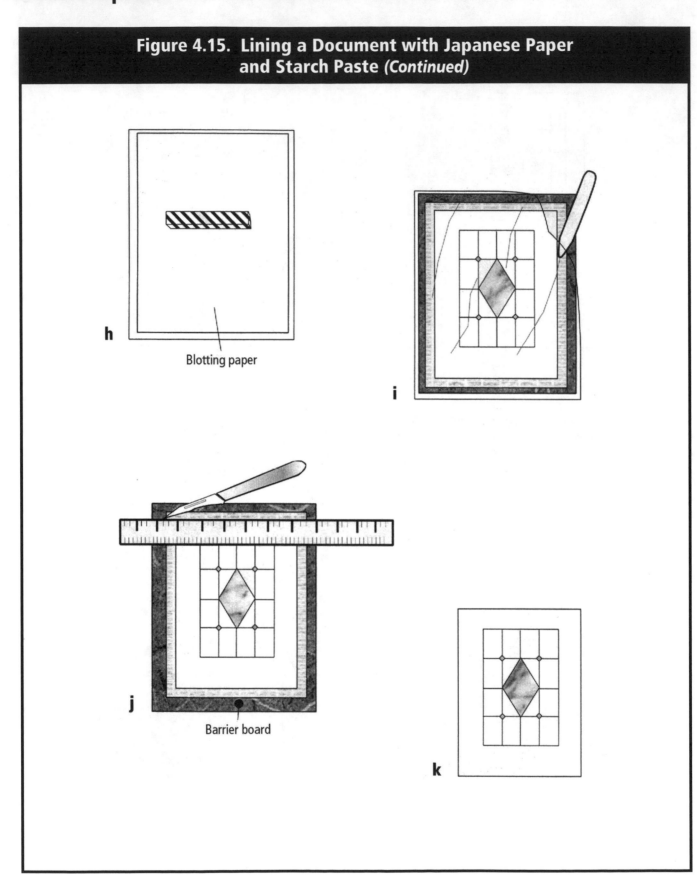

h

Blotting paper

i

j

Barrier board

k

adhere the pasted-out liner to the back of the object. (See Figure 4.15g.)

10. Place a piece of blotting paper on top and a weight on top of that (see Figure 4.15h). Allow to dry for 2 hours. After 1 hour replace the polyester and the blotting paper with clean dry pieces. Replace again if necessary.

11. When the lining is thoroughly dry, turn the package over and place it on a piece of barrier board. Remove the polyester film from the front of the object. Since you have pasted out beyond the borders of the object (see step 5), it is likely that the film will stick to the lining. Gently insert a bone folder between them to help separate the polyester film. (See Figure 4.15i.)

12. Place a ruler up against the top edge of the object and cut away the excess lining with a scalpel (see Figure 4.15j). Repeat for each side of the object.

13. The finished object may be stored in a folder or may be encapsulated for further protection (see Figure 4.15k).

Resources

Repairing Simple Tears

Glue and Paste Mends

Greenfield, Jane. *Books and Their Care*. New York: H.W. Wilson, 1983.
Schechter, Abraham. *Basic Book Repair Methods*. Littleton, CO: Libraries Unlimited, 1999.

Tape or Heat-Set Tissue

Morrow, Carolyn Clark, and Carole Dyal. *Conservation Treatment Procedures: A Manual of Step-by-Step Procedures for the Maintenance and Repair of Library Materials*. 2nd ed. Littleton, CO: Libraries Unlimited, 1986.
Schechter, Abraham. *Basic Book Repair Methods*. Littleton, CO: Libraries Unlimited, 1999.

Japanese Paper and Starch Paste

Greenfield, Jane. *Books and Their Care*. New York: H.W. Wilson, 1983. See pp. 77–79.
Kyle, Hedi. *Library Materials Preservation Manual*. New York: Nicholas T. Smith, 1983. See pp. 54–58.
Morrow, Carolyn Clark and Carole Dyal. *Conservation Treatment Procedures: A Manual of Step-by-Step Procedures for the Maintenance and Repair of Library Materials*. 2nd ed. Littleton, CO: Libraries Unlimited, 1986. See pp. 105–112.
Ritzenthaler, Mary Lynn. *Archives & Manuscripts: Conservation*. SAA Basic Manual Series. 2nd ed. Chicago: Society of American Archivists, 1993. See pp. 102–105.
Schechter, Abraham. *Basic Book Repair Methods*. Littleton, CO: Libraries Unlimited, 1999. See pp. 14–17.

Repairing Losses

Repairing Losses with Japanese Paper and Starch Paste

Greenfield, Jane. *Books and Their Care*. New York: H.W. Wilson, 1983. See "Filling in Lacunae," pp. 71–72 and 80–81.

Young, Laura S. *Bookbinding and Conservation of Books by Hand*. New Castle, DE: Oak Knoll Press, 1995. See pp. 60–62.

Tipping-In and Hinging-In Leaves and Sections

Greenfield, Jane. *Books and Their Care*. New York: H.W. Wilson, 1983. See pp. 91–103.

Kyle, Hedi. *Library Materials Preservation Manual*. New York: Nicholas T. Smith, 1983. See pp. 59–65.

Middleton, Bernard C. *The Restoration of Leather Bindings*. 3rd ed. New Castle, DE: Oak Knoll Press, 1998. See pp. 102–105.

Schechter, Abraham. *Basic Book Repair Methods*. Littleton, CO: Libraries Unlimited, 1999. See pp. 29–36.

Young, Laura S. *Bookbinding and Conservation of Books by Hand*. New Castle, DE: Oak Knoll Press, 1995. See pp. 55–56.

Backing and Lining Paper

Kyle, Hedi. *Library Materials Preservation Manual*. New York: Nicholas T. Smith, 1983. See pp. 66–70.

Young, Laura S. *Bookbinding and Conservation of Books by Hand*. New Castle, DE: Oak Knoll Press, 1995. See pp. 62–66.

Hinge and Spine Repair

The hinges and spines of books are particularly susceptible to damage from frequent use, careless handling, and even from book drops. Such treatment results in damage to both inner and outer hinges and to the spine itself. When this damage occurs in casebound books with cloth bindings, it can be repaired easily and inexpensively. This also has the advantage of retaining as much of the original binding as possible. Other book structures, such as the traditional hand-bound or the variety of side-sewn methods, are best left to a conservator or bindery because of their complexity.

Most library vendors offer a variety of materials for the repair of hinges and spines. These materials include items like rolls of buckram strips, which are very useful for replacing spines, and hinging tape in both single- and double-stitched versions. Because these tapes are made of a heavy tape and adhesive that will be attached to the paper of the textblock, however, they will eventually cause the paper to break along the edge of the tape. They are thus not recommended for books you wish to keep permanently in your collections.

This chapter is divided into four sections: (1) binding and sewing structures; (2) repair of casebound books; (3) reinforcement of paperbound books; and (4) reinforcement and binding of pamphlets.

Decisions

Specific Factors

Extent of damage to hinge(s) and spine
Type of binding and structure
Overall condition of binding
Importance of the original cover

A note about the figures: Figure 5.1a–e depict the most common sewing or adhesive structures found in casebound books. They are grouped together to help you better understand the structure of the

Figure 5.1. Sewing and Adhesive Structures

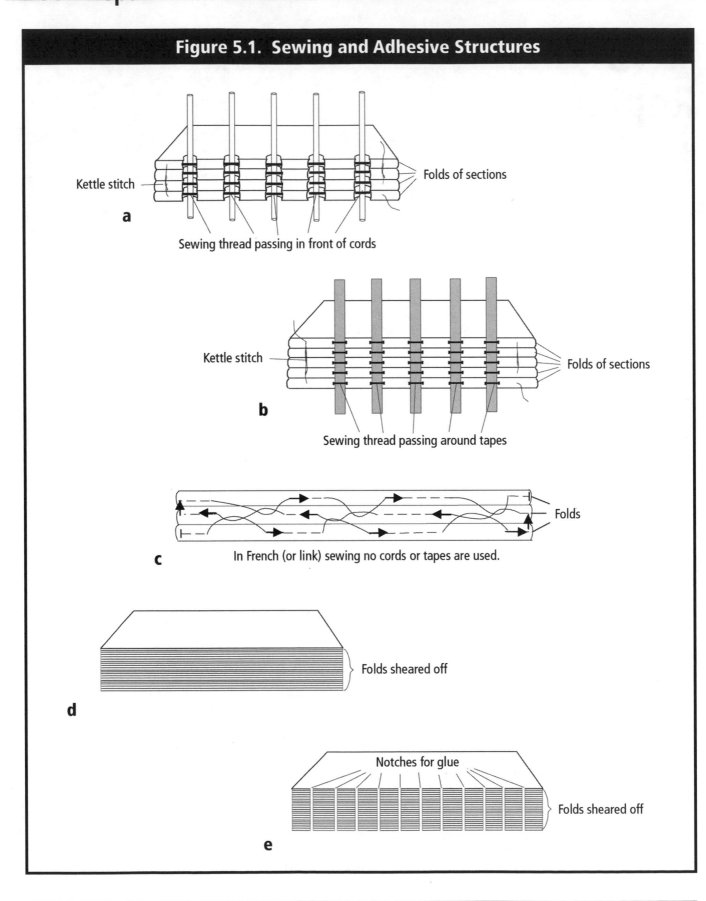

Kettle stitch — Folds of sections

a

Sewing thread passing in front of cords

Kettle stitch — Folds of sections

b

Sewing thread passing around tapes

Folds

In French (or link) sewing no cords or tapes are used.

c

Folds sheared off

d

Notches for glue

Folds sheared off

e

textblock. Figure 5.2a–g shows a diagram of the typical case cover and the methods of attachment of the individual sewing and adhesive structures. They are grouped together to help give you a better understanding of the most common hinging structures found in library books.

Binding and Sewing Structures

Most of the hardbound books in your library will have a case binding; that is, the two boards, the spine, and the covering material have been made as a single unit and then attached to the textblock (see Figure 5.2a). Most of these bindings utilize some type of book cloth for the cover, although both paper and leather have also been used. The paper and leather bindings should be left to a conservator or bindery, but the cloth-covered books can usually be repaired within the library.

Before beginning the actual repair of a casebound book, it is important to understand how the book has been put together. The first main consideration is whether the textblock is made up of gatherings with the folds intact or whether these folds have been sheared off to produce a "perfect" binding. Within the first category there are three primary methods by which the textblock can be sewn together and then attached to the case binding. With each of these, if the paper is still good, there is always the option of resewing the textblock to approximate or enhance its original structure. If the paper is brittle, however, the best treatment is a protective enclosure.

Recessed Cords

After the textblock has been gathered, collated, and folded, it is put into a clamp and vertical slits are sewed into the folds to contain the cords. The individual gatherings are then sewn to these cords (see Figure 5.1a). These ends of the cords are then usually frayed out and glued to the underside of each board, with the endpapers and super being laid down on top of them (see Figure 5.2b–c). The preservation problem most often encountered with this type of structure arises from the inherent weakness of the cords themselves. Because very thin cords had to be used to fit into the sewn slits, they deteriorate quickly at the hinges, particularly with thick or heavy books. In addition, it was usual to cut off two of the cords at the spine of the textblock, so the stress on the remaining three is even greater. If the cords have deteriorated all across the spine, the textblock will need to be reinforced or completely resewn.

Tapes

After the textblock sections have been gathered, collated, and folded, they are then sewn individually around these tapes (see Figure 5.1b). The ends of the tapes are then glued to the underside of each board, with the endpapers and super being laid down on top of them (see Figure 5.2d–e). Preservation problems occur when the tapes are no

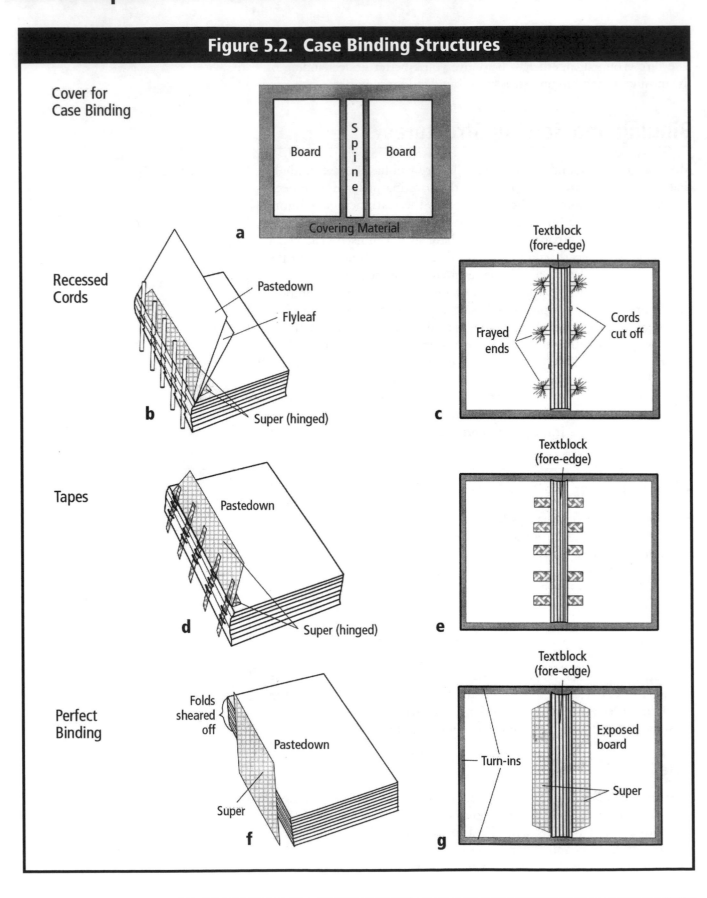

Figure 5.2. Case Binding Structures

Cover for Case Binding

Board | Spine | Board

Covering Material

a

Recessed Cords

Pastedown
Flyleaf
Super (hinged)

b

Textblock (fore-edge)
Frayed ends
Cords cut off

c

Tapes

Pastedown
Super (hinged)

d

Textblock (fore-edge)

e

Perfect Binding

Folds sheared off
Pastedown
Super

f

Textblock (fore-edge)
Turn-ins
Exposed board
Super

g

longer strong enough to act as hinges or they are no longer able to hold the sections of the book together. If the tapes have deteriorated all across the spine, the textblock will need to be reinforced or completely resewn.

French or Link Sewing

After the textblock sections have been gathered, collated and folded, they are then sewn together through a series of linked stitches (see Figure 5.1c). The threads are sewn into the endpapers, which act as the hinges of the book. Preservation problems usually arise because the thread has deteriorated and no longer holds the sections together. The textblock will need to be reinforced or completely resewn. A variant of this style of structure is created by the Smythe sewing machine and is used extensively in rebinding library books and periodicals.

Perfect Binding

Increasingly, hardbound books are actually "perfect bound"; that is, the folds of the sections are sheared off, the spine of the textblock glued up, the super affixed to the spine, and the textblock laid into the case. In many instances, however, there is actually no super at all; the textblock is simply glued up and attached to the case binding by reinforced endpapers (see Figure 5.1d–e and Figure 5.2f–g). This structure has all of the problems that are encountered with paperback books, particularly those of loose pages and broken spines, but because of its weight, it is, in addition, much more susceptible to torn hinges.

Repair of Casebound Books

The treatments needed to repair casebound books depend upon the extent of the damage and the structure of the sewing and case attachment. If the original paper or cloth is weak but still intact, then a reinforcement procedure may be adequate. If they are torn, however, then you will need to use a replacement treatment. The structure of the textblock and the method of attachment are also important in determining which procedures will give the best support to the book you are repairing.

Tightening Loose Hinges

This procedure is useful when the textblock is sagging in the boards, but the hinges have not torn away.

Supplies

PVA
Knitting needle
Glue brush
Bone folder
Wax paper

Procedure

1. Stand the book on the table with the boards spread wide enough to hold the book up. Gently pull the textblock away from the spine, but do not tear the hinges. (See Figure 5.3a.)

2. Dip the knitting needle into the glue bottle, being sure to coat the needle well.

3. Carefully avoiding the spine, insert the knitting needle into the gap between the loose endsheet and the board of the case (see Figure 5.3b). If both hinges are loose, repeat this process for the second hinge.

4. Close the book, lay it flat, and use the bone folder to smooth the outer hinges down in the joint (see Figure 5.3c). Turn the book over and repeat for the other hinge if necessary.

5. Place wax paper between the boards and the textblock and place the book under weights. A knitting needle can be placed in the outer groove of any hinge that was tightened to help keep it stable while it dries. Be sure, however, to use a clean knitting needle. (See Figure 5.3d.)

Replacing Endsheets

Often you will have books with tears in one or both endsheets along the inner hinge (see Figure 5.4). These books can be repaired by replacing the torn endsheets with new paper. Although endsheets are available in prefolded, precut sizes, it is cheaper and better to cut your own. Make sure, however, that the grain is parallel to the spine of the textblock. See Chapter 1 for more information regarding paper for endsheets.

Supplies

Paper for endsheets
PVA
Glue brush
Micro-spatula
Straightedge
X-Acto or Olfa knife or scalpel
Boards
Wax paper
Waste paper
Weights

Optional Supplies

Japanese paper (medium weight: Sekishu)
Rice or wheat starch paste
Sandpaper (220 grit)
Spun polyester

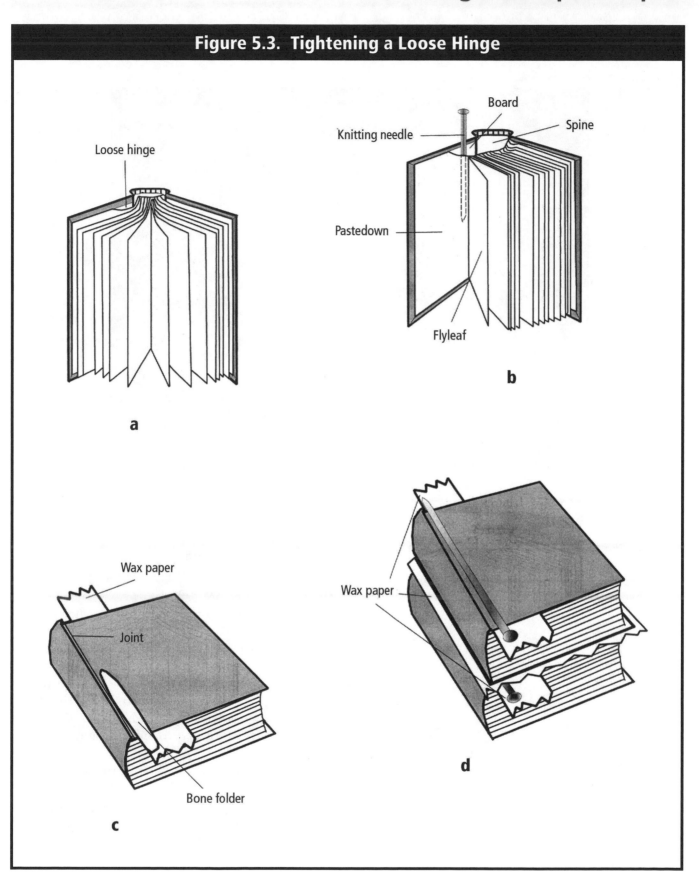

Figure 5.3. Tightening a Loose Hinge

a

b

Loose hinge

Knitting needle

Board

Spine

Pastedown

Flyleaf

Wax paper

Joint

Bone folder

c

Wax paper

d

Figure 5.4. Torn Endsheet

Book with a torn endsheet.

Procedure

1. Remove the torn endsheet by gently pulling the tipped-in fly leaf away from the textblock, being careful not to tear the page to which it is attached (see Figure 5.5a).

2. (Optional) If the original pastedown is partially detached from the board, you can remove it by gently peeling the attached portion of the pastedown away from the board with a rounded scalpel or micro-spatula, being careful not to damage the super. Making shallow 1-inch cuts along the edge of the turn-ins (see Figure 5.5b) will help you to start pulling up the pastedown. If the pastedown is difficult to remove after this, make shallow cuts along the edges of the turn-ins around the entire board. After the pastedown has been pulled off, remove any scraps of endsheet still attached to the board with a micro-spatula (see Figure 5.5c).

3. Lay the book on the table, open one cover, and place enough plywood or other boards under the open cover to support it.

4. (Optional) Sand the inside of the board to provide a smooth surface for the new endsheet.

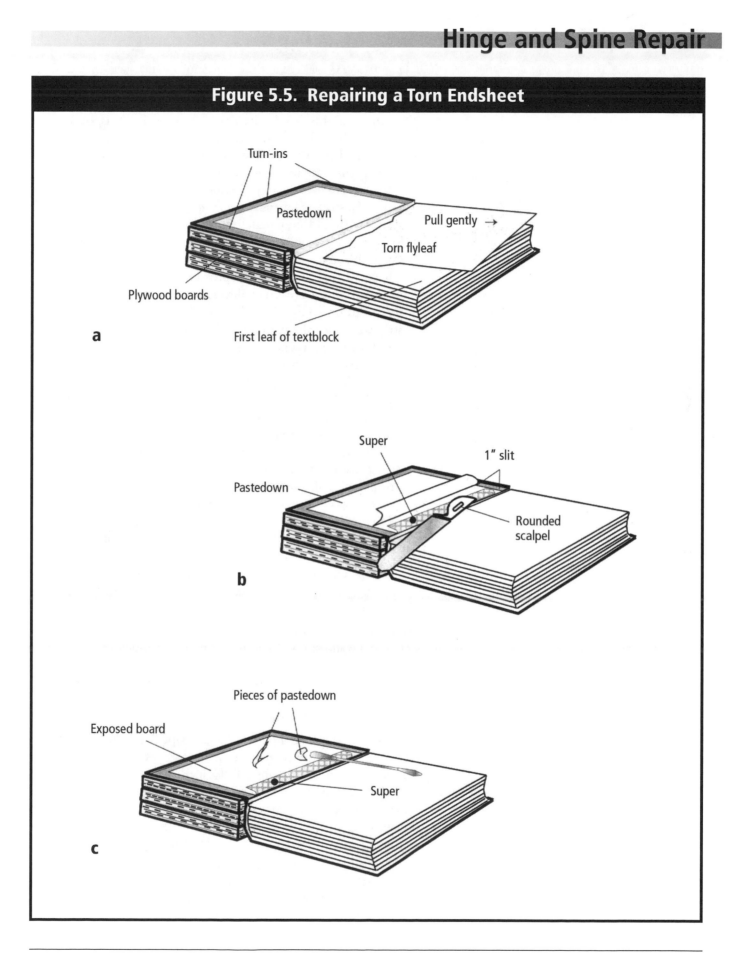

Figure 5.5. Repairing a Torn Endsheet

a

Turn-ins

Pastedown

Pull gently →

Torn flyleaf

Plywood boards

First leaf of textblock

b

Super

1″ slit

Pastedown

Rounded scalpel

c

Pieces of pastedown

Exposed board

Super

5. If the other endsheet needs to be replaced as well, repeat this process. When both boards are ready, continue with step 6 or 7.

6. (Optional) If this book circulates frequently, it is best to strengthen the fold of the endsheets with Japanese paper (a process called *guarding*). This is not necessary, however, for books that circulate infrequently. If extra strength is desired in the endsheet, follow the steps below:

    a. Tear off a strip of Japanese paper approximately 1 inch wide. The tear should be parallel to the chain lines of the paper. Methods of tearing Japanese paper are discussed in Chapter 1.

    b. Paste the strip with starch paste, as described below (see Chapter 1 for paste recipe). Spread paste evenly over a piece of wax paper or polyester film. Lay the mending strip in the paste and brush lightly with a thin layer of paste. Allow the strip to absorb the paste (it will change color as it does so). Gently lift the mending strip out of the paste using the micro-spatula or tweezers. (See Figure 5.6a–d.) Do not lift too quickly or the strip will stretch, causing the mend to wrinkle as it dries. If less moisture is desired on the mending strip, place it between a "sandwich" of blotting paper and spun polyester (see Figure 5.6e) and rub with a bone folder.

    c. Lay the strip on a piece of wax paper or spun polyester, and then place the fold of the endsheet along the center of the strip, tapping it into place (see Figure 5.6f).

    d. Pull the wax paper or spun polyester up and around the fold of the endsheet, pressing gently along the fold (see Figure 5.6g). This will fold the strip of Japanese paper around the fold of the endsheet.

    e. Place the endsheets between the sheets of spun polyester and blotting paper, and then place the endsheets under weights and allow to dry (see Figure 5.6h).

7. Trim the endsheets to the height of the textblock, using the straightedge and scalpel. This is accomplished much more easily *before* the endsheet is attached to the textblock rather than afterward. Because it is easy to forget this step, however, an illustration is included for trimming the endsheet *after* it has been attached (see Figure 5.9b).

8. Place the endsheet on a piece of waste paper or scrap polyester film. Then place another piece of waste paper on top of the endsheet, leaving approximately ⅛ inch of the folded edge of the endsheet extending beyond the top piece of waste paper. Carefully spread glue along the exposed edge of the endsheet, brushing from the top waste sheet over the exposed edge of endsheet onto the bottom waste sheet. (See Figure 5.7a.)

9. Being careful to align the edges of the endsheet with the edges of the textblock, place the endsheet on the textblock, glued side down, and gently push the folded edge into the curve of the shoulder with a bone folder (see Figure 5.7b).

Figure 5.6. Making a Guard for an Endsheet

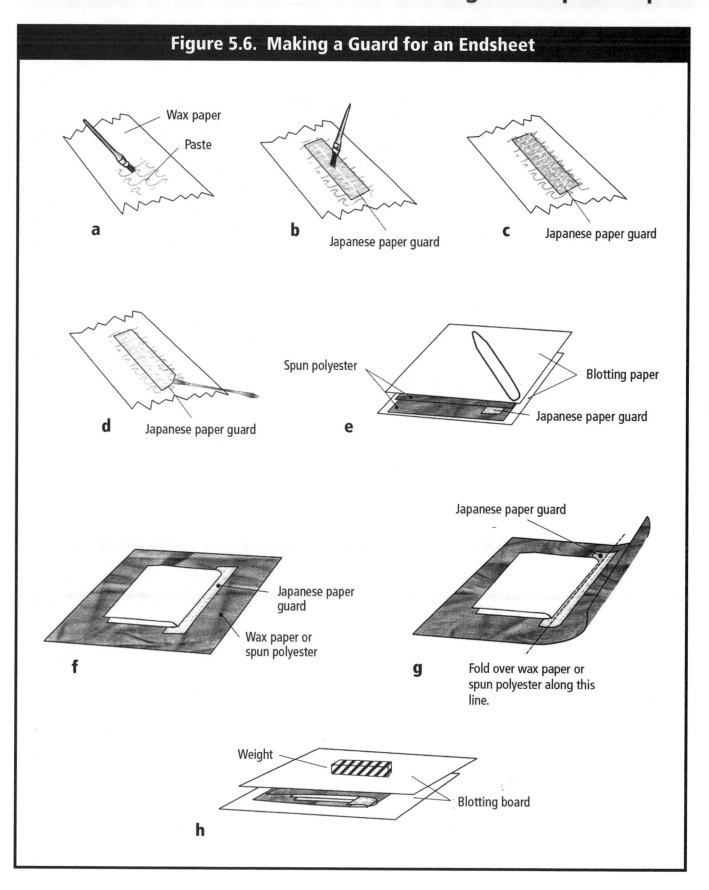

a — Wax paper / Paste

b — Japanese paper guard

c — Japanese paper guard

d — Japanese paper guard

e — Spun polyester / Blotting paper / Japanese paper guard

f — Japanese paper guard / Wax paper or spun polyester

g — Japanese paper guard / Fold over wax paper or spun polyester along this line.

h — Weight / Blotting board

Figure 5.7. Tipping in an Endsheet

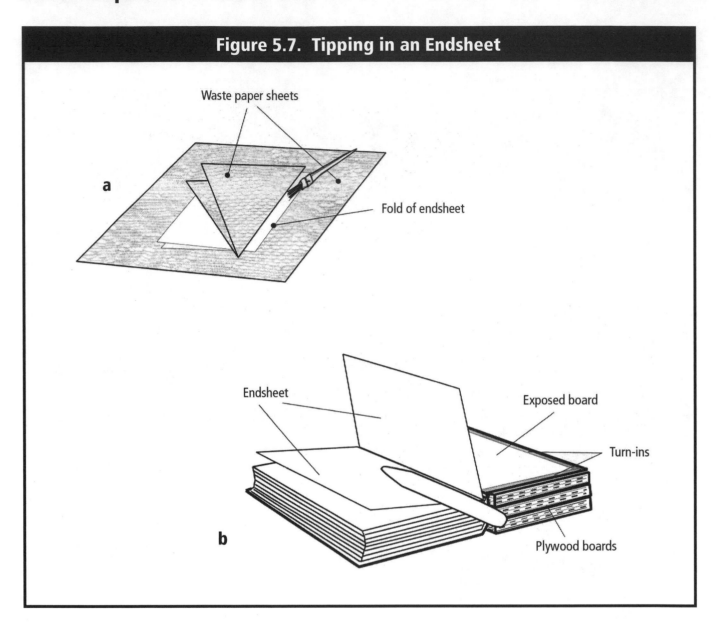

Waste paper sheets

a

Fold of endsheet

Endsheet

Exposed board

Turn-ins

b

Plywood boards

10. Place a strip of wax paper between the endsheets, close the cover, and gently rub the outer hinge with the bone folder (see Figure 5.3c for example).

11. (Optional) For greater flexibility and strength, a hinge of Japanese paper may be attached to the fold of the endsheet.

   a. Tear off a strip of Japanese paper approximately 1 inch wide. The tear should be parallel to the chain lines of the paper. Make a crease in the middle of the strip lengthwise.

   b. Brush out a thin layer of paste on a piece of wax paper. Lay half of this hinging strip on the paste and rub lightly with a bone folder. Then brush out with a thin layer of paste. (See Figure 5.8a–b.)

   c. Gently lift the hinging strip out of the paste using the micro-spatula or tweezers. Do not lift too quickly or the strip will stretch, which will cause the hinge to wrinkle as it dries. If less moisture is desired on the hinging strip, place it between a "sandwich" of blotting paper and spun polyester, and rub with a bone folder.

d. Place the hinging strip on a piece of spun polyester and line up the fold of the endsheet with the crease in the hinge. Smooth down with a bone folder to adhere the Japanese paper to the endsheet. (See Figure 5.8c.)

e. Dry between sheets of spun polyester and blotting paper under a weight (see Figure 5.6h).

f. After the hinge has dried, trim the endsheet to the height of the textblock. This step is accomplished much more easily *before* the endsheet has been attached to the textblock. Because it is easy to forget this step, however, an illustration is included for trimming the endsheet *after* it has been attached (see Figure 5.9b).

g. Unfold the hinging strip and apply a thin layer of paste to the free half of the strip (see Figure 5.8d).

h. Being careful to align the edges of the endsheet with the edges of the textblock, push the pasted hinge into the curve of the shoulder and, with a bone folder, attach the hinge to the textblock (see Figure 5.8e).

i. Place a strip of wax paper between the hinge and the endsheet, close the cover, and gently rub the outer hinge with the bone folder.

12. Trim the fore-edge of the endsheet to the size of the textblock. To do this, lay the book on the table with the repaired side down. Place a piece of scrap board between the endsheet and the cover. Place the ruler between the endsheet and the textblock, lining up the ruler's edge and the textblock's fore-edge. Then cut along the edge of the ruler with the knife. (See Figure 5.9a.)

13. Turn the book over so that the repaired side is up. Open the cover and support it with plywood boards. Place a piece of waste paper or scrap polyester film inside the folded endsheet. Then, starting in the center of the page near the folded edge, carefully spread glue over the endsheet. (See Figure 5.10a.) Some conservators prefer to dilute the glue with water for this process. The usual mixture is 3 parts glue to 1 part water.

14. Gently lift the glued endsheet just enough to replace the waste paper and make sure the fold of the endsheet is completely down in the hinge of the book. Then lay the endsheet back down and close the cover of the book, pressing gently to adhere the endsheet to the cover. Again, gently rub the outer hinge with the bone folder. (See Figure 5.10b.)

15. Open the cover, and remove the waste paper. The endsheet should be attached to the board. Supporting the cover with plywood boards, smooth the endsheet by covering it with a fresh

Figure 5.8. Hinging in an Endsheet

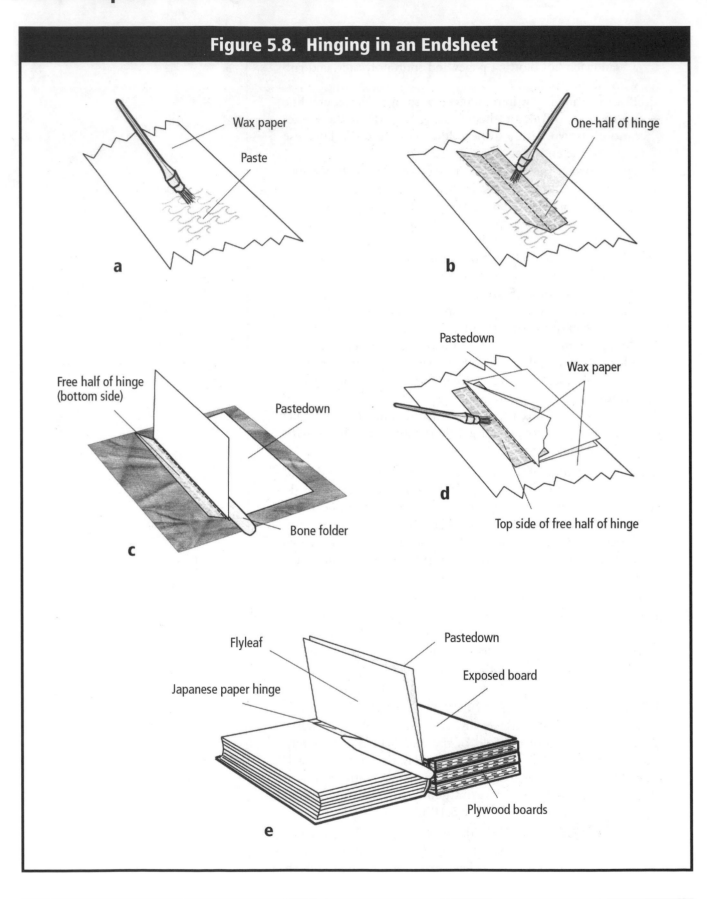

a — Wax paper / Paste

b — One-half of hinge

c — Free half of hinge (bottom side) / Pastedown / Bone folder

d — Pastedown / Wax paper / Top side of free half of hinge

e — Flyleaf / Pastedown / Exposed board / Japanese paper hinge / Plywood boards

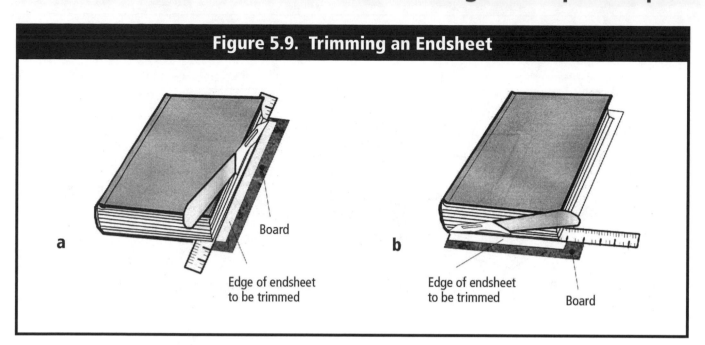

Figure 5.9. Trimming an Endsheet

a — Board / Edge of endsheet to be trimmed

b — Edge of endsheet to be trimmed / Board

piece of waste paper or scrap spun polyester and rubbing it with the bone folder through this protective layer. When the endsheet is smooth, remove the waste paper or spun polyester. (See Figure 5.10c.)

16. Place wax paper inside the fold of the new endsheet and place the book in a book press or under weights, with a knitting needle in the groove of any outer hinges that were repaired (see Figure 5.10d).

17. If the other endsheet is being replaced also, repeat steps 5 through 15 for the other endsheet. Before placing the book under weights, put a piece of wax paper inside the fold of the new endsheet.

Repairing Broken Back of Textblock

An unfortunate development has been the decision of major publishers to bind hardback books with a "perfect" binding. This method was seen first with art books and children's books but now has become widespread across publishing genres. Most recently, however, hardback books have appeared that are perfect-bound without any super. This means that the textblock is held together only by its glue and that it is attached to the boards only by stiffened endpapers. The most common preservation problems are that the pages "pop out" and the textblock breaks apart wherever it is forced or held open (see Figure 5.11a). The first problem can be solved through simple "tipping in" methods (see "Tipping in Single Leaves," p. 84). The second problem, though more complex, may be satisfactorily addressed using the following procedures, which are shown for a book that is broken in one place and whose hinges are intact. If there are multiple breaks in the textblock, it is best

Figure 5.10. Gluing down an Endsheet

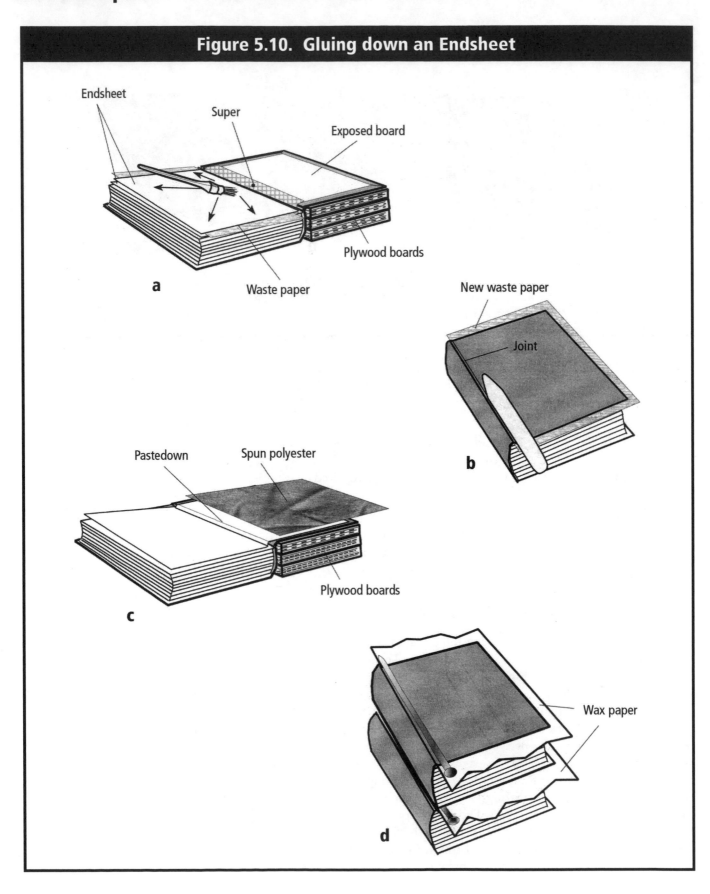

to cut through one hinge, glue up and reinforce the textblock with a piece of super, and create a new hinge.

Supplies

Japanese paper (medium weight; e.g., Sekishu)
Rice or wheat starch paste
Wax paper
Cloth for the super
PVA
Bone folder
Boards
Weights

Procedure

1. Tear off a strip of Japanese paper approximately 1 inch wide and $\frac{1}{2}$ inch shorter than the textblock (see Figure 5.11b). The tear should be parallel to the chain lines of the paper. Methods of tearing Japanese paper are discussed in Chapter 1.

2. Paste out half of this strip with a 1:1 mixture of PVA and starch paste (rice, wheat) or methyl cellulose, as described below. Spread paste evenly over a piece of wax paper or polyester film. Lay the mending strip in the paste and brush lightly with a thin layer of paste. (See Figure 5.11c.)

3. Place a piece of wax paper over the mending strip and gently rub the paper with a bone folder to coat the Japanese paper with paste.

4. Remove wax paper, and gently lift the mending strip out of the paste using the micro-spatula or tweezers (see Figure 5.6c–d). Do not lift too quickly or the strip will stretch, which will cause the hinge to wrinkle as it dries. If less moisture is desired on the hinge, place it between a "sandwich" of blotting paper and spun polyester (see Figure 5.6e) and rub with a bone folder.

5. Place strips of wax paper along the spine of the cover and beneath the top page of side B of the textblock. Carefully place the pasted-out half of the hinge on this page, with the fold facing the spine. (See Figure 5.11d.)

6. Place another strip of wax paper on top of the pasted-out half and smooth down with a bone folder. Place a piece of blotting paper and a weight on top and allow to dry. (See Figure 5.11e.)

7. Cut a piece of super the width of the spine and $\frac{1}{8}$ inch shorter than the textblock.

8. Paste out the spine of side B of the textblock and attach the super to it, rubbing with a bone folder to make sure it adheres well to the spine (see Figure 5.11f).

9. Remove the strip of wax paper from side B and bring side B into an upright position.

Figure 5.11. Repairing the Broken Back of a Textblock

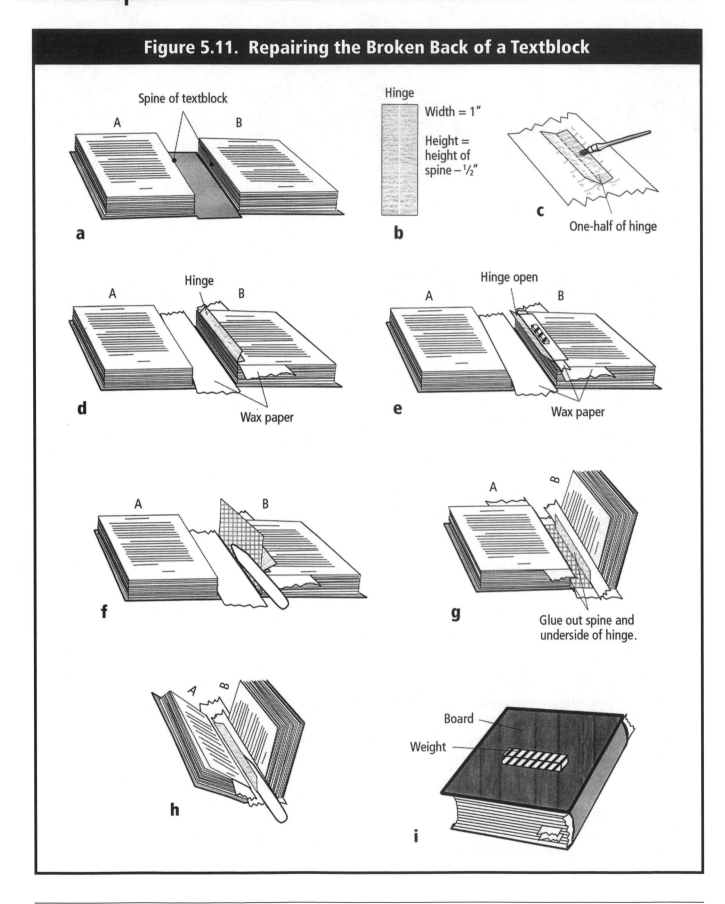

10. Place a strip of wax paper under the top page of side A. Place another strip of wax paper under the hinge. Paste out the underside of the hinge and the spine of side A. (See Figure 5.11g.)

11. Carefully bring side A upright, making sure that the two halves of the book are aligned properly. Use a bone folder to smooth out the hinge if necessary. (See Figure 5.11h.)

12. Close the book and put a board and weight on it (see Figure 5.11i).

13. After the repairs have dried, carefully remove the three pieces of wax paper by opening the book. Because the pages are now glued to the strip of super, you have in effect created a hollow-back binding. If the wax paper sticks in the spine area, open both covers back until a space appears between the wax paper strip and the spine of the cover. Use a bone folder or a micro-spatula to separate the wax paper from the spine of the textblock.

If the textblock of a sewn book breaks, it is best to leave the repair to a conservator or binder, since this often involves a complete recasing and replacement of the sewing structure.

Replacing the Spine

When books are given weak or inadequate covering material in the original binding, the piece of material covering the spine can become weakened, if not torn (see Figure 5.12). This same type of damage can occur because of thoughtless handling, inappropriate shelving, or even from frequent use. The method of repair depends on the strength of the joints and the spine piece. If only one joint is torn and the spine piece is still strong and intact, there is an easy method of repair. If the spine is weak or if both joints are torn, however, it is best to completely remove the original spine and reinforce it with a new spine piece. In each case the original spine is kept, either as part of the original cover or glued onto a new spine piece. (If the original spine piece is completely missing, either imprint directly on the new spine piece or create new paste-on labels.) Wherever possible, the book cloth used for this new spine piece should be of approximately the same weight and color as the original. Publishers, however, have used a wide variety of covering materials, and it is not always feasible, or even possible, to match the original material.

Supplies

Book cloth
Cotton or linen
PVA
Glue brush
Bristol board or card stock
(Optional) Cotton cord
Small scissors
Bone folder
Straightedge

Figure 5.12. Torn Spine

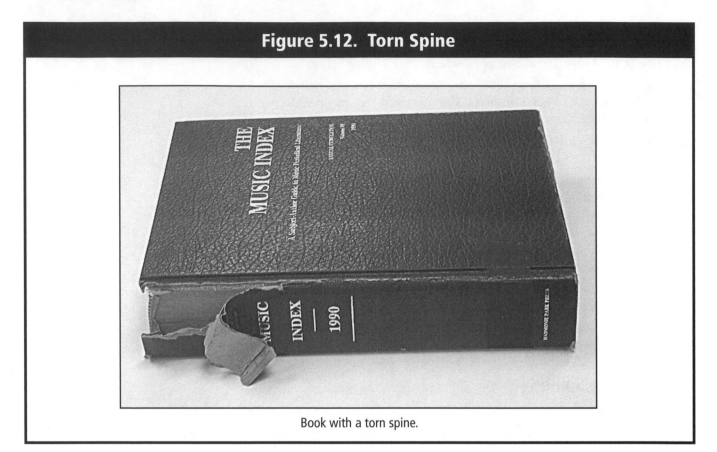

Book with a torn spine.

X-Acto or Olfa knife or scalpel
Micro-spatula
Waste paper or polyester film scraps
Wax paper
Weights
Knitting needles

Procedure

The following preliminary steps for replacing outer hinges (joints) apply to both categories of damage.

1. Cut through the damaged joint with the X-Acto or Olfa knife or scalpel. In order not to cut through the inner hinges of the book, keep the blade turned up. (See Figure 5.13a.) Repeat for second joint if the spine piece is to be completely removed.

2. Use a ruler or straightedge to make a cut ⅛ inch in from the edge of the board. This will give a neater mend and will help in lifting up the cover cloth from the board. (See Figure 5.13b–c.) Do this for both covers of the book if the entire spine is to be replaced. If the spine is in fairly good shape, it can be saved, trimmed, and glued back in place on top of the new spine.

3. Using the knife or scalpel, slice through the original cover at the top and bottom edge of the board. These slits should be

approximately 1 inch long. (See Figure 5.13c.) Do this for both boards of the book if entire spine is to be replaced.

4. Gently peel back the covering material with a rounded scalpel or micro-spatula, beginning at the spine edge of the board and ending on a line even with the slits made at the top and bottom edges of the boards (see Figure 5.13d).

5. (Optional) If the paper liner or super on the back of the textblock is weak or disintegrating, clean the spine and attach new paper or super to it. If necessary, the old adhesive may be softened by spreading a thin layer of paste on it and letting it soak in for a few minutes. Gently scrape off the paper or super with a micro-spatula and clean the folds of the gatherings as carefully as possible. Glue on the new super or paper liner, using a bone folder to make sure that the paper or cloth adheres well. (See Figure 5.14a–d.)

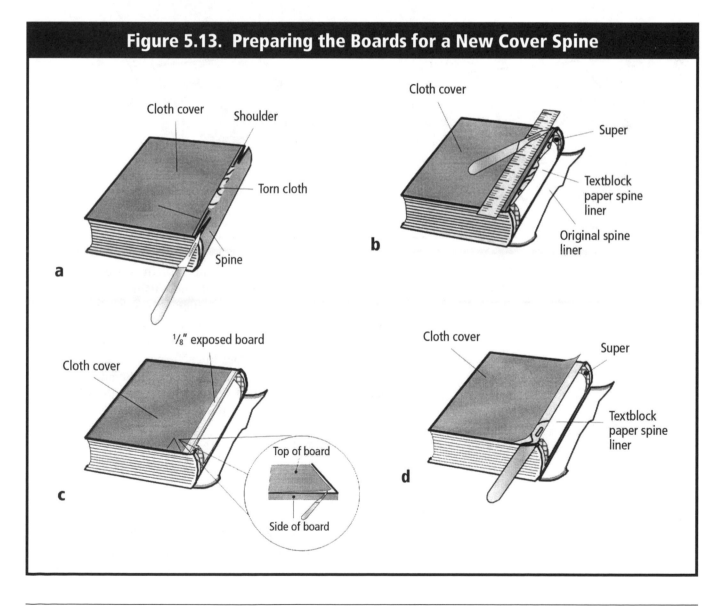

Figure 5.13. Preparing the Boards for a New Cover Spine

Figure 5.14. Preparing and Lining the Spine of the Textblock

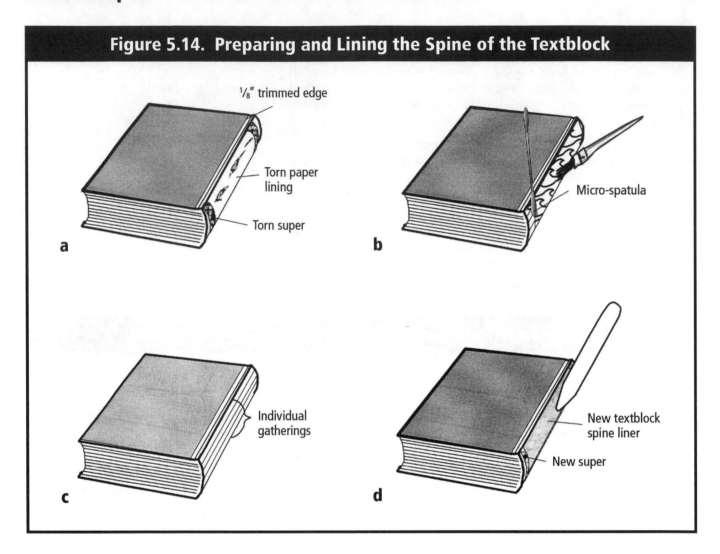

a — ⅛″ trimmed edge; Torn paper lining; Torn super

b — Micro-spatula

c — Individual gatherings

d — New textblock spine liner; New super

6. (Optional) If the paper and cloth liners for the cover spine are weak, it is best to replace them with new paper and cloth. If necessary, the old adhesive may be softened by spreading a thin layer of paste on it and letting it soak in for a few minutes. Gently scrape off the paper or super with a micro-spatula and glue on the new super or paper liner, using a bone folder to make sure that the paper or cloth adheres well. Scrape off only so much of the original liner as will come off easily in order not to damage the weak cloth. (See Figure 5.15a–c.)

Category 1

Use this procedure when one joint is torn, but the other joint and the spine itself are strong and intact.

Procedure

1. Trim the edge of the original spine piece (see Figure 5.16a).

2. Cut a piece of book cloth that is the height of the textblock and wide enough to cover the spine plus 1 inch. The grain of this

Figure 5.15. Lining the Old Cover Spine

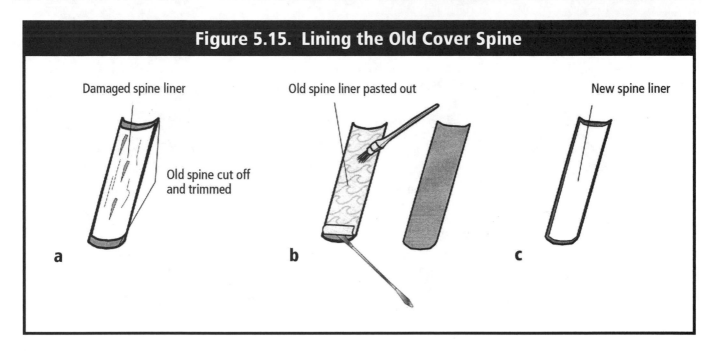

Damaged spine liner

Old spine cut off and trimmed

Old spine liner pasted out

New spine liner

a

b

c

piece of book cloth should be parallel to the spine of the book. To measure this piece, place a strip of scrap paper into the joint and mark where it comes to the end of the board slits. (See Figure 5.16b–c.)

3. Put the new spine piece into place, fitting it snugly down into the joint and curving it around the spine of the textblock (see Figure 5.16d).

4. Glue out the original spine and attached it to this new spine piece. Rub down with a bone folder. Do *not* glue the new spine piece to the back of the textblock. (See Figure 5.16d–e.) Let dry until set.

5. Open up the new spine piece and glue out the exposed board (see Figure 5.16f). Fit the new spine piece in place and rub down with a bone folder (see Figure 5.16g).

6. Glue out the underside of the peeled-back cover, smooth back down with a bone folder, and place a piece of wax paper under the board (see Figure 5.16h–i).

7. Place a board and weight on the book and let dry (see Figure 5.16j).

Category 2

Use this procedure when one joint is torn and the spine is weak or when both joints are weak or torn.

Procedure

Original spine piece

1. Cut through both joints following the procedures outlined above (see Figure 5.13a–d).

Figure 5.16. Repairing a Spine: Category 1

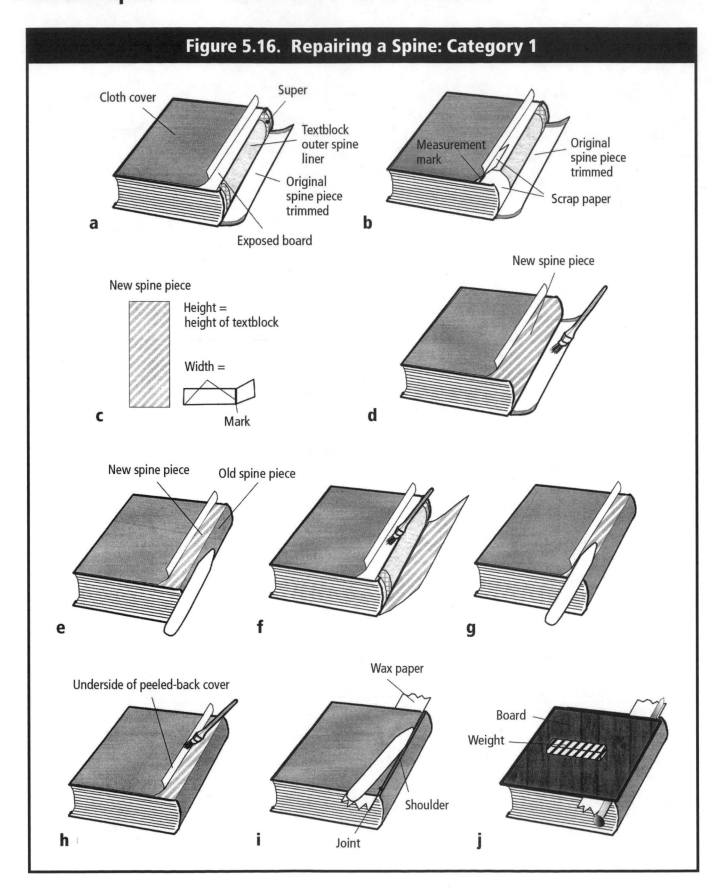

2. Remove the spine piece and trim the edges. If the spine is still strong and intact, it may be attached as is to the new spine piece.

3. If the spine cloth is deteriorated, it is best to back it with heavy paper or cloth. Gently pull the original liner away from the cloth and clean the spine piece. Applying a thin layer of starch paste will help remove the lining paper. Glue out a new piece of paper or cloth and attach to the spine piece, smoothing with a bone folder. (See Figure 5.15a–c.) Let dry.

New spine piece

1. Cut a piece of book cloth that is 1½ inches longer than the book is tall and 2 inches wider than the spine of the book. The grain of this piece of book cloth should be parallel to the spine of the book. To measure the spine, wrap a piece of scrap paper around the spine and mark the edges of the spine on this paper. Then measure the distance between these two marks. (See Figure 5.17a–b.)

2. (Optional) If time, money, and materials allow, you may reinforce the new spine piece with an inlay of Bristol board or card stock, which can be cut from a stiff manila file folder, and an inner lining of linen or cotton cloth. The inlay should be exactly the width of the spine and the height of the boards. The linen liner should be the height of the boards, but ½ inch wider than the spine. Glue the linen liner to the center of the book cloth strip; then glue the inlay to the liner, centered on the book cloth. (See Figure 5.17c.)

3. (Optional) Another refinement of this repair is the addition of small cords to strengthen the head and tail of the new spine. This is accomplished by gluing a piece of cotton string or cord along each end of the inlay. These cords should be exactly as long as the spine inlay is wide. Then make two cuts on each end of the new spine. Begin at the ends of the cords and angle slightly toward the center of the new spine piece as you cut toward the edge of the book cloth. Spread glue on the center tabs formed by these cuts and fold these tabs over the cords. (See Figure 5.17d–e.)

4. Clean spine of textblock and replace paper liner and super if necessary (see Figure 5.14a–d).

5. Spread glue on the exposed area of the board and place the side flap of the new spine piece on this glue under the original cover. If you are using the inlay for extra support, be sure that the top and bottom edges of the inlay are lined up with the top and bottom edges of the boards. Use the bone folder to smooth the new book cloth into place. (See Figure 5.18a–c.)

6. Spread glue on the underside of the raised original cloth and gently rub it back down with the bone folder (see Figure 5.18d). Place a piece of wax paper under the board and a waste sheet or spun polyester on top while doing this (see Figure 5.18e).

Figure 5.17. Making a New Spine Piece

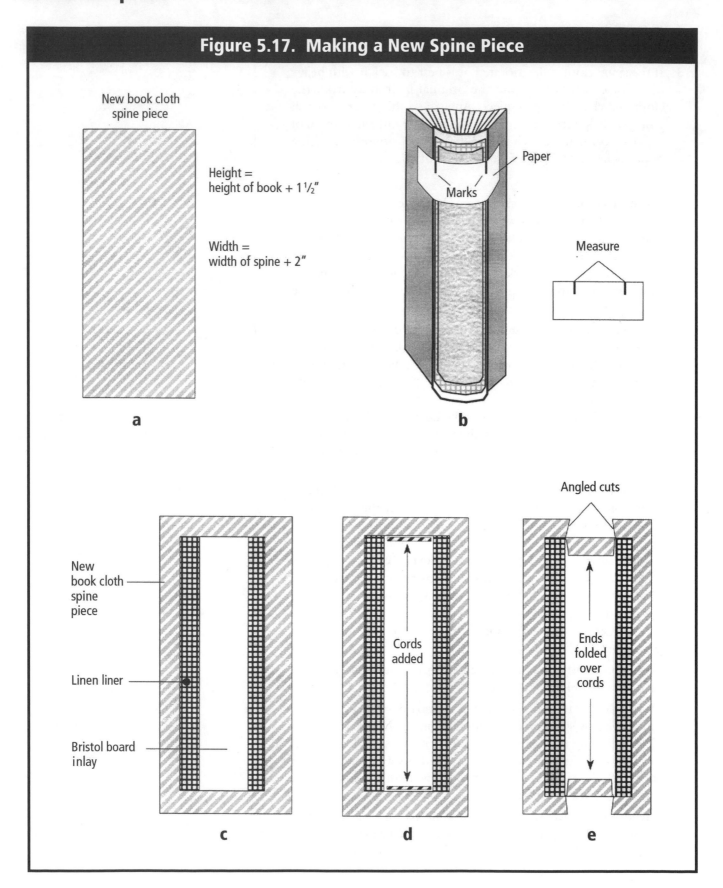

New book cloth
spine piece

Height =
height of book + 1 ½"

Width =
width of spine + 2"

a

Paper

Marks

Measure

b

New
book cloth
spine
piece

Linen liner

Bristol board
inlay

c

Cords
added

d

Angled cuts

Ends
folded
over
cords

e

Figure 5.18. Repairing a Spine: Category 2

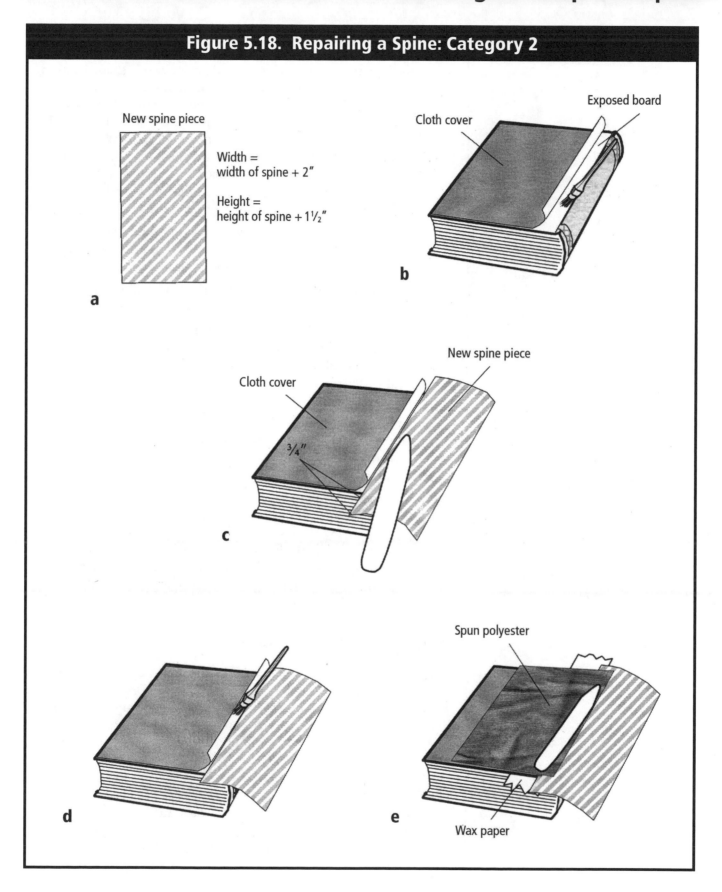

New spine piece

Width =
width of spine + 2″

Height =
height of spine + 1½″

a

Cloth cover

Exposed board

b

Cloth cover

New spine piece

3/4″

c

d

Spun polyester

e

Wax paper

7. Repeat steps 5 and 6 for the other side of the new spine.

8. Stand the book on its spine and gently open the boards. Using the X-Acto or Olfa knife or scalpel, make two V-shaped cuts in the book cloth at both the head and tail of the book. Begin the first cut at the corner of the board and angle slightly *toward the center of the spine* as you cut toward the edge of the book cloth. Begin the next cut in the same place as the first and angle slightly *toward the board*. Remove the small triangle piece. (See Figure 5.19a–b.) If you have added the optional steps above, you have already made these cuts and folded and glued the center tab before you attach the new spine to the boards.

9. Spread glue on the center tab of the book cloth and, using the bone folder, tuck it under the spine of the book (see Figure 5.19c). Repeat this process for the other end of the book.

10. Glue the remaining tabs of book cloth and fold them over the top and bottom edges of the boards (see Figure 5.19d).

11. (Optional) Lift the pastedowns up from the boards, glue the tabs to the boards, and reglue the pastedowns over the tabs. This effectively hides the tabs of the new spine piece. (See Figure 19e–f.)

12. Place wax paper inside the boards and weight the book between plywood boards or other books. Lay the knitting needles in the grooves of the outer hinges. If you are stacking books on top of each other, place pieces of wax paper between them. (See Figure 5.3d, p. 111.)

13. To attach the original spine to this new spine, spread glue on the inside of the original spine and place it on the new spine, gently rubbing with a bone folder. It is wise to double-check the orientation of the book to be sure you are putting the spine on right-side up. If the old spine has difficulty in sticking to the new book cloth, wrap an elastic bandage (e.g., Ace bandage) around the book to hold the spine in place while it dries.

Reinforcing an Inner Hinge

When the inner hinge is torn only at the fold of the endpapers, it may be repaired with Japanese paper. Since this is a reinforcement and not a replacement, the super must be intact, strong enough to act as the hinge, and firmly attached to the spine. The Japanese paper makes a good reinforcement and will help prevent the further deterioration of the hinges.

Supplies

Medium-weight Japanese paper (e.g., Sekishu)
PVA
Rice or wheat starch (see formula in Chapter 1)
Glue brush

Figure 5.19. Attaching a New Spine

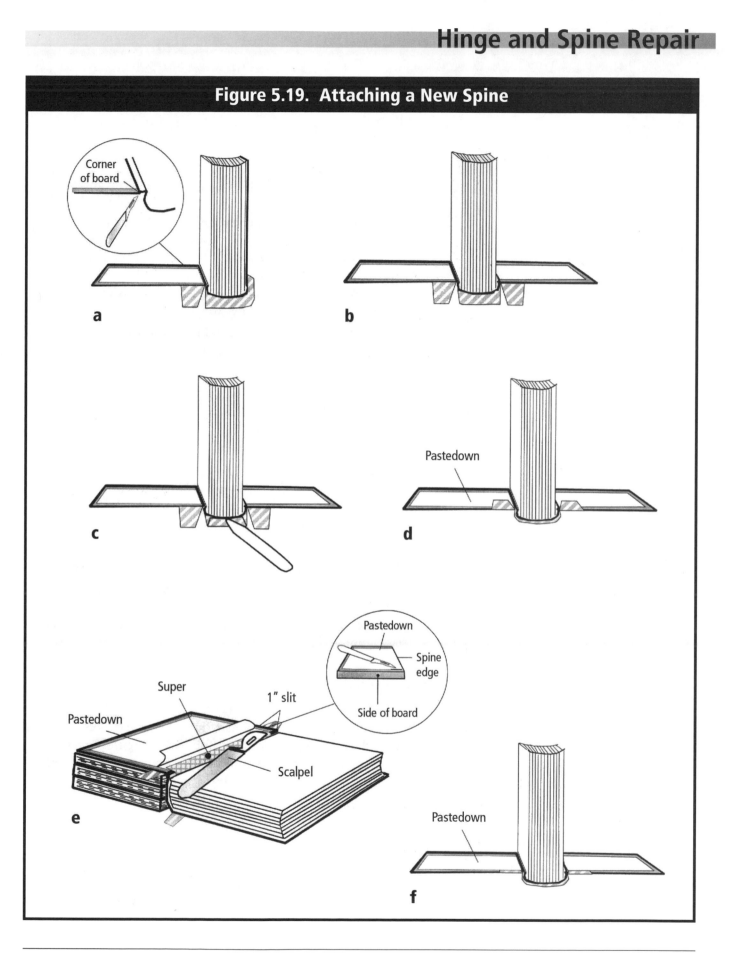

Bone folder
Micro-spatula
Wax paper
Plywood or other stiff boards

Procedure

1. Open the book at the torn hinge and support the cover with boards (see Figure 5.20a).

2. Cut a strip of Japanese paper the height of the textblock and 1 inch wide, or wide enough to accommodate at least a ¼-inch overhang onto the pastedown and the flyleaf. The grain should be parallel to the long side. Medium weight should suffice for most books. For large or heavy books, use a heavier weight of paper or several layers of lighter-weight paper.

3. Make a 50/50 mixture of PVA and rice or wheat starch.

4. Paste out a strip of wax paper and lay the Japanese paper on it (see Figure 5.20b).

5. Cover with another strip of wax paper, and rub down lightly with a bone folder (see Figure 5.20c).

6. Remove the Japanese paper with a micro-spatula, being careful to stretch it as little as possible (see Figure 5.20d).

7. Lay this strip over the torn fold area, place a strip of wax paper over it, and rub down with a bone folder (see Figure 5.20e). Be sure that the Japanese paper adheres to all parts of the hinge area.

8. Insert a clean strip of wax paper into the new Japanese paper hinge (see Figure 5.20f).

9. (Optional) If both hinges need reinforcement, cut two pieces of Japanese paper, paste them out, and proceed with steps 7 and 8 for each hinge.

10. Close the cover, put a weight on it, and let dry for several hours (see Figure 5.20g).

Replacing One Inner Hinge

Frequently one or both hinges of a book have become almost or completely separated from the textblock. If the book has only one torn hinge, and if the case is still intact, one of the following three methods of reattachment is recommended. If both hinges are torn, it is recommended that you recase the book (see pp. 143–150).

Supplies

Cotton or linen
PVA
Glue brush
Straightedge
X-Acto or Olfa knife or scalpel
Scissors

Figure 5.20. Reinforcing an Inner Hinge

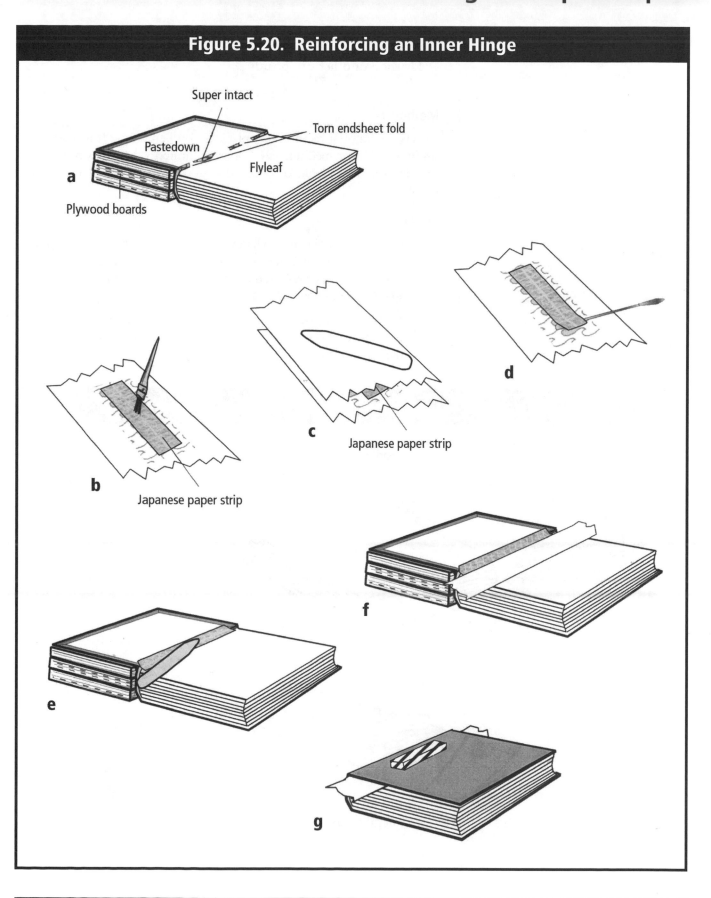

Super intact

Torn endsheet fold

Pastedown

Flyleaf

a

Plywood boards

b

Japanese paper strip

c

Japanese paper strip

d

e

f

g

Wax paper
Waste paper or scrap polyester film
Plywood or other stiff boards
Weights

Method 1

This is the simplest method of replacing a broken hinge. It is particularly useful on thin or medium-size books of limited value. It is not recommended for thick books or books that get heavy use, such as reference books.

Procedure

1. Carefully cut through whatever is left of the broken hinge and the super, avoiding the cloth of the outer case. If the book was sewn on tapes or recessed cords, cut them off at the edge of the spine. (See Figure 5.21a.)

2. Support the loose cover with plywood or other stiff boards and trim any excess material on the spine edge of the boards and on the edge of the spine (see Figure 5.21b).

Figure 5.21. Cutting and Trimming an Inner Hinge

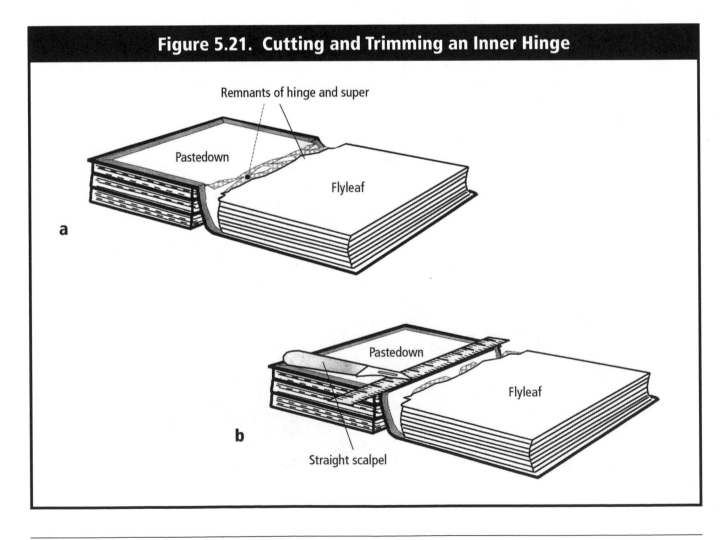

3. Cut a piece of cotton or linen cloth that is ⅛ inch shorter than the textblock and 1½ inches wide (see Figure 5.22a). This cloth will form the new hinge.

4. Place the cloth on a piece of waste paper and place another piece of waste paper on top of the cloth. One long edge of the cloth should extend ⅛ inch beyond the top piece of the waste paper. Then glue the ⅛-inch strip that is exposed, starting on the upper waste sheet, down across the exposed edge and onto the lower waste sheet. (See Figure 5.22b.)

5. Turn the hinge over, and place the glued edge down into the shoulder of the textblock. Using a bone folder, gently rub the glued section of cloth into place in the shoulder of the book. Make 45-degree angled cuts at each end of the new hinge. (See Figure 5.22c.)

6. Place a piece of wax paper underneath the new hinge and glue out with PVA (see Figure 5.22d). Replace the used piece of wax paper with a new one.

7. Lift the cover board and bring the spine edge over the shoulder and down into the gutter (see Figure 5.22e). The shoulder of the textblock *must* fit into the shoulder of the cover.

8. Close the cover and rub down the outer joint with a bone folder, which will attach the cover firmly into the shoulder of the textblock (see Figure 5.22f).

9. Place a board and a weight on the book and let dry. A knitting needle will help keep the joint formed correctly. (See Figure 5.22g.)

Method 2

This method provides additional strength to the hinge and is particularly useful when pictorial endpapers must not be covered up. This method may also be used in recasing a volume.

Procedure

1. Follow steps 1–4 in Method 1 of creating a new hinge.

2. Make shallow 1-inch cuts along the edge of the turn-ins starting at the spine edge of the board (see Figure 5.23a).

3. Insert a rounded scalpel or a micro-spatula between the board and the strip of super still attached to the pastedown. Use this strip of super to lift up the pastedown and gently peel it back 1 inch to expose the board. (See Figure 5.23b.)

4. If the ends of the tapes or the cords are still attached to the board, they should be removed. Use the rounded end of a micro-spatula to lift up the tape ends, or use the pointed end to dig under and lift up the threads of the cords (see Figure 5.23c–d).

Figure 5.22. Replacing an Inner Hinge: Method 1

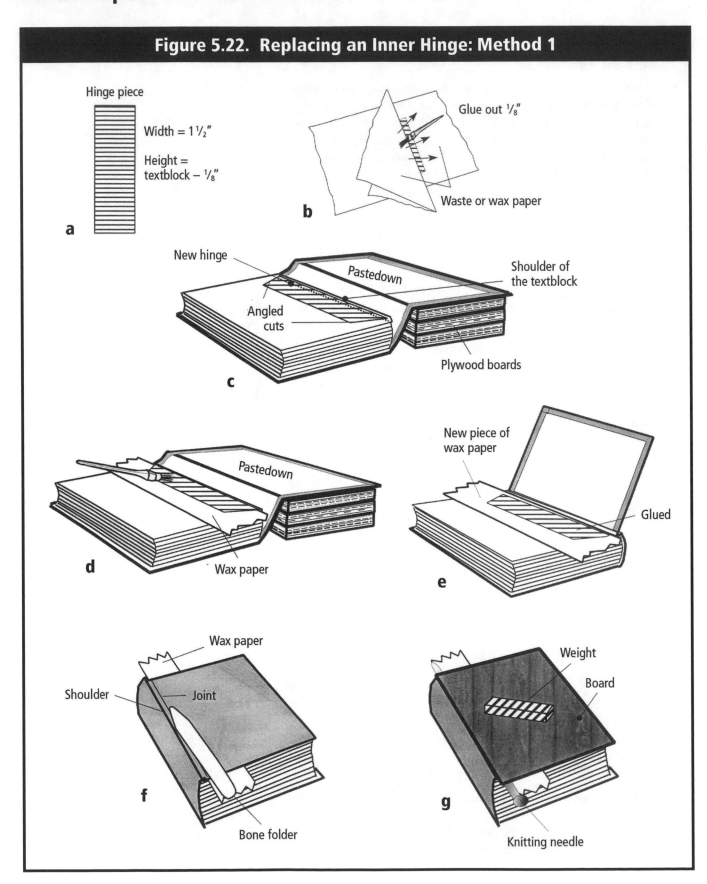

a — Hinge piece
Width = 1½"
Height = textblock − ⅛"

b — Glue out ⅛"
Waste or wax paper

c — New hinge
Pastedown
Shoulder of the textblock
Angled cuts
Plywood boards

d — Pastedown
Wax paper

e — New piece of wax paper
Glued

f — Wax paper
Shoulder
Joint
Bone folder

g — Wax paper
Weight
Board
Knitting needle

Figure 5.23. Replacing an Inner Hinge: Method 2

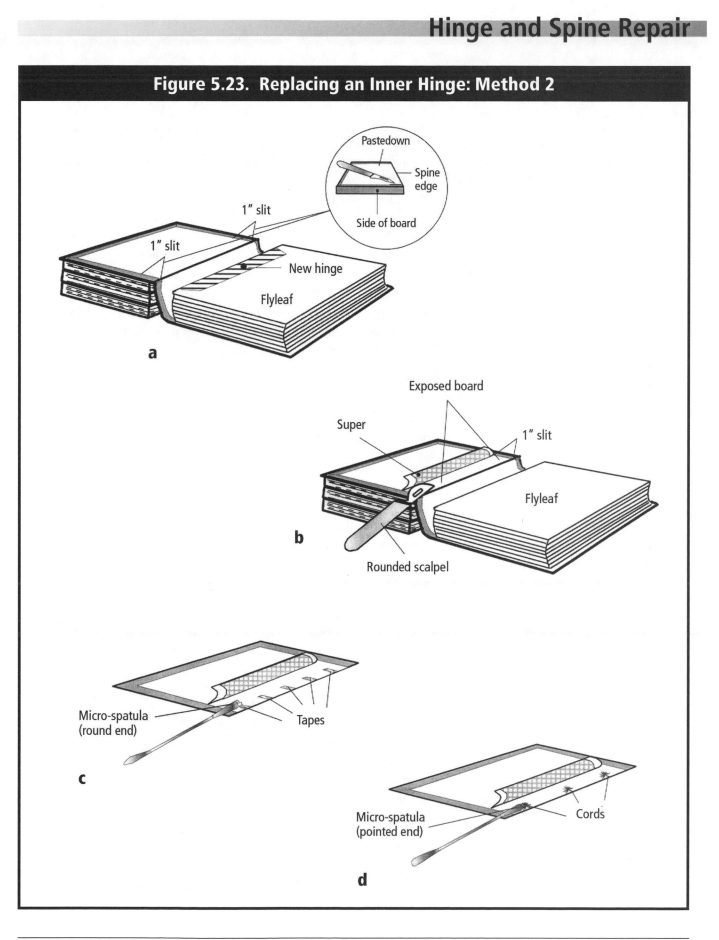

5. Glue out the exposed board with PVA. Bring the board down into the gutter and adhere the new hinge to it by smoothing with a bone folder. (See Figure 5.24a–b.)

6. Glue out the underside of the peeled-back pastedown, place it back down onto the new hinge, smooth down with a bone folder, and place a piece of wax paper between the board and the textblock (see Figure 5.24c).

7. (Optional) If the edge of the pastedown is ragged or torn, it may be trimmed ⅛ inch with a straightedge and scalpel (see Figure 5.9a, p. 119, for this technique).

8. Close the cover and rub down the outer joint with a bone folder, which will attach the cover firmly into the shoulder of the textblock (see Figure 5.24d).

9. Place a board and a weight on the book and let dry. A knitting needle will help keep the joint formed correctly. (See Figure 5.16j, p. 128.)

Method 3

This method involves sewing the hinge to the textblock and thus is particularly important for thick or heavy books that receive a lot of use. This method may also be used in recasing a volume.

Supplies

Dissecting needle or ice pick
Linen thread
Sewing needles (e.g., candlewicking needles)
Beeswax

Procedure

1. Follow steps 1–4 in Method 1 of creating a new hinge.

2. Place five marks on the spine where you will punch holes for the sewing. These holes should begin ½ inch from the head or tail and proceed at approximately 1½-inch intervals, ending ½ inch from the opposite end. On tall books, more than 5 holes may be needed. This is acceptable, but be sure to mark out an odd number of holes and not to allow the holes to be closer together than 1 inch. (See Figure 5.25a.)

3. Using the dissecting needle or ice pick (see Figure 5.25b–c), punch holes at the marks made in step 2. You should gently push the dissecting needle from the inside of the shoulder (i.e., the gutter), coming out through the spine. The angle of these holes should alternate, beginning with a shallow-angled hole, continuing with first a more deeply angled hole, then another shallow hole. (See Figure 5.25d.)

4. Cut a piece of linen thread 3 times the length of the book, and wax the thread with beeswax. Thread one end of it through a sewing needle, and thread the other end through a needle as

Figure 5.24. Replacing an Inner Hinge: Method 2, Continued

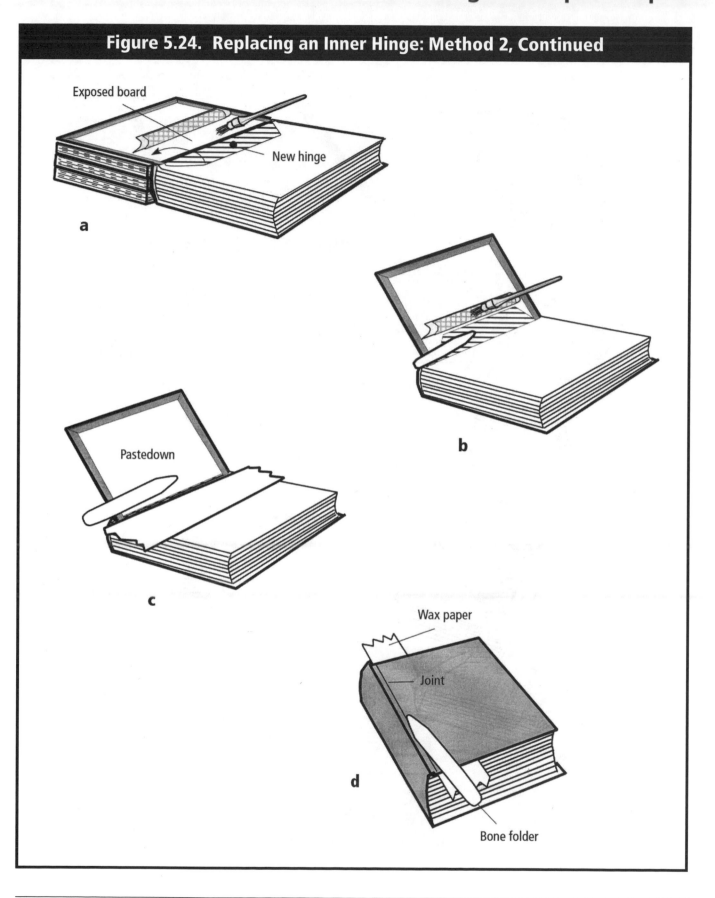

Exposed board

New hinge

a

b

Pastedown

c

Wax paper

Joint

Bone folder

d

Figure 5.25. Replacing an Inner Hinge: Method 3

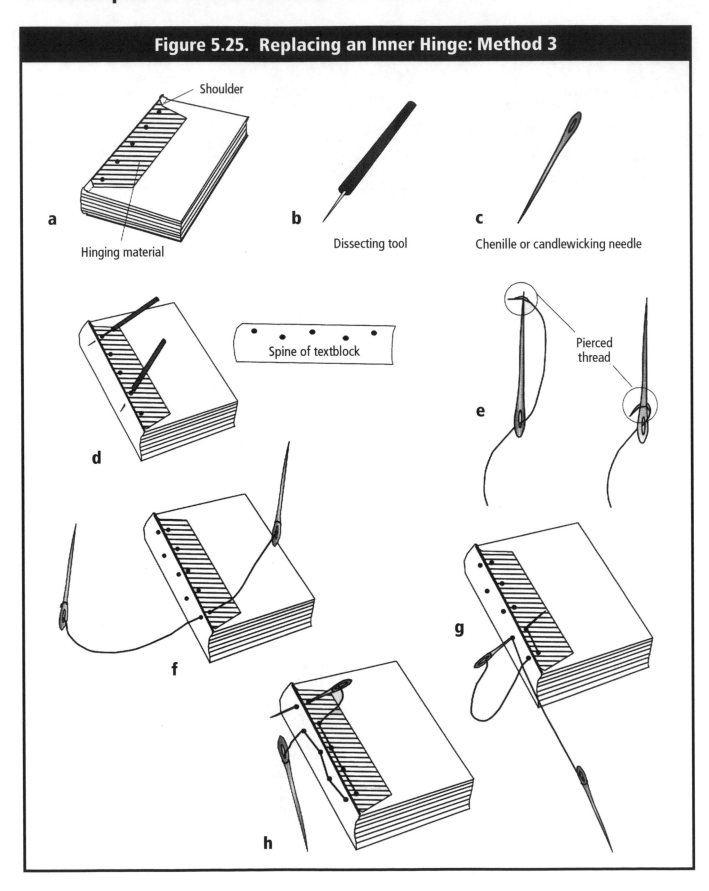

a   Shoulder
Hinging material

b   Dissecting tool

c   Chenille or candlewicking needle

d

Spine of textblock

e   Pierced thread

f

g

h

well. A good way to anchor the thread is to pierce it at each end. (See Figure 5.25e.)

5. Put one needle through the first hole at one end of the textblock and draw it through until equal lengths of thread extend on each side, as if beginning to lace a shoe (see Figure 5.25f).

6. Take the needle on the shoulder side of the hole and put it through the second hole from the shoulder side. Take the other needle (on the spine side) and put it through the second hole from the spine side, being sure to pull the first thread taut back toward you. (See Figure 5.25g.)

7. Continue to lace the thread through the holes until you come to the last hole. On the final hole, run only the shoulder side thread through the hole. (See Figure 5.25h.) Use a square knot to tie the two ends of the thread together as near the second hole from the end as possible. The beeswax should help hold the thread as you tie it.

8. Continue with steps 2–9 of Method 2.

Recasing the Textblock

Damage to the spine and hinges can become particularly severe when it is coupled with torn endsheets. In the worst cases, the textblock becomes completely separated from the case (see Figure 5.26). This type of damage can be repaired only by recasing the textblock. In many instances, the original case can be reattached to the textblock. Recasing actually involves more than one procedure. For example, you will need to replace the endsheets (described earlier) when you recase a book. You can also strengthen the hinges of the original case by lining the spine (described below) in preparation for recasing.

Supplies

Bookcloth
Endsheets
PVA
Glue brush
Bone folder
Small scissors
Straightedge
X-Acto or Olfa knife or scalpel
Linen or cotton cloth
Bristol board or card stock
Waste paper or polyester film scraps
Wax paper
Sand paper (220 grit)
Plywood or other stiff boards
Weights
Knitting needles

Figure 5.26. Textblock Separated from Its Case

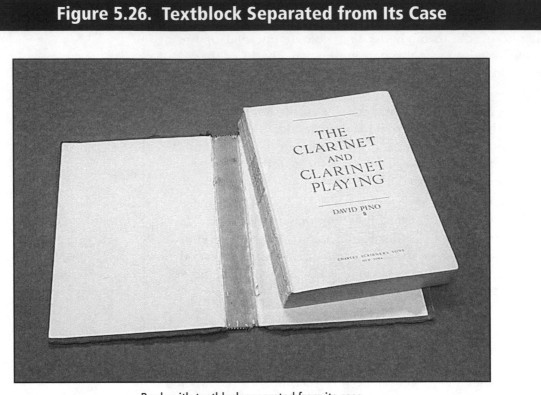

Book with textblock separated from its case.

Optional Supplies

Japanese paper
Rice or wheat starch paste

Procedure

1. Remove the cover from the textblock, without cutting the cloth of the outer hinge. This may involve carefully cutting through partially torn endsheets, super, and remnants of tapes if the book was sewn on tapes. You may also have to remove the flyleaf side of the original endsheet. (See Figure 5.27a–b.)

2. (Optional) If this book circulates frequently, it is best to strengthen the fold of the endsheets with Japanese paper (see under "Replacing Endsheets," step 6 [guarding], p. 114). This is not necessary, however, for books that circulate infrequently.

3. Attach the endsheets to the textblock, following the instructions given in the earlier section of this chapter "Replacing Endsheets."

4. Cut a piece of cotton or linen cloth that is ¼ inch shorter than the spine and 2 inches wider than the spine (see Figure 5.28a). This piece of cloth will be the new super and will form the hinges that will hold the textblock to the case.

5. Spread PVA on the spine of the textblock and center the new super on the spine with approximately 1 inch of the super

Figure 5.27. Removing the Textblock from Its Case

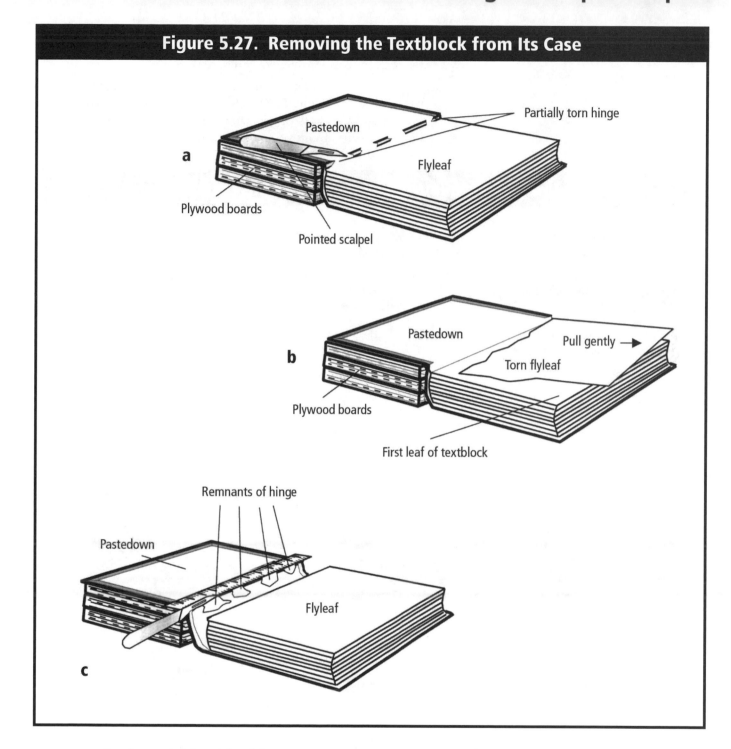

extending beyond either side of the spine. You may make center marks on the spine lining and the super to help you place the super down correctly. Rub the super into place with the bone folder. (See Figure 5.28g.)

6. Cut a piece of paper that is ⅛ inch shorter than the spine and as wide as the spine. This paper can be brown craft paper or left-over endsheet paper; the grain should run parallel to the spine.

7. Spread PVA on one side of this paper and position it on the spine (see Figure 5.28h). Rub it down with the bone folder. Set the textblock aside while you prepare the case.

8. Make slits along the turn-ins on the board and peel back the pastedown (see Figure 5.29a). Remove the old super from the boards and the ends of the tapes or cords, if necessary (see Figure 5.29b). Remove any remaining pastedown fragments

Figure 5.28. Making a New Super for the Textblock

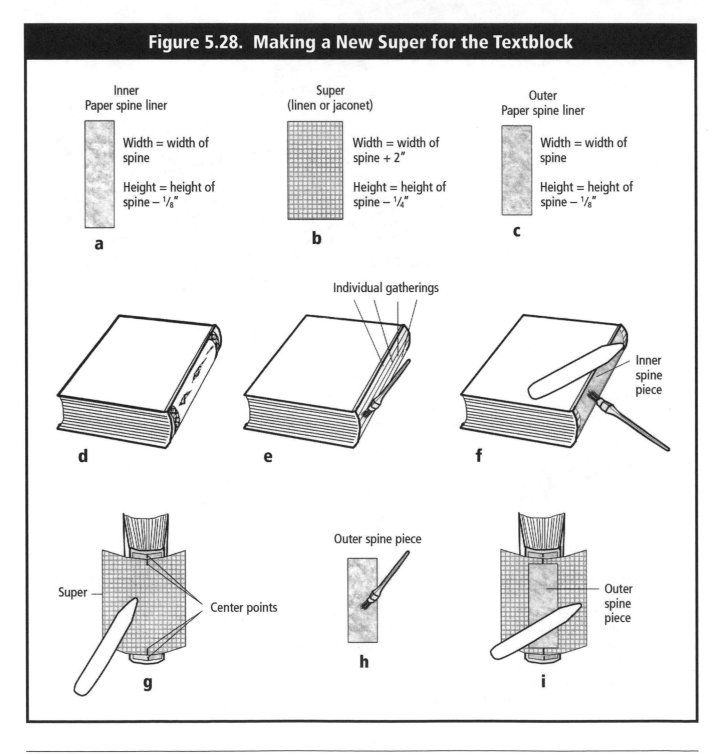

Inner
Paper spine liner

Width = width of spine

Height = height of spine − 1/8″

a

Super
(linen or jaconet)

Width = width of spine + 2″

Height = height of spine − 1/4″

b

Outer
Paper spine liner

Width = width of spine

Height = height of spine − 1/8″

c

d

Individual gatherings

e

Inner spine piece

f

Super

Center points

g

Outer spine piece

h

Outer spine piece

i

with a micro-spatula. If any rough surface has been left on the boards, it should be lightly sanded off.

9. If the spine liner is torn or weak, spread a thin layer of paste on it and let it soak in (see Figure 5.29c). Gently remove this liner with a micro-spatula, being careful not to tear the original cloth (see Figure 5.29d). Glue on a new spine liner (see Figure 5.29e).

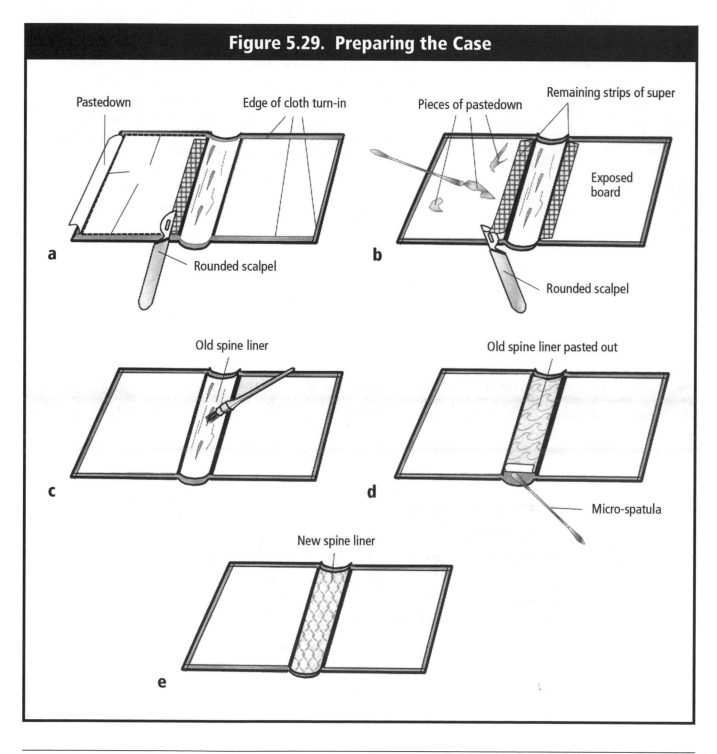

Figure 5.29. Preparing the Case

10. (Optional) If the cloth of the case is particularly worn or even torn in the hinge area, you can line the spine with book cloth. To begin this process, you will have to slice through the turn-ins 1 inch from the spine edge of the boards and gently peel up the flaps made by these cuts (see Figure 5.30a). Carefully peel away the original inlay from the spine.

11. (Optional) You will also have to peel the original cloth away from the boards, beginning at the spine edge and ending on a line even with the cuts made in the turn-ins (see Figure 5.30b).

12. (Optional) Cut a piece of book cloth that is 2 inches wider than the spine and 2 inches longer than the height of the boards. Carefully spread a thin layer of PVA on the inside of the original spine and adjacent areas of cloth that were peeled up from the boards. (See Figure 5.31a–b.) (If the cloth of the original cover is particularly worn or fragile in the spine area, you should spread the glue on the new book cloth lining instead. To glue the book cloth, lay it face up on the table with a piece of waste paper covering 1 inch of the book cloth at each end. Weight the waste paper and spread glue on the exposed portion of the book cloth.)

13. (Optional) Place one edge of the new book cloth lining between one board and the glued cloth. The face of the book cloth should be against the glue. Continue to lay the lining onto the glue and place the other edge under the other board. The new lining should extend approximately 1 inch beyond the head and tail of the case. Lay the case flat and rub the lining down with the bone folder. Then turn the case over, smooth

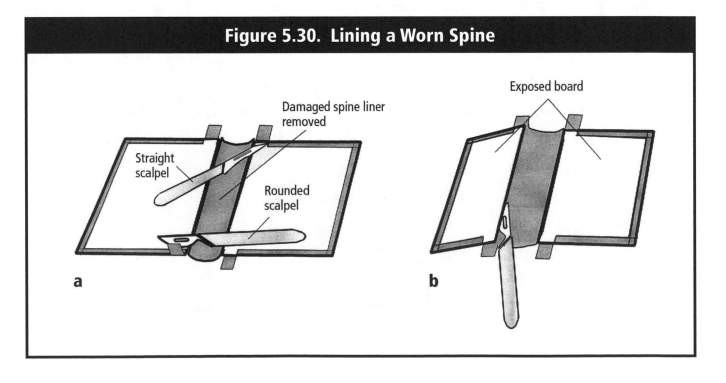

Figure 5.30. Lining a Worn Spine

Damaged spine liner removed

Straight scalpel

Rounded scalpel

a

Exposed board

b

out any loose material or bubbles, and remove any excess glue with a fingertip. If you glued the new book cloth instead of the original case, spread a small amount of PVA under the top and bottom of the original spine piece of the case and rub it down.

14. (Optional) Turn the case back over so that the inside of the case is facing up and spread glue on the boards where the original cloth was peeled away. Press the boards down onto the liner and rub with a bone folder. Turn the case over again and rub the cloth down on the glued area of the boards.

15. (Optional) Cut an inlay of Bristol board or other card stock that is as long as the boards and exactly as wide as the spine. Glue the inlay and place it in the center of the inside of the new spine lining. Rub the inlay with the bone folder. (See Figure 5.31c.)

Figure 5.31. Lining a Worn Spine, Continued

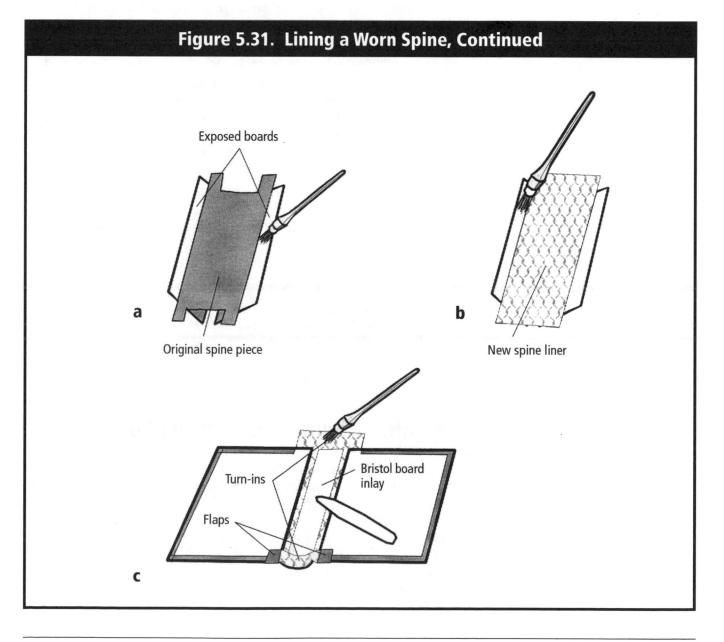

16. (Optional) Trim the ends of the lining so that they are even with the original turn-ins. You may want to glue a piece of cotton string or cord along each end of the inlay to strengthen the folds at the head and tail of the lining. These cords should be exactly as long as the spine inlay is wide. Spread PVA on the ends of the lining. Then fold these tabs and the new turn-ins over the ends of the inlay and board edges. Rub them down with the bone folder. (See Figure 5.17c–e, p. 130, for this technique.)

17. With the case open, place the textblock on the back board. Be sure to put the textblock in right-side up. Check the fit of the case by folding the spine and front board around the textblock. If the spine of the textblock is curved, you may need to shape the spine of the case by gently bending it around a pipe or broom handle.

18. Place a piece of waste paper under the new pastedown and spread PVA between the hinge and pastedown. Rub the hinge down, gluing it to the pastedown. Glue out the exposed side of the hinge and the rest of the pastedown. (See Figure 5.32a–c.)

19. Remove the waste paper and carefully close the cover, bringing the spine of the cover up against the spine of the textblock and then laying the board down on the glued hinge and pastedown. The spine edge of the board *must* fit down into the gutter of the textblock. Rub down the outer hinges with the bone folder. (See Figure 5.32d.)

20. Lift the textblock so that it is resting on its spine and gently open the cover you have just glued into place. Cover the pastedown with spun polyester and rub it carefully with a bone folder to remove any bubbles or wrinkles. (See Figure 5.33a–b.)

21. Repeat steps 18–20 for the back cover (except that the textblock will now be resting on the front board).

22. Place wax paper inside the boards and weight the book under a plywood board or other books. Lay knitting needles in the grooves of the outer hinges. If you are stacking books on top of each other, place pieces of wax paper between them. Allow the glue to dry overnight. (See Figure 5.33c.)

Reinforcement of Paperbound Books

Paperback books present a rather difficult problem. They are the least expensive type of book, but they are also the least durable type of book, with inherently weak spines and hinges. While their price makes them very desirable, their instability makes them very difficult to keep for any length of time. There are, however, a number of ways to strengthen the hinges and spines of paperback books without adding too much to their overall cost. Most library vendors offer several products for strengthening paperbacks. The simplest of these products is book tape, which can be applied to the spine of a paperback. Pressure-sensitive laminate films are

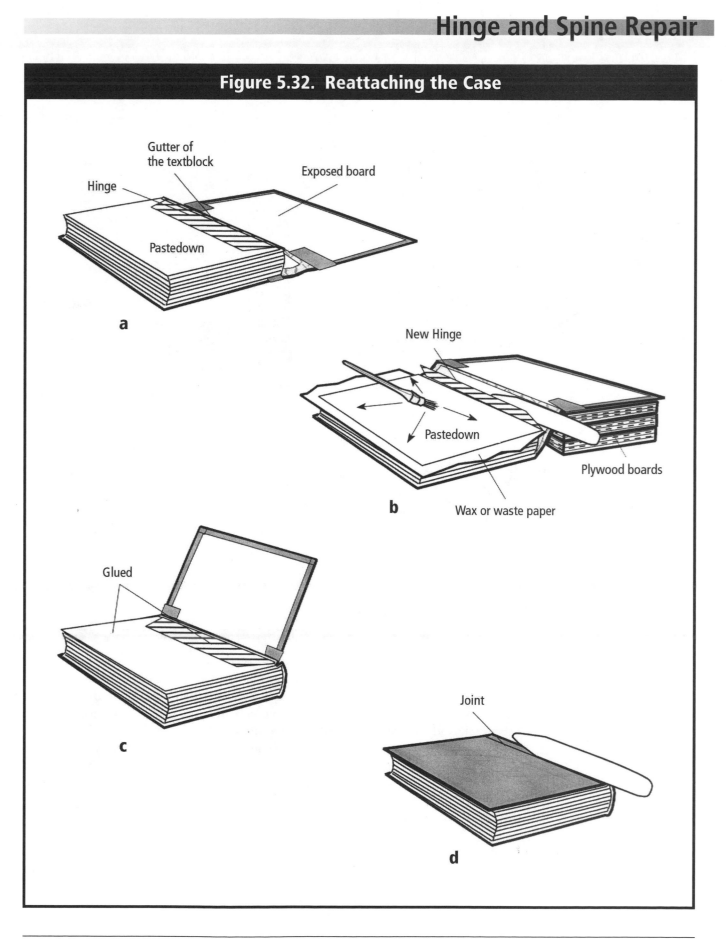

Figure 5.32. Reattaching the Case

a

Hinge

Gutter of the textblock

Exposed board

Pastedown

b

New Hinge

Pastedown

Plywood boards

Wax or waste paper

c

Glued

d

Joint

Figure 5.33. Reattaching the Case, Continued

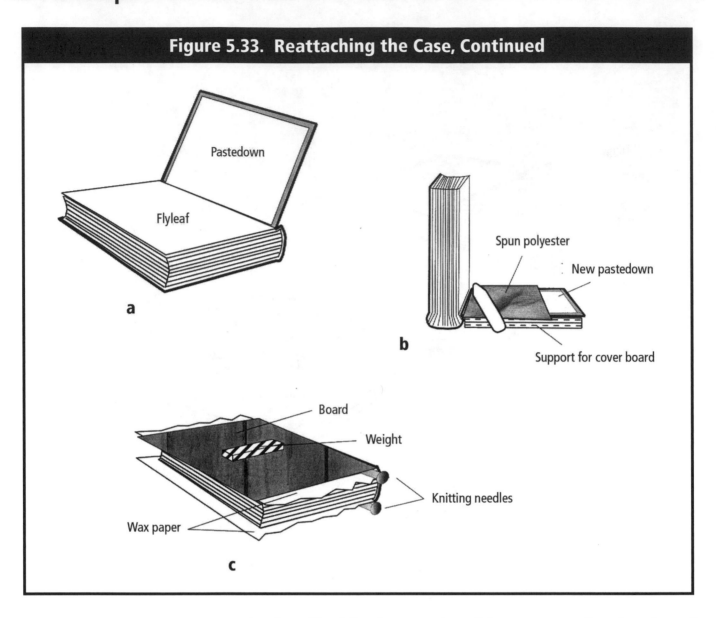

also offered for the protection of the covers as well as the spines of paperbacks. These are usually available in precut sizes or in rolls and in a variety of weights. These book tapes and laminate films are, however, acidic and irreversible. Some companies also offer clear, nonadhesive, adjustable covers that can be reused.

If you opt for one of the commercially available methods of strengthening paperbacks, it is suggested that you use one of the laminates that allow a portion of the film to fold over the edges of the cover like the turn-ins on a clothbound book. These laminates protect the edges of the paper cover as well as its outer surface. The heavier, rigid laminates should be used only on books that will not be kept for a great length of time, since these covers can ultimately pull the cover away from the textblock. The exceptions are laminates that are rigid over the covers but are flexible where they wrap around the spine. These covers can be very useful and are less likely to pull the cover away from the textblock.

Paperback books can also be reinforced with cloth hinges and boards. The various methods of performing this procedure differ in the weight of the boards used and in the treatment of the cover. Some methods retain the original cover, and others hide or replace the original cover. Two such methods are discussed in the following sections.

Pamphlets are also paperback publications that need support. However, most preservation issues stem from the fact that they have been irreversibly glued into acidic folders and are deteriorating because of these enclosures. Many pamphlet binders are offered by library suppliers and are easy and inexpensive to use. Simple procedures are given in a later section that take advantage of these products while at the same time provide a safer environment for these paper documents.

Reinforcing a Paperback Book with Boards

The covers and spines of paperbacks may be strengthened using cloth and a thin board. Of the two methods discussed here, the first reinforces the paperback with inner hinges, utilizes a thinner board, and allows the original cover to show. The second method reinforces the paperback with outer hinges, utilizes a thicker board, and hides the original cover, which is retained but is no longer visible without lifting the new outer cover. These two procedures are discussed separately in the following sections.

These procedures provide a stronger cover for the book, whereas the use of tape or laminate serves only to protect the original cover. Large-format paperbacks or paperback reference books are good candidates for reinforcement with boards. Perfect-bound paperbacks are best preserved by adding inner hinges, as the addition of outer hinges and heavier boards can cause the cover to separate from the textblock. The addition of inner hinges is also the best alternative when it is important that the original cover remain visible, which may be the case with art books. Reference books might best be preserved by adding outer hinges and heavier boards, since they are used so frequently.

Reinforcing a Paperback Cover with Inner Hinges

Supplies

Bristol board (.010 or .030 inch)
Linen or cotton cloth
PVA
Glue brush
Scissors
Straightedge
X-Acto or Olfa knife or scalpel
Bone folder
Waste paper or polyester film scraps
Wax paper
Plywood boards
Weights

Procedure

1. Cut two pieces of Bristol board precisely the height of the book and ¼ inch narrower than the book is wide (see Figure 5.34a). The grain of these boards should run parallel to the spine of the book.

2. Cut two pieces of cloth the height of the book and 1 inch wide (see Figure 5.34b).

3. If the cover is tipped onto the first and last leaves of the book, carefully separate the cover from the inner edge of these leaves. Do not separate the cover from the spine, just from the first and last leaves of the textblock. (See Figure 5.34c–d.)

4. Open the book, spread PVA evenly on one piece of cloth, glued side down, and position this piece of cloth along the inner hinge of one cover. Half of the cloth strip should rest on the cover and half on the first leaf of the textblock. Use the bone folder to rub the cloth tightly into place. (See Figure 5.34e.)

5. Spread PVA evenly on a piece of Bristol board and place it, glued side down, on the inside of the cover, aligning the fore-edge, top, and bottom of the board with the fore-edge, top, and bottom of the original cover (see Figure 5.34f).

6. Place a piece of wax paper between the cover and first page, close the book, and rub the cover with a bone folder over a piece of polyester film or spun polyester (see Figure 5.34g).

7. Turn the book over and repeat steps 4–6 for the back cover of the book.

8. Allow the glue to dry overnight under weights.

Reinforcing a Paperback Cover with Outer Hinges

Supplies

Pressboard or barrier board (up to 0.060 inch)
Linen or cotton cloth
Book cloth
PVA
Glue brush
Scissors
Straightedge
X-Acto or Olfa knife or scalpel
Bone folder
Sandpaper (220 grit)
Spun polyester or polyester film scraps
Wax paper
Plywood boards
Weights

Figure 5.34. Reinforcing a Paperback with Inner Hinges

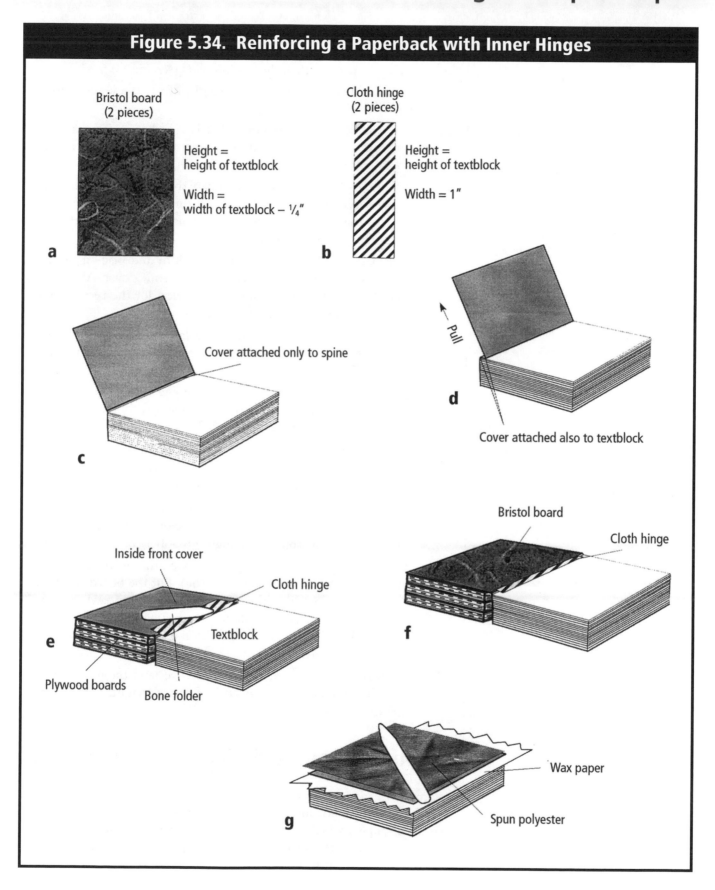

a Bristol board (2 pieces)

Height = height of textblock

Width = width of textblock − ¼″

b Cloth hinge (2 pieces)

Height = height of textblock

Width = 1″

c Cover attached only to spine

d Pull

Cover attached also to textblock

e Inside front cover

Cloth hinge

Textblock

Plywood boards

Bone folder

f Bristol board

Cloth hinge

g Wax paper

Spun polyester

Procedure

1. Cut two pieces of board that are as long as the book is tall and ¼ inch narrower than the book is wide (see Figure 5.35a).

2. Cut two pieces of cloth to the height of the book and 1 inch wide (see Figure 5.35b).

3. Cut one piece of book cloth that is 2 inches wider than the spine of the book and 2 inches longer than the height of the book (see Figure 5.35c).

4. (Optional) If you are covering a paperback that has a shiny or glossy cover, you can lightly sand a ½-inch strip along the spine edge of the front and back covers. This will allow the glue to adhere better to the cover.

5. Spread PVA evenly on one piece of cloth and place it, glued side down, along the spine edge of the front cover. Attach ⅜ inch to ½ inch of the cloth to the cover; let the rest extend beyond the spine (see Figure 5.35d).

6. Fold the cloth back over itself on a line even with the spine, leaving the unattached portion of the glued side facing up (see Figure 5.35e).

7. Place a board on the glued cloth, aligning the fore-edge, top, and bottom of the board with the fore-edge, top, and bottom of the original cover (see Figure 5.35f).

8. Repeat steps 5–7 for the back cover of the book.

9. Spread PVA on the spine of the book and position it in the center of the piece of book cloth (see Figure 5.36a).

10. Make two cuts in the tabs of book cloth that extend beyond the head and tail of the book. These cuts should be on a line with the corners of the spine. (See Figure 5.36b.)

11. Spread PVA on one side flap of book cloth and turn the flap over onto the cover (see Figure 5.36c). Lift the board and fold the tabs at head and tail over the inside of the board. Repeat this process for the other side flap, and trim the remaining flap at head and tail so that it is even with the top and bottom of the spine. (See Figure 5.36c–d.)

12. Put wax paper between the original cover and the new boards and allow the glue to dry overnight under weights (see Figure 5.36e).

Reinforcement and Binding of Pamphlets

Pamphlets may be reinforced before attaching them to pamphlet binders. In the following procedures, the pamphlet is sewn to an extra sheet of paper, which is then glued into the pamphlet binder. The sewing reinforces the structure of the pamphlet, while the paper wrap keeps the document from being directly adhered to the binder.

Figure 5.35. Reinforcing a Paperback with Outer Hinges

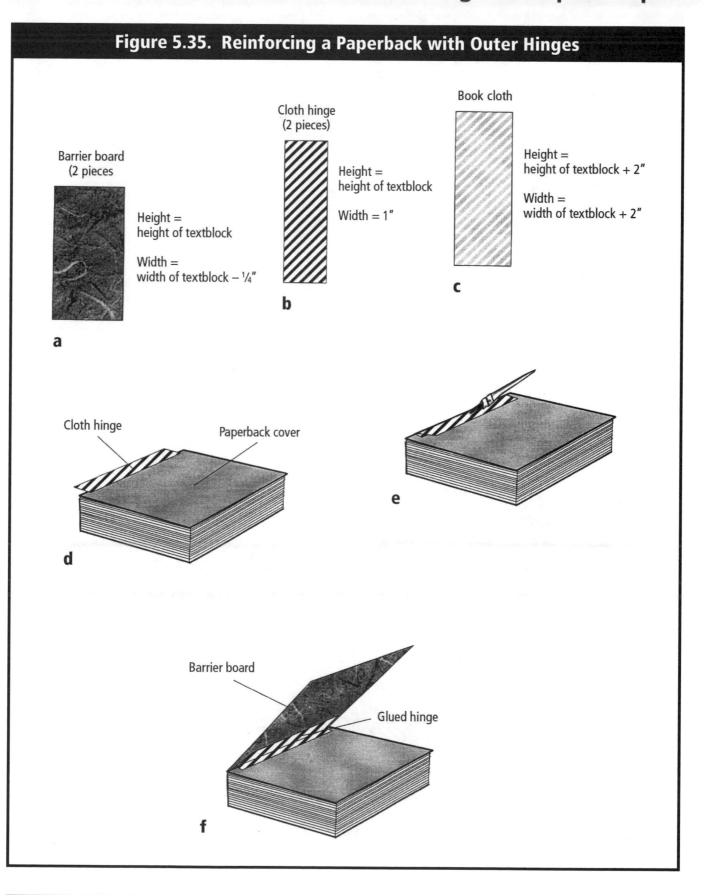

Barrier board
(2 pieces

Height =
height of textblock

Width =
width of textblock − ¼"

a

Cloth hinge
(2 pieces)

Height =
height of textblock

Width = 1"

b

Book cloth

Height =
height of textblock + 2"

Width =
width of textblock + 2"

c

Cloth hinge

Paperback cover

d

e

Barrier board

Glued hinge

f

Figure 5.36. Reinforcing a Paperback with Outer Hinges, Continued

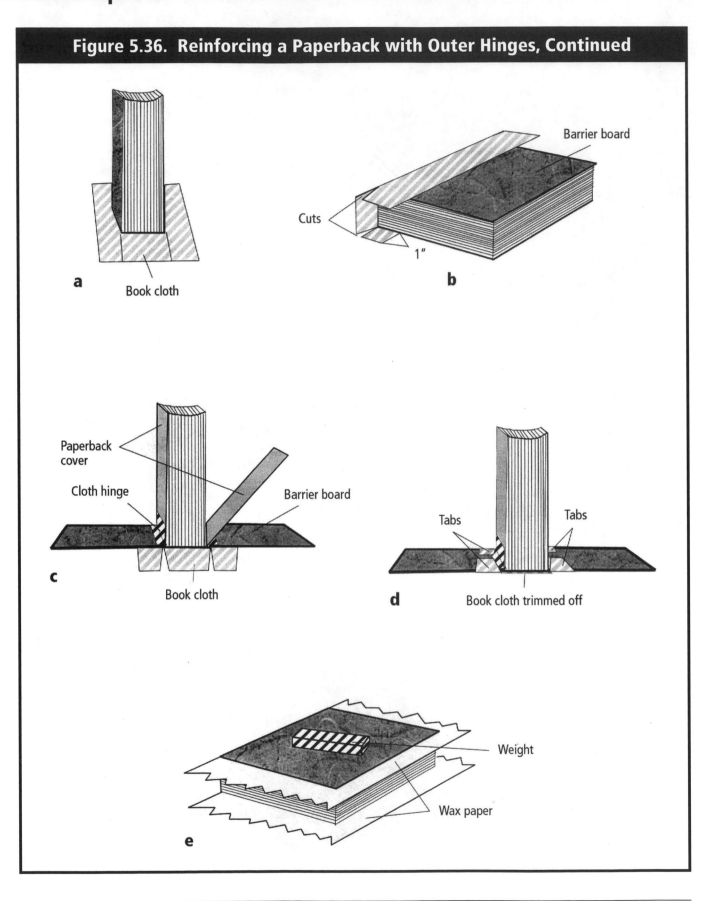

a — Book cloth

b — Barrier board — Cuts — 1"

c — Paperback cover — Cloth hinge — Barrier board — Book cloth

d — Tabs — Tabs — Book cloth trimmed off

e — Weight — Wax paper

Reinforcing a Pamphlet

Supplies

Sheet of white paper, preferably acid-free and buffered
Dissecting tool or ice pick
Linen thread
Chenille or candlewicking needle
Beeswax
Micro-spatula

Procedures

1. Open the pamphlet and lay it flat.

2. Carefully lift up the ends of the staples with a bone folder (see Figure 5.37a).

3. Turn the pamphlet over, and carefully remove any staples from the spine with a micro-spatula.

4. Cut a piece of white paper, preferably acid-free and buffered, the exact size of the pamphlet cover. Wrap this around the outside of the pamphlet.

5. Make five evenly spaced holes with a dissecting tool or an ice pick (see Figure 5.37b). Small pamphlets may need only three holes, and very large ones seven holes. In all cases, however, there *must* be an odd number of holes.

6. Cut a piece of linen thread three times the length of the pamphlet. Wax the thread thoroughly with beeswax.

7. Thread a chenille or candlewicking needle and secure the thread at one end by piercing it (see Figure 5.25e, p. 142).

8. Starting with the middle hole, draw the needle and thread through to the spine of the pamphlet. To keep the free end of the thread from coming through, either secure it with your thumb or wrap it around a small paper clip. Pull the needle through the next hole up (i.e., the fourth hole) in toward the gutter of the textblock. Draw the needle through the top hole back toward the spine again, then through the next hole (i.e., the fourth hole) toward the gutter again, being careful not to pierce the thread that you already have pulled through. The sewing should be kept taut as you go along. Continue in this manner until you have pulled the thread through the second hole toward the gutter. (See Figure 5.37c.)

9. Making sure that the sewing is taut, remove the needle (and paper clip if you have used one) from the thread. Tie a tight square knot as close to the second hole as possible so that the bulge will fit into the hole. (See Figure 5.37d.) The beeswax should help hold the thread in position as you make your knot. Clip off the ends of the thread as short as possible.

10. Attach the pamphlet, with its paper wrap now sewn in place, into the appropriate commercial pamphlet binder.

Figure 5.37. Reinforcing a Pamphlet

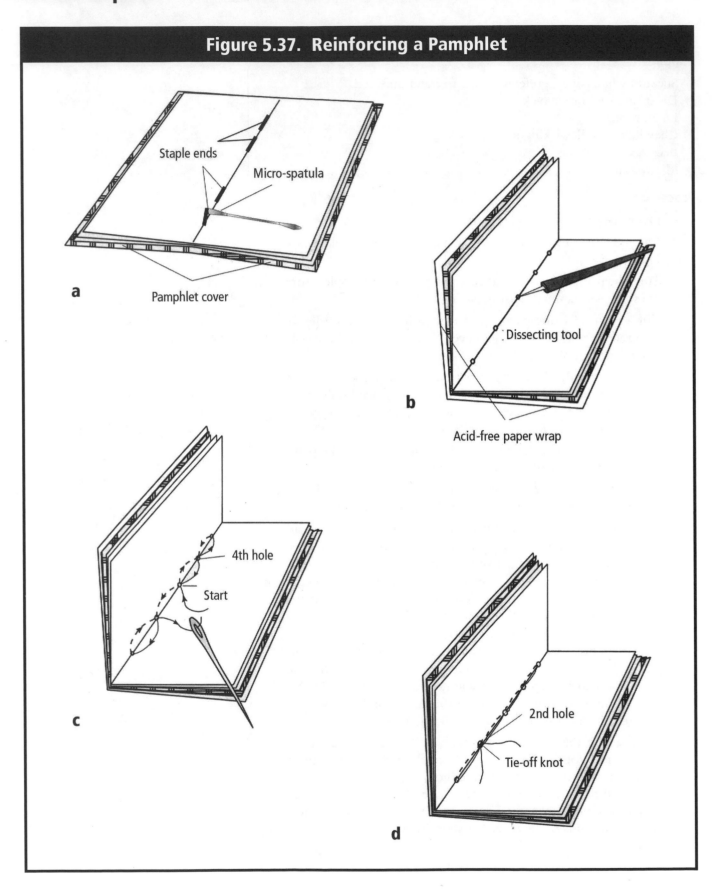

Making a Pamphlet Binder

You may choose to make your own pamphlet binder. This procedure is relatively easy and inexpensive and allows you the choice of materials appropriate to the document.

Supplies

Barrier board (60 point)
Linen hinging tape
PVA
Glue brush
Bone folder
Wax paper
Weight

Procedure

1. Cut two pieces of barrier board the height of the pamphlet plus ¼ inch and the width of the pamphlet plus ¼ inch (see Figure 5.38a).

2. Cut two strips of linen tape the height of the pamphlet and 2 inches wide (see Figure 5.38b).

3. Measure the thickness of the sewn pamphlet and align the two pieces of barrier board exactly this far apart. Position a strip of linen tape equidistant onto the outside of the two boards. Adhere using a bone folder. (See Figure 5.38c.)

4. Turn this cover over and attach the second strip of linen tape across the middle and onto the boards. Be sure to rub it down with a bone folder so that it adheres well to both the tape and the boards. (See Figure 5.38d.)

5. Glue out one side of the paper wrap and place this, glued side down, onto one of the pieces of barrier board. The spine of the pamphlet should line up with the edge of the board. Open the pamphlet and smooth down the paper with a bone folder. (See Figure 5.38e.) Place a piece of wax paper between this endpaper and the pamphlet cover. Glue out the second endpaper. (See Figure 5.38f.) Carefully fold the pamphlet binder over onto the endpaper, aligning the fore-edges of the two pieces of board. Open the board and smooth the endpaper down with a bone folder. Place a piece of wax paper between this endpaper and the pamphlet cover. Close the pamphlet binder, place a weight on it, and let it dry. (See Figure 5.38g.)

Alternative Conservation Suggestions

All of the procedures discussed in this chapter will extend the life of a book or pamphlet, but some will not necessarily be permanent. For example, if you tighten the hinges of a casebound book that receives

Figure 5.38. Making a Pamphlet Binder

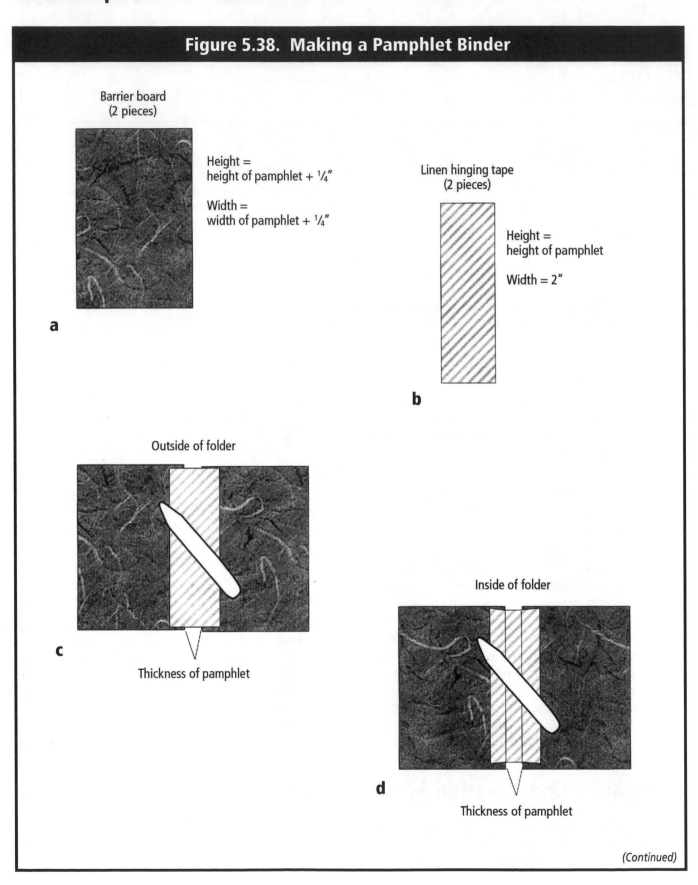

Barrier board
(2 pieces)

Height =
height of pamphlet + ¼"

Width =
width of pamphlet + ¼"

a

Linen hinging tape
(2 pieces)

Height =
height of pamphlet

Width = 2"

b

Outside of folder

c

Thickness of pamphlet

Inside of folder

d

Thickness of pamphlet

(Continued)

Figure 5.38. Making a Pamphlet Binder *(Continued)*

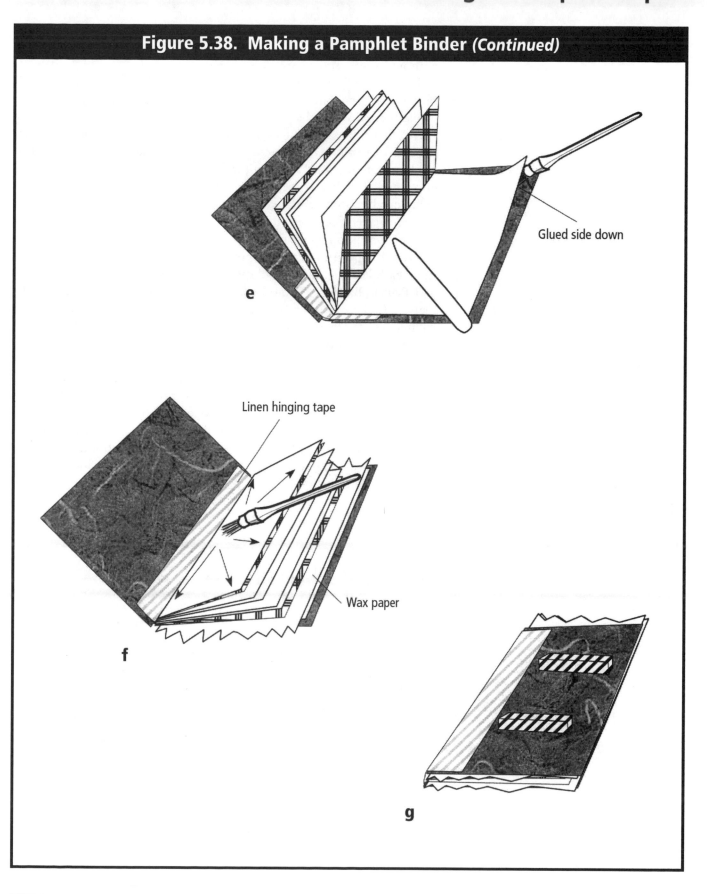

Glued side down

e

Linen hinging tape

Wax paper

f

g

heavy use, its hinges will eventually begin to give way again. It is important to note that the procedures discussed in this chapter cannot be reversed without causing some harm to the object.

For books of artistic or historic value that need hinge and spine repair but are not candidates for full restoration, the use of Japanese paper is a viable alternative. In the preceding treatments for hinge repair (with the exception of the sewn hinge), it may be used instead of jaconet or other material. In spine replacement treatments, it may be used instead of buckram or other book cloth. One of the most common problems encountered is that of loose boards for leather books. A very effective technique has been developed for repair of weakened leather joints using Japanese paper. See Don Etherington, "Japanese Paper Hinge Repair for Loose Boards on Leather Books," *The Abbey Newsletter* 19, no. 3 (1995): 48–49. Another type of technique for reattaching the boards of tight-back leather-bound books is joint tacketing. See Robert Espinosa and Pamela Barrios, "Joint Tacketing: A Method of Board Reattachment," *Book and Paper Group Annual* (1991): 78–83. Both of these techniques may be successfully accomplished with training and practice.

If you have books of greater artistic, bibliographic, or historic value, they should be treated or restored by a professional conservator. If full restoration is not within your budget, a protective enclosure should be made for such items. Some of the enclosures discussed in Chapter 6 might be considered as alternative procedures for these books. Book wraps may be made for books with weak joints if the books do not circulate frequently; phase boxes may be made for books that have damage to the hinges or spine; clamshell boxes may be made for books of value that need added protection.

Resources

Binding and Sewing Structures

Johnson, Arthur W. *The Thames and Hudson Manual of Book Binding*. London: Thames and Hudson, 1978. See pp. 93–157 and 194–203.

Middleton, Bernard C. *The Restoration of Leather Bindings*. 3rd ed. New Castle, DE: Oak Knoll Press, 1998. See pp. 100–113.

Young, Laura C. *Bookbinding & Conservation by Hand*. New Castle, DE: Oak Knoll Press, 1995. See pp. 5–10.

Repair of Casebound Books

Greenfield, Jane. *Books and Their Care*. New York: H.W. Wilson, 1983. See pp. 129–156.

Kyle, Hedi. *Library Materials Preservation Manual*. New York: Nicholas T. Smith, 1983. See pp. 71–94.

Morrow, Carolyn Clark, and Carole Dyal. *Conservation Treatment Procedures: A Manual of Step-by-Step Procedures for the Maintenance and Repair of Library Materials*. 2nd ed. Littleton, CO: Libraries Unlimited, 1986. See pp. 15–80.

Schechter, Abraham. *Basic Book Repair Methods*. Littleton, CO: Libraries Unlimited, 1999. See pp. 25–28, 37–49, 51–69, and 71–74.

Reinforcement of Paperbound Books

Greenfield, Jane. *Books and Their Care*. New York: H.W. Wilson, 1983. See pp. 129–156 and 156–158.

Kyle, Hedi. *Library Materials Preservation Manual*. New York: Nicholas T. Smith, 1983. See pp. 71–94.

Morrow, Carolyn Clark, and Carole Dyal. *Conservation Treatment Procedures: A Manual of Step-by-Step Procedures for the Maintenance and Repair of Library Materials*. 2nd ed. Littleton, CO: Libraries Unlimited, 1986. See pp. 15–80 and 93–104.

Schechter, Abraham. *Basic Book Repair Methods*. Littleton, CO: Libraries Unlimited, 1999. See pp. 25–28, 37–49, 51–69, and 71–74.

Reinforcement and Binding of Pamphlets

Dartmouth College. *A Simple Book Repair Manual*. Hanover, NH: Dartmouth College, 2000. http://www.dartmouth.edu/~library/preservation/repair/index.html.

Greenfield, Jane. *Books and Their Care*. New York: H.W. Wilson, 1983. See pp. 109–128.

Kyle, Hedi. *Library Materials Preservation Manual*. New York: Nicholas T. Smith, 1983. See pp. 119–135.

Morrow, Carolyn Clark and Carole Dyal. *Conservation Treatment Procedures: A Manual of Step-by-Step Procedures for the Maintenance and Repair of Library Materials*. 2nd ed. Littleton, CO: Libraries Unlimited, 1986. See pp. 81–92.

Protective Enclosures

Many books in your library are probably in such a deteriorated state that the covers either already have separated or are about to separate from the textblock. You may also have several odd sizes of AV materials, or large flat objects like posters or maps. You may even have photo albums or videotapes. All of these items are candidates for protective enclosures. These enclosures can serve two purposes—to hold together an item with several parts, whether a book with loose boards or a filmstrip and its accompanying audiotape; and to protect special items, such as fragile books of historical importance or books with fine bindings.

Many types of enclosures are available commercially, including polyester film envelopes, acid-free folders, and precut phase box kits. Some of these items are a bit more costly than the do-it-yourself methods offered here, but often they can save enough time to more than offset the expense. Of course, there are other considerations as well. For example, the precut phase box kits are actually cheaper than the board recommended for phase box use. However, these kits also use a 20-point board, about the same thickness as a standard catalog card. While this board is heavy enough for books that still have their boards loosely attached or that do not circulate much, it is not heavy enough to protect a more severely deteriorated book or one that circulates frequently.

Several of the protective enclosures discussed in this chapter utilize polyester film, such as Melinex. This is not simply because polyester film is an extremely versatile material, useful in many preservation procedures. It also offers simple, cost-effective solutions to many preservation problems and is available in a variety of forms, including envelopes, precut encapsulation units, sheets, and rolls. Some suppliers even offer polyester film envelopes with a tab along one side, punched with holes for storage in a photo album or other three-ring binder.

Because one type of object can usually be treated with more than one type of enclosure, this chapter will be divided into two sections. The first will discuss enclosures for two-dimensional objects, such as maps and letters. The second will discuss three-dimensional objects, such as pamphlets and books.

Decisions

The following factors will influence your decision regarding the most appropriate repair treatment.

Specific Factors

Condition of this object
Degree of protection required for this object
Projected use of this object
Intrinsic value of this object
Further treatment plans for this object

Enclosures for Two-Dimensional Objects

The most common preservation enclosures for two-dimensional objects are folders, encapsulation, and mats. Selection among these enclosures depends upon the level of support needed and the intended use of the object.

Making an Acid-Free Folder

A folder is the simplest form of enclosure for two-dimensional objects. It can be made from virtually any type of acid-free, and preferably lignin-free, buffered board. In general, a wide range of board weights, or thicknesses, is acceptable. The board must be strong enough and stiff enough to protect the object from abrasion and accidental creasing or folding. The thinnest available board that meets these criteria is usually best because it will take up less room in your flat file storage area. Light- or medium-weight Bristol board, 2-ply mat board, and light-weight barrier board can all be used to make an acid-free folder.

A more important consideration is the acid content of the board. The preferred board in any case will be acid-free and lignin-free; however, some boards are buffered with an agent that allows the board to absorb a certain amount of acid before it becomes acidic itself. This means that the board will last longer when it is adjacent to an acidic object, such an old letter or newspaper clipping. While buffering is good for the storage of almost all paper objects, it is not always good for photographs, particularly for albumen, dye transfer, or chromogenic prints. If you have any old photographs that you are concerned about, contact a photograph conservator.

Most library vendors offer a full line of acid-free folders, ranging from file folders for small objects to map and poster folders for objects as large as 32 by 40 inches. Many vendors even offer both buffered and nonbuffered versions of these folders. Depending upon your resources, these commercially available folders can be a very good alternative to creating your own folders.

The primary disadvantage in using folders for storage is that their two flaps are joined on only one side. While this allows easy access, it does not protect the object as well as encapsulation would. For example, when a folder is moved too quickly, the object inside can slide partially or completely out of the folder. Since it is possible for the object to move around inside the folder, it is possible for the object to get damaged. This often happens when maps of different sizes are housed in folders of the same size all stored in the same drawer. One other disadvantage is that folders take up slightly more space than would encapsulated objects. Of course, in some situations, it is best to use a combination of encapsulation and acid-free folders. For example, several related and individually encapsulated objects might all be kept in one acid-free folder. This combination does not take up as much room as keeping each item in its own folder, yet it gives the added protection of encapsulation to each object.

Procedures follow for making folders for single-sheet or thin objects and for matted or other thick objects. The former include maps, letters, documents, and prints. These objects may also be encapsulated. The latter include works mounted on board, works that have already been matted, or a stack of related works that you want to keep together.

Supplies

Acid-free board
Linen hinging tape
Bone folder
Ruler or straightedge
X-Acto or Olfa knife or scalpel
Linen hinging tape (optional)

Procedure

Measuring and Scoring a Folder for a Single Sheet of Paper

1. Measure the height and width of the object. Add 6 inches to the length, allowing 3 inches of border on both sides. Double the height of the object and add 6 inches. The grain of the board should be parallel to the long side. (See Figure 6.1a.) This is not always possible, however, with larger objects.

2. Cut a piece of board for the folder to the above measurements.

3. Score the board in the middle lengthwise with a bone folder (see Figure 6.1b).

4. If the board is too thick to bend, you will need to score it and then cut it. At the middle point of the short side, place a straightedge and score the board by running the *tip* of your bone folder along this line (see Figure 6.1c). Turn the board over and make a cut with a scalpel exactly on the reverse side of the score you have just made (see Figure 6.1d). Be very careful to cut only the outside layer of the board.

5. Bend the board again at the crease, with the cut being on the outside. When the board folds easily, close the folder and rub

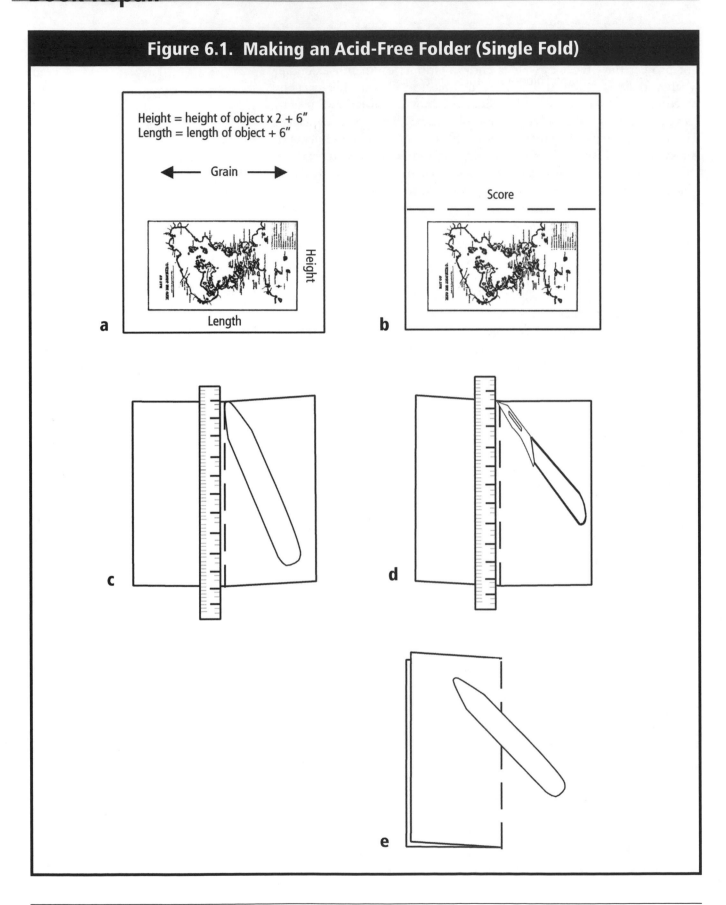

Figure 6.1. Making an Acid-Free Folder (Single Fold)

Height = height of object x 2 + 6"
Length = length of object + 6"

Grain

Height

Length

a

Score

b

c

d

e

the outside of the crease with a bone folder (see Figure 6.1e). You may reinforce the fold with linen hinging tape.

Measuring and Scoring a Folder for a Thick Object

1. Measure the height, width, and depth of the object. Add 6 inches to the width to form the *length* of the board. Double the height of the object, and add the depth plus 6 inches. This will be the measurement of the *height* of the board. The grain of the board should be parallel to the long side. (See Figure 6.2a.) This is not always possible, however, with larger objects.

2. Cut a piece of board for the folder to the above measurements.

3. Find the midpoint on the height edge of the board. Take your depth measurement and add ¼ inch. Divide this total in half. (See Figure 6.2b.)

4. Draw one line this distance above the midpoint and one below the midpoint mark. (For a ½-inch mat the lines will be ⅜ inch above and below the midpoint mark.) Score these lines with a straightedge and bone folder (see Figure 6.2c). The additional ¼ inch will keep the object from binding in your creases.

5. Turn the board over and make a cut with a straightedge and scalpel exactly on the reverse side of each score you have just made (see Figure 6.2d). Be very careful to cut only the outside layer of the board.

6. Bend the board again at the creases, with the cuts being on the outside. When the board folds easily, close the folder and rub the outside of the creases with a bone folder (see Figure 6.2e).

Encapsulation

Encapsulations are made of two pieces of polyester film, one behind the object and one in front, that are attached along two or more edges. The edges of this package may be sealed with heat or sonar welders, but these machines are expensive. Double-sided tape is inexpensive, readily available, and easy to use; thus, it is the most common method employed for encapsulation. Flat items, such as documents, maps, posters, or prints, that are damaged, brittle, or wanting overall protection and that are frequently used are perfect candidates for encapsulation. This type of enclosure is also particularly useful for items that have printing on both sides. There are three basic types:

1. **Two-sided encapsulation**: This format is very useful for fragile or large documents that need to be consulted frequently. Leaving the top corner open allows easy access to the material. This enclosure is also good for items that need to be kept in a ring binder or a post-binding album.

2. **Three-sided encapsulation**: This format is an important type of holder for documents and photographic prints and negatives that are going to be stored in archival folders or boxes. The

Figure 6.2. Making an Acid-Free Folder (Double Fold)

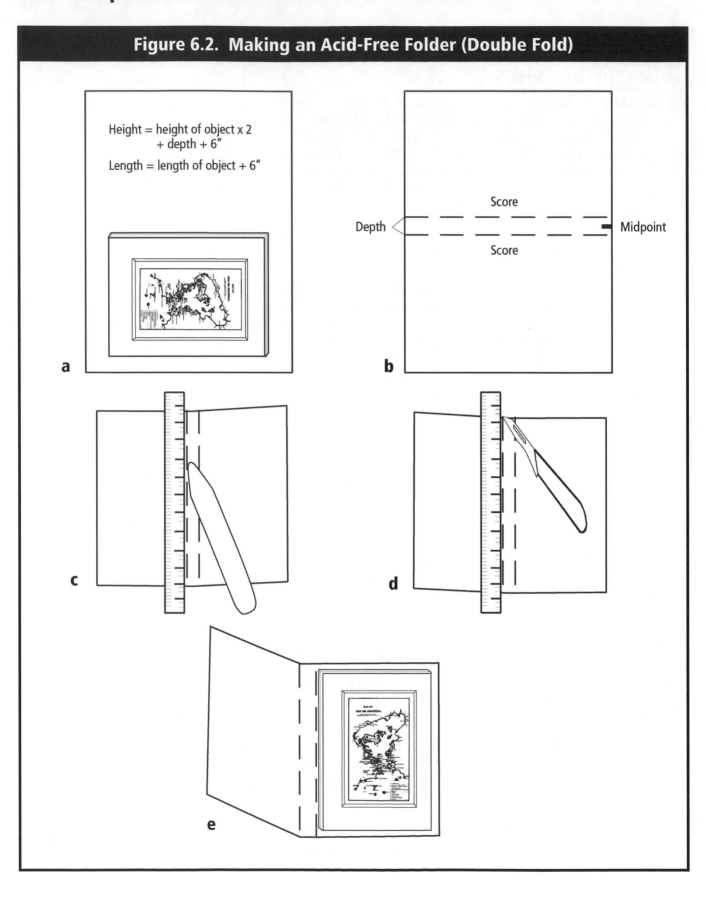

Height = height of object x 2
+ depth + 6″

Length = length of object + 6″

a

Score

Depth

Score

Midpoint

b

c

d

e

attached three sides make a very sturdy enclosure, although it can sometimes be difficult to remove the object easily and cleanly.

3. **Four-sided encapsulation**: This format is the archival alternative to lamination. It is especially useful for large items that are handled frequently, such as maps and posters. A modification using polyester tab supports enables objects to be safely hung vertically for exhibit.

Encapsulation is safe for most flat objects, although static electricity may cause problems with some types of media. Encapsulation should not be used on charcoal, graphite, or pastel drawings, as these items have very loose pigments that can be pulled off the surface of the paper by the static electricity of the polyester film. The same caution applies to objects that have been water-colored, such as illustrations and maps. If testing reveals that there are no pigments lying on the surface of the paper and only the dye remains in the paper, then it is safe to encapsulate the object. When in doubt, it is best not to allow the image to come into contact with the polyester film. This caution is also important when using film as a protective cover in mats.

If the item selected for encapsulation is in a condition that could benefit from cleaning, it is wise to do so before it is encapsulated. If deacidification is needed, then it, too, should be done prior to encapsulation. These steps are particularly important for objects receiving four-sided encapsulation.

Supplies

Melinex
Double-sided tape (1/4-inch 3M Scotch Brand 415)
Bone folder
Weight
Spun polyester
Soft bristled brush (such as a hake brush or a photography brush)
Metal ruler
X-Acto or Olfa knife or scalpel

Optional supplies

Measuring grid
Squeegee
Brayer
Scissors
Cotton glove
Encapsulation machine

Polyester Film

Polyester film attracts through static electricity; thus, care must be taken that your hands are clean and dry and the workspace clean and free of dust. Throughout this procedure, it is preferable that the polyester film be handled only on the extreme edges, which will not come into contact with the item itself. When working in other areas of the polyester film, it is best to wear cotton gloves or place another protective layer of film or spun polyester under your hand.

Polyester film can also be difficult to handle. The 3-mil thickness used for encapsulation, for example, is "springy," and the piece of film can go awry if it is not guided well. It is thus recommended that when laying down the top piece of film you use a bone folder, squeegee, or brayer to help guide the piece down smoothly (see Figure 6.3a–c). This procedure also helps to expel the air throughout the encapsulation.

It is important that the pieces of film are squared and of exactly the same size. This allows you to line up the edges with each other, making the encapsulation neater and easier to complete. Polyester film is also very sharp, and thus you may want to round the corners after you have finished your encapsulation. This may be done with a corner rounder or a scalpel. This step is particularly important if the item is not going to receive a further enclosure, such as a folder or mat.

Figure 6.3. Tools for Encapsulation

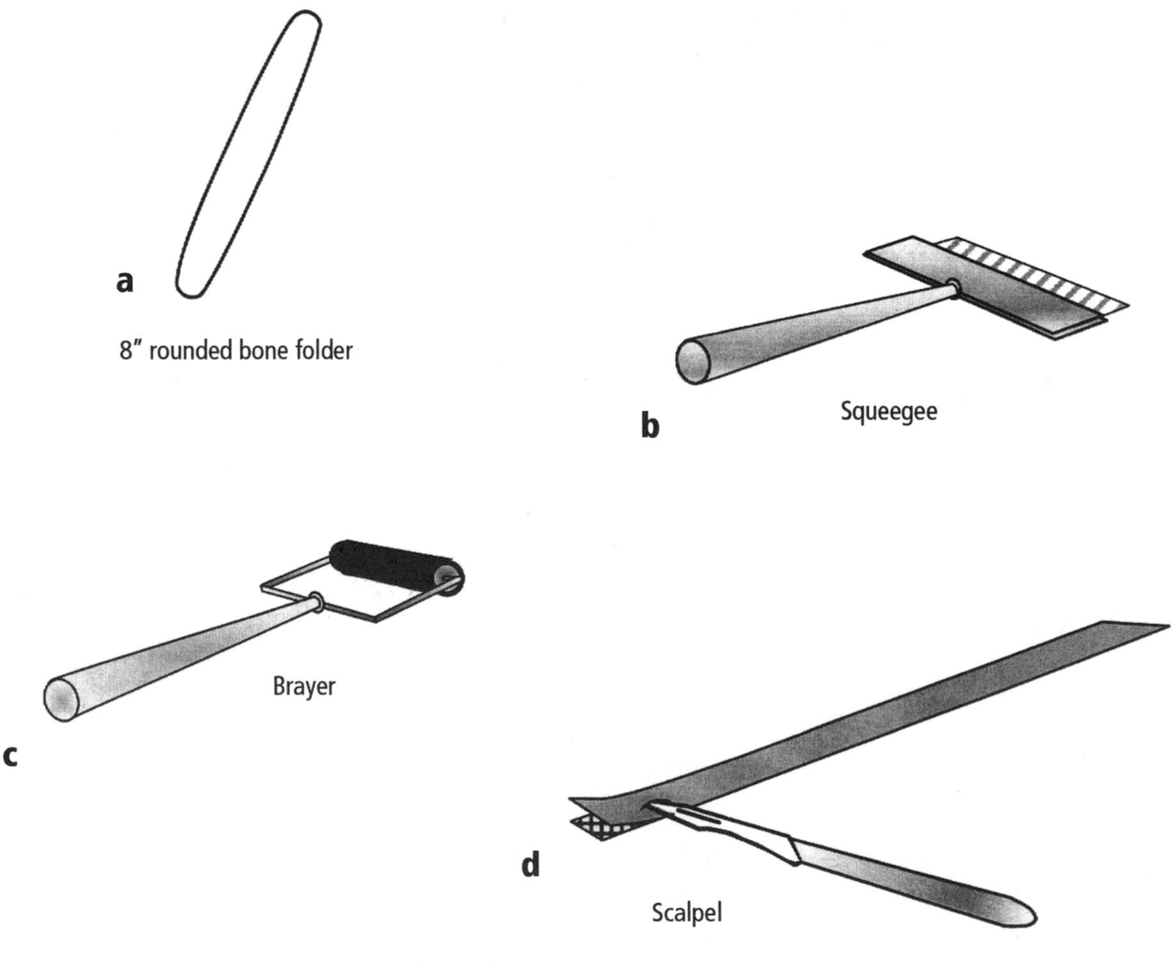

a
8″ rounded bone folder

b
Squeegee

c
Brayer

d
Scalpel

Double-Sided Tape

Only 3M Scotch Brand 415 tape is suitable for preservation work. It is available in various widths, but the ¼-inch tape is the best to use for encapsulation. This tape is very sticky and is difficult to remove from polyester film. Once you have placed a strip where you want it, rub it down with a bone folder. This will adhere the tape firmly to the film and will allow you to remove the paper backing easily. If you have difficulty lifting up this backing with your fingers, pierce it with a scalpel and pull it off (see Figure 6.3d). Because of its stickiness, the tape should not be right on the edge of the encapsulation film and should *never* touch the object itself. Leaving a ¼-inch space between the tape and the outside edge of the encapsulation allows enough space that the tape will remain clean; leaving a ¼-inch space between the tape and the object allows enough space that the object, unless shaken severely, will not slip into the tape. Over a period of years, however, the adhesive of the tape will soften, and the pieces of film will no longer bond together through static electricity.

Grids

A variety of grids are available from art and drafting supply stores and other companies, or you can make your own. Self-healing cutting mats with grids are also very useful for cutting squared pieces of film. The grids with ¼-inch squares are the most useful for encapsulation because they allow you to lay the strips of tape precisely in place and to maintain the distance between the edges of the film and the tape and between the tape and the object (see Figure 6.4a). Once you have done your measurements on a grid, you may lay down the strips of tape without using the object itself, thus minimizing any possible harm to the object (see Figure 6.4c–d).

Two-Sided Encapsulation

Separate Enclosures

Procedure

1. Lay the item out on a smooth, clean, dry surface and lightly dust the item with a soft bristled brush. Turn the item over and dust the back in the same manner.

2. Measure the item; then cut two pieces of polyester film approximately 2 inches larger than the item in both directions, and lay one of them on a clean, dry surface or on a grid with ¼-inch squares (see Figure 6.4a).

3. Lay the object on this piece of polyester film with 1 inch of film extending beyond the object's edges on all sides. Place a piece of spun polyester and a small weight in the center of the item to hold it in place. (See Figure 6.4b.)

4. If you are using a grid, place pieces of double-sided tape on the polyester film ¼ inch away from and parallel to the bottom and left sides of the object. Leave small ⅛-inch spaces between the

ends of the strips of tape. (See Figure 6.4b.) If you are not using a grid, place strips of tape ½ inch from the bottom and the left edges of the polyester film (see Figure 6.4e). Position the object ¼ inch from both pieces of tape, and place a piece of spun polyester and small weight in the center of the item to hold it in place.

5. Once you are certain that the strips of tape are positioned correctly, smooth them down with a bone folder.

6. Remove the weight and protective layer and place the second piece of polyester film on top of the item. Replace the weight and protective layer, making sure the object is still square on the film between the strips of tape.

7. While gently holding one corner of the top piece of polyester film, remove the backing from the tape on two adjacent sides of the object (see Figure 6.5a).

8. Let the film drop slowly into place, guiding it with a brayer or bone folder. Smooth down the exposed tape with a bone folder. (See Figure 6.5b.)

9. Trim the edges of the polyester film to within approximately ¼ inch of the tape. Trim the corners of the polyester to a round shape with a scalpel or corner rounder to avoid damaging other items (or yourself) with the sharp corners. This last step is particularly important if the encapsulation is not going to be further protected by a folder or mat and is going to receive heavy use. Smooth down the tape with a bone folder. (See Figure 6.5c.)

Encapsulation for Post-Binding Albums

Procedure

1. Lay the item out on a smooth, clean, dry surface and lightly dust the item with a soft bristled brush. Turn the item over and dust the back in the same manner.

2. Measure the item; then cut two pieces of polyester film approximately 1 inch larger than the item on the top, bottom, and right sides, and 2½ inches larger on the left side. Lay one of them on a clean, dry surface (see Figure 6.6a) or on a grid with ¼-inch squares.

3. Place a strip of tape ½ inch in from the left side of the polyester film piece. This strip should reach to ½ inch from the top and bottom edges of the film. Lay another strip of tape the same length as the first 1½ inches to its right. Place your object ¼ inch away from the edge of the second strip of tape and 1 inch from the bottom edge of the polyester film piece. Place a piece of spun polyester and small weight in the center of the object to hold it in place. Lay another strip of tape ½ inch from the bottom edge, ⅛ inch from the edge of the second piece of tape, and long enough to accommodate the width of your

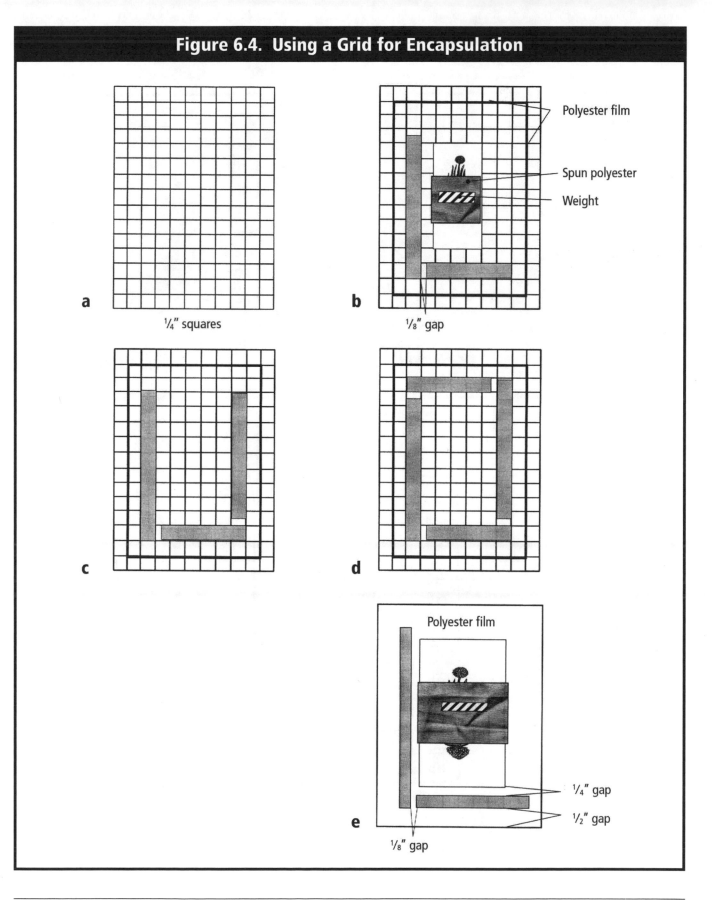

Figure 6.4. Using a Grid for Encapsulation

a — ¼" squares

b — Polyester film / Spun polyester / Weight / ⅛" gap

c

d

e — Polyester film / ¼" gap / ½" gap / ⅛" gap

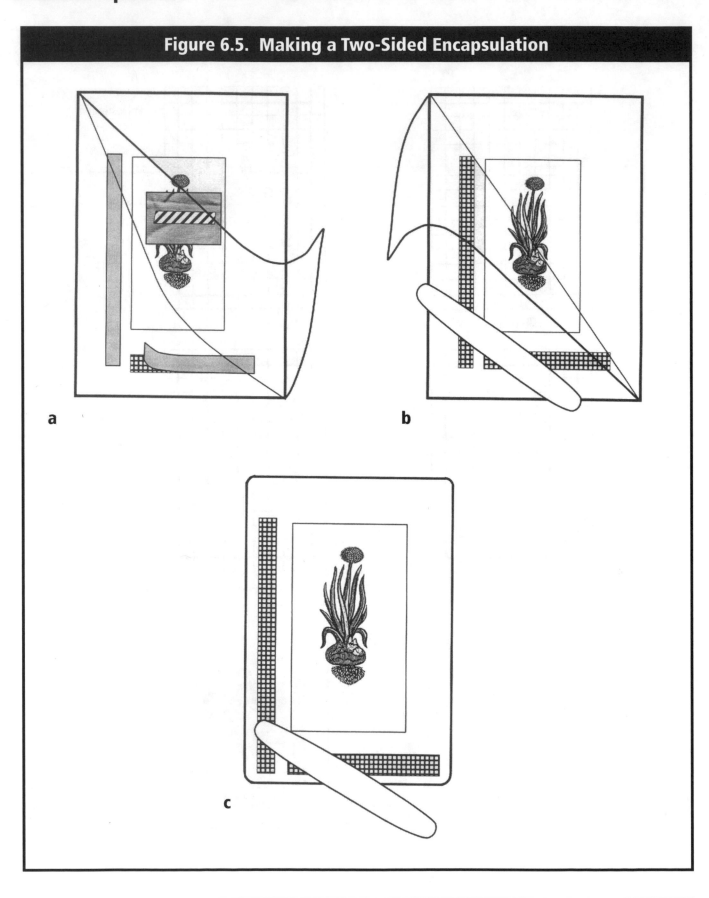

Figure 6.5. Making a Two-Sided Encapsulation

a

b

c

object. Smooth these strips down with a bone folder. (See Figure 6.6a).

4. Remove the weight, protective layer, and the object; place the second piece of polyester film on top of the first, making sure that they are square with each other. Replace the weight and protective layer.

5. Lift up the left side of the top piece of polyester film, and pull off the paper backing layer from the strip of tape. Smooth down with a bone folder. (See Figure 6.6b–c.)

6. Remove the weight and spun polyester, and remove the backing from the other two strips of tape. Holding the edge of the top polyester film piece, slowly guide down and over with a brayer or a bone folder. Smooth the tape down with a bone folder. Make the three holes in the space between the two long strips of tape. Trim the edges of the polyester film piece, allowing ¼ inch between the edges and the strips of tape. (See Figure 6.6d.)

7. Place the encapsulation over the posts (or rings) of your binder (see Figure 6.6e).

8. Lift back the top piece of polyester film and carefully insert the object until it is ¼ inch from both strips of tape (see Figure 6.6f).

Three-Sided Encapsulation

Procedure

1. Perform steps 1–3 above for two-sided encapsulation of separate enclosures.

2. If you are using a grid, place pieces of double-sided tape on the polyester film ¼ inch away from and parallel to the bottom, left, and right sides of the item. The strips on the two sides should be even in height. Leave small ⅛ inch spaces between the ends of the strips of tape. If you are not using a grid, place these strips of tape ½ inch from the bottom, left, and right edges of the polyester film.

3. Once you are certain that the strips of tape are positioned correctly, smooth them down with a bone folder.

4. Place the second piece of polyester film on top of the first, making sure that they are both square with each other. Place a weight and protective layer on top.

5. Gently roll up the bottom edge of the top piece of polyester film and remove the paper backing from the strip of tape (see Figure 6.7a).

6. Let the top piece down slowly; then smooth out with a bone folder over the exposed tape (see Figure 6.7b).

7. Remove the weight and protective layer. Gently roll down the top piece of polyester film until it exposes the two side strips of tape. (See Figure 6.7c.)

Figure 6.6. Making a Two-Sided Encapsulation with a Post Binding

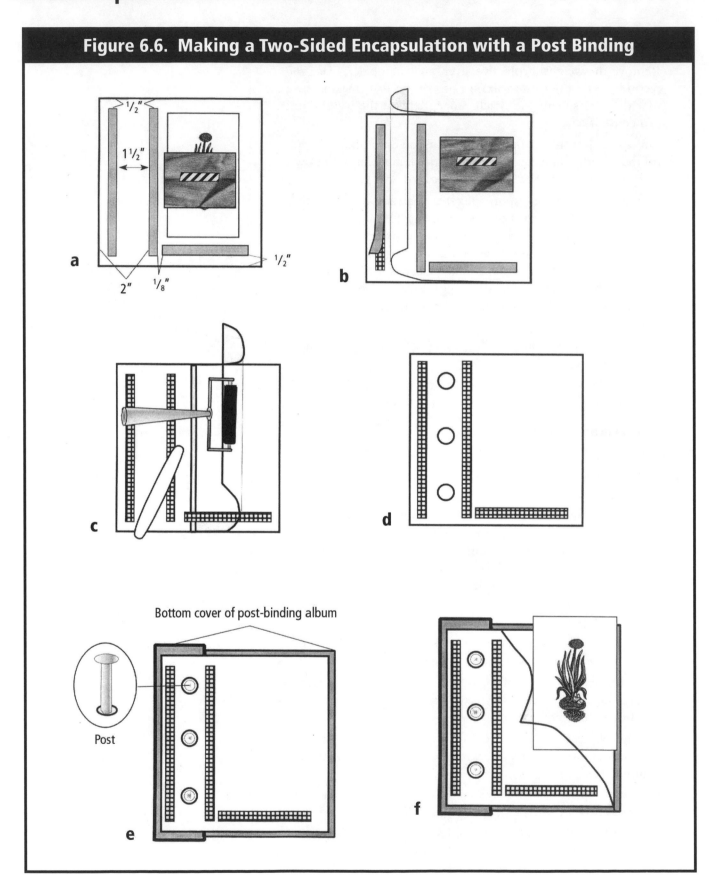

Bottom cover of post-binding album

Post

Figure 6.7. Making a Three-Sided Encapsulation

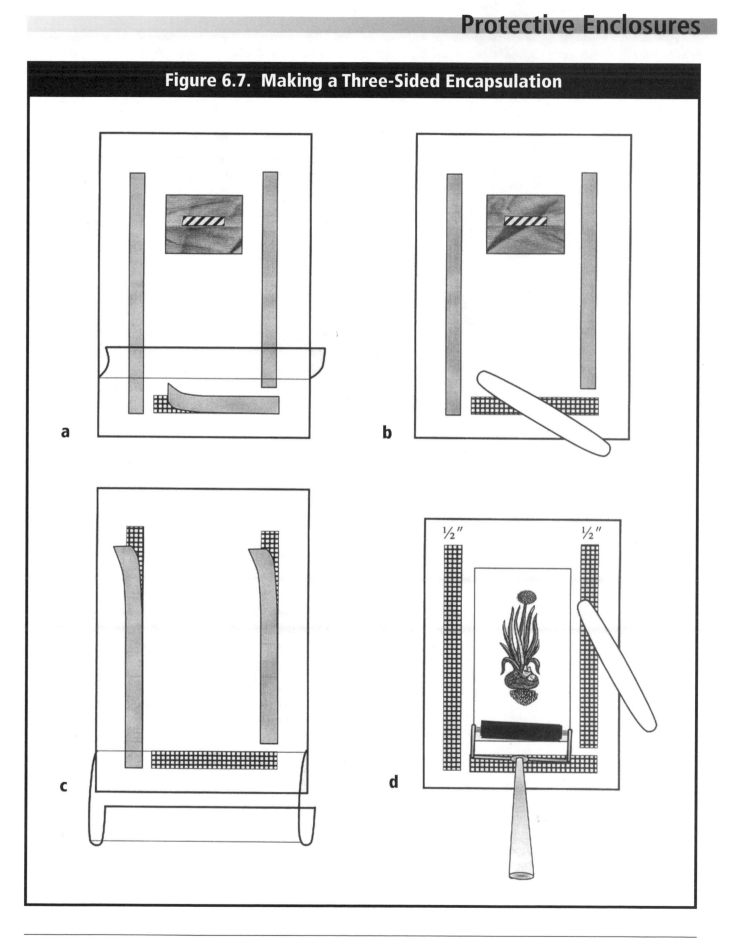

8. Remove the paper backing and slowly roll back the top piece of film; use a brayer to help you put the film back down evenly. Smooth down the strips of tape. There should be at least ½ inch between the ends of the tape and the top edge of the polyester film. Place the object in the encapsulation. (See Figure 6.7d.)

9. The corners may be rounded, although most often this polyester document holder will be housed within an archival folder or box.

Four-Sided Encapsulation

Separate Enclosures

Procedure

1. Perform steps 1–3 for two-sided encapsulation of separate enclosures.

2. If you are using a grid, place pieces of double-sided tape on the polyester film ¼ inch away from and parallel to each of the four sides of the item. Leave small ⅛ inch spaces between the ends of the strips of tape. If you are not using a grid, place strips of tape ½ inch from the four edges of the polyester film. Position the object ¼ inch from the pieces of tape, and place a piece of spun polyester and small weight in the center of the item to hold it in place.

3. Once you are certain that the strips of tape are positioned correctly, smooth them down with a bone folder.

4. Remove the weight and protective layer and place the second piece of polyester film on top of the item. Replace the weight and protective layer, making sure the item is still square on the film between the strips of tape.

5. While gently holding one corner of the top piece of polyester film, remove the backing from the tape on two adjacent sides of the item (see Figure 6.8a). If the shape of the enclosure is tall or unwieldy, however, follow the steps listed for a three-sided encapsulation, and roll the polyester film from the bottom to the top (see Figure 6.7a–d).

6. Let the film drop slowly into place. Smooth down the exposed tape with a bone folder. (See Figure 6.8b.)

7. Pull back the opposite corner, and remove the backing from the two remaining strips of tape. While slowly lowering the top piece of polyester film, use a brayer or large bone folder to help you lay the film down evenly and to expel the air through the gaps between the strips of tape. (See Figure 6.8c.)

8. Trim the edges of the polyester film to within approximately ¼ inch of the tape. Trim the corners of the polyester to a round shape with a scalpel or corner rounder, to avoid damaging other items (or yourself) with the sharp corners. This last step is particularly important if the encapsulation is not going to be further

Figure 6.8. Making a Four-Sided Encapsulation

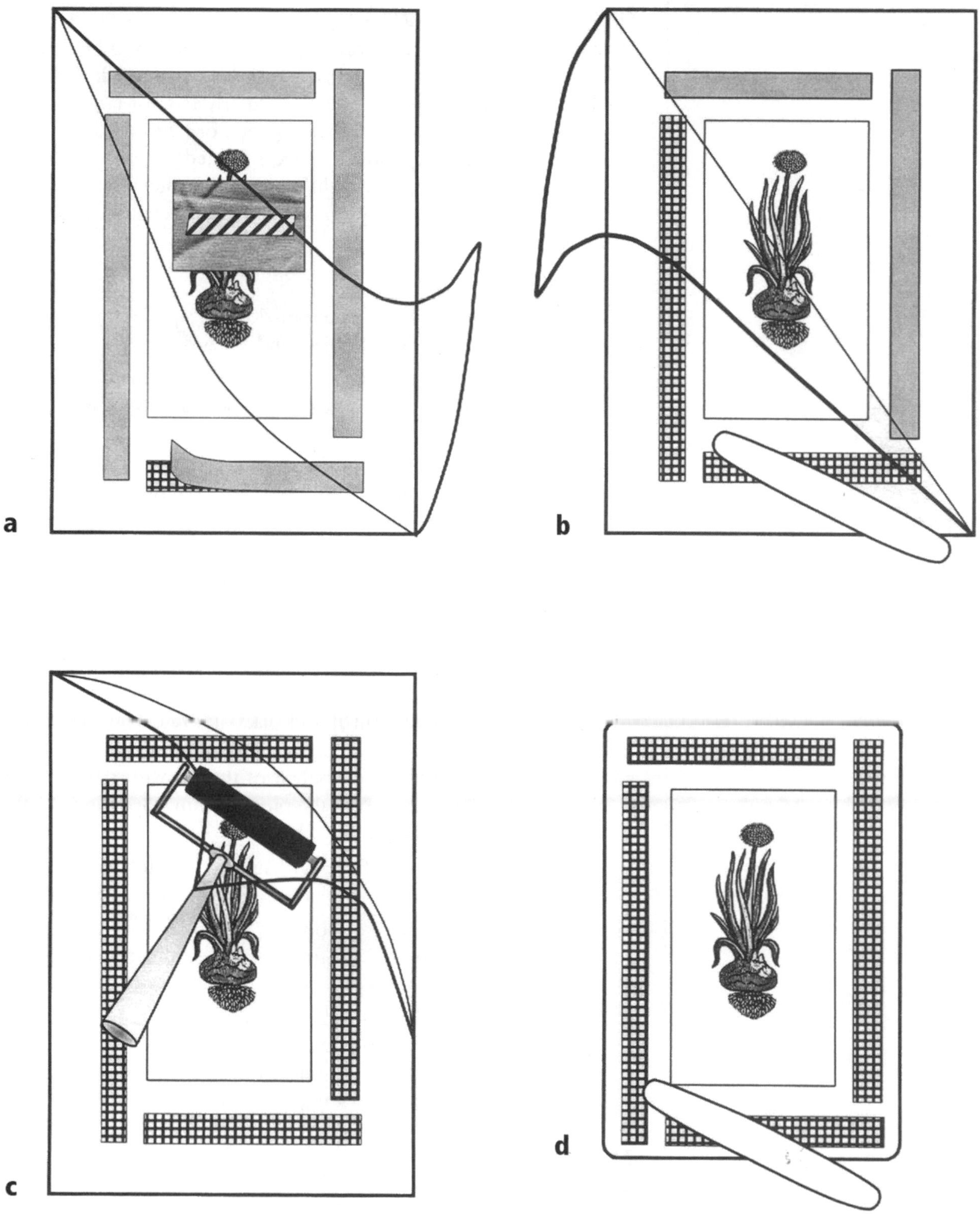

protected by a folder or mat and is going to receive heavy use. Smooth out any bubbles that still appear in the tape. (See Figure 6.8d.)

Encapsulation for Matting or Exhibit

When an object encapsulated with polyester film and tape is hung vertically, either matted or by itself, there is the real danger of it falling down into the bottom strip of tape. This is particularly true of large horizontal objects such as maps, works on heavy paper, or items encapsulated long enough for the tape adhesive to have softened. A simple addition of folded tabs of polyester film will keep this problem from occurring. These tabs can serve the same purpose, of course, even if the encapsulation is kept lying flat.

Procedure

1. Follow steps 1–3 above for a four-sided encapsulation of separate enclosures. Remove the object and set aside.

2. Place a ruler or straightedge along the bottom of the object. Make a mark at this point on the paper backing of each of the side strips of tape. (See Figure 6.9a.)

3. Cut tabs 1 by 1 inch from pieces of 3-mil polyester film. The number of tabs depends on the needs of the object, although it is never fewer than two. Horizontal maps, for example, may require three or four tabs to provide the proper support. Crease the tab in half, and affix a piece of double-sided tape to the back side of one half of the tab, making sure that there is a border around the tape (see Figure 6.9b). Repeat for the other tab(s).

4. Remove the tape from the backside of one of the tabs. With the straightedge still in place on the marks you have made, position this tab where you want it and place its crease on the edge of the ruler. Be sure that the taped backside is against the piece of polyester film. Rub the back half of the tab with a bone folder to firmly adhere the tab to the piece of film. (See Figure 6.9c.) Repeat for the other tab(s).

5. Bring the front half of the tabs up and crease again. Lay the object into the creases you have made. (See Figure 6.9d.)

6. Place the second piece of polyester film on top of the item and proceed with steps 4–8 for four-sided encapsulation of separate enclosures.

7. Your finished encapsulation will have the object held firmly by the tabs, which are almost invisible (see Figure 6.9e). The corners may be rounded, although this is rarely done for an item to be hung by itself, with a backing, or in window mat.

Mats

Mats are most often thought of as a pretty way to set off framed prints and photographs. They come in many striking colors and may be purchased

Figure 6.9. Making a Four-Sided Encapsulation with Tabs

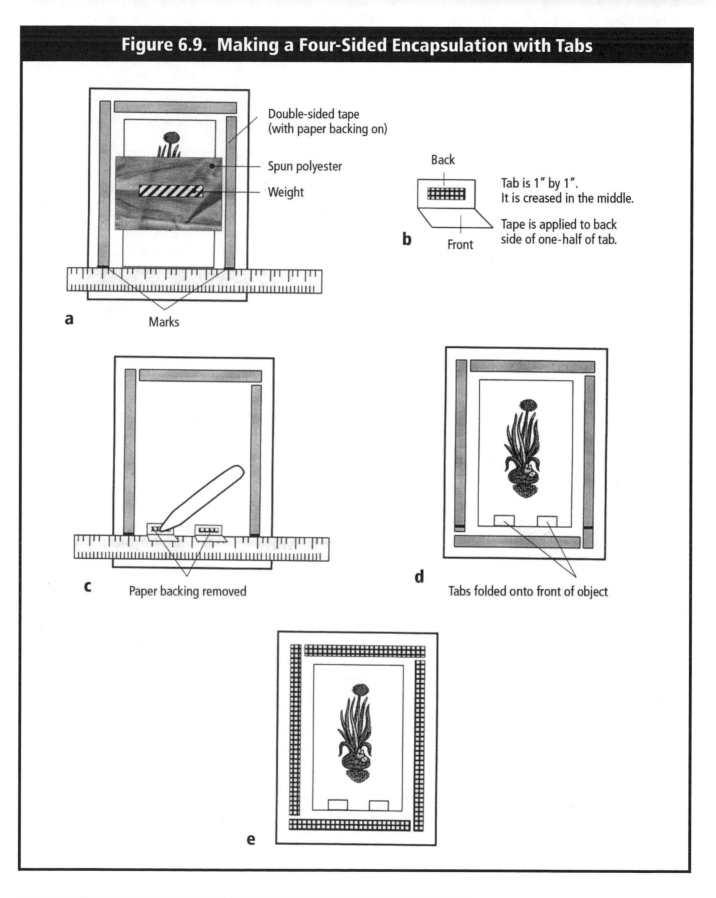

Double-sided tape (with paper backing on)

Spun polyester

Weight

a Marks

Back

Front

b

Tab is 1″ by 1″. It is creased in the middle.

Tape is applied to back side of one-half of tab.

c Paper backing removed

d Tabs folded onto front of object

e

as part of a professional framing job or bought separately from art supply and hobby stores. Mats can, however, also be made part of a preservation program to fulfill two important functions: providing support for documents, maps, photographs, and prints on exhibit; and providing protection for these and other flat objects in storage. To this end, the proper materials must be chosen and the appropriate treatment procedures must be followed.

Three basic types of mats are important for conservation work. Each of these has many variations, such as the addition of onlays of colored board or a solid front board, but the basic structure remains the same.

1. **Standard window mat**: This format consists of two pieces of archival-quality board, one with a window cut in it, that are hinged together to enclose the flat object. The object is hinged to the back board with a T-hinge; the window mat covers the edges of the object and the hinges. (See Figure 6.10a–b.)

2. **Floating window mat**: This format consists of two pieces of archival-quality board, one with a window cut in it, that are hinged together to enclose the flat object. The object is hinged to the back board with a V-hinge; the window mat does not cover the edges of the object, and the hinges are hidden behind the object itself. This format is important when the image comes all the way to the edges of the object and you do not want the window board to cover any of it. (See Figure 6.10c–d.)

3. **Sink mat**: A more complex type of mat akin to a shadow box. Side pieces are mounted on the back board around the edges of the object; they rise above the level of the object to protect it from the window mat or front board. It is particularly useful for warped or very thick objects. Instructions on making a sink mat may be found in *Matting and Hinging Works of Art on Paper*, listed in the Resources at the end of this chapter.

It is very important that only the best archival-quality materials actually touch the object itself. Much damage has been done to irreplaceable works of art on paper through the use of acidic materials such as colored board, cloth matting, tape hinges, cardboard backing, and wood frames. The conditions are exacerbated when the object is housed in such an enclosure permanently, for exhibit or for storage.

The mat board (colored or white) that is widely available for commercial or do-it-yourself framing projects is very acidic. It begins to deteriorate within a few years, leeching acid into the object it is in contact with. It is most often 4-ply board and colored on only one side. Conservation mat board is often termed "museum mounting board" to distinguish it from this acidic type. It is generally found in shades of white (e.g., bright, soft, ivory) and in 2-ply or 4-ply thicknesses. Since many terms are associated with conservation board, it is perhaps best to list the standards accepted by the Library of Congress and most museums:

Figure 6.10. Basic Elements of Matting

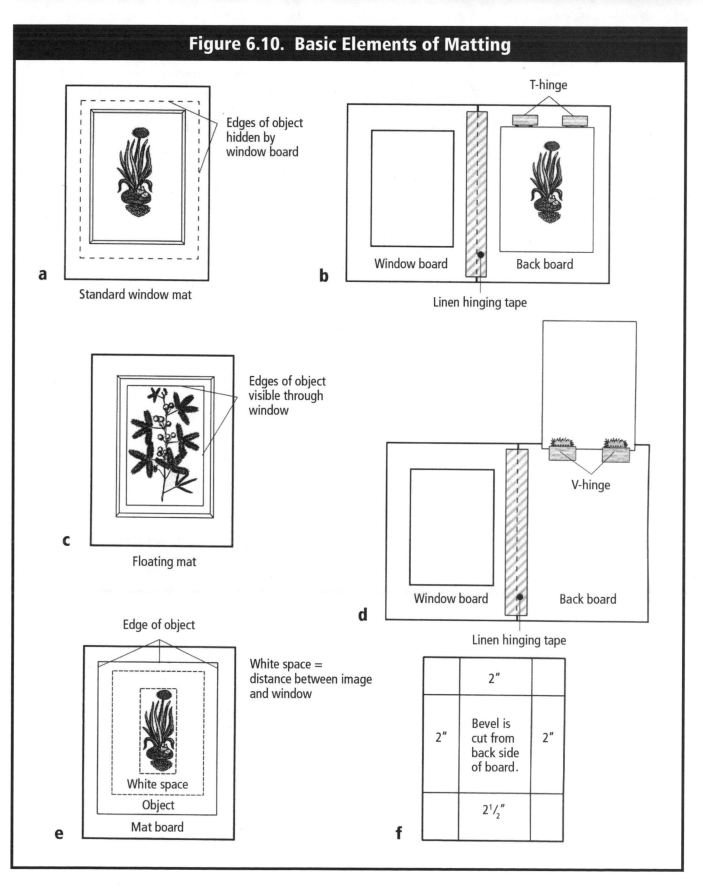

a Standard window mat

Edges of object hidden by window board

b Window board — Back board — T-hinge — Linen hinging tape

c Floating mat

Edges of object visible through window

d Window board — Back board — V-hinge — Linen hinging tape

e Edge of object — White space = distance between image and window — White space — Object — Mat board

f 2″ — 2″ — Bevel is cut from back side of board. — 2″ — 2½″

Made of 100 percent rag (i.e., cotton) or highly refined wood pulp

Acid-free and lignin-free

Buffered with a 2–3 percent alkaline reserve (generally of calcium carbonate) with pH of 8.5

Buffered board or paper is *not* to be used with some types of photographic prints (e.g., albumen, dye transfer, chromogenic) and textiles (e.g., silk, wool)

Adhering to these standards will ensure that the board you use to protect your objects for exhibit or storage will not harm them. It is particularly important that all boards which touch the object be of this quality.

Supplies

Conservation board (4–ply)
Linen hinging tape (1 inch)
Medium-weight Japanese paper
Rice or wheat starch
Spun polyester (or wax paper)
Blotting paper
Small, light weights

Tools

Bone folder
Mat cutter
Straightedge (or ruler)
Tweezers
Print-mounting positioner (optional)

Measuring

Making a good mat that both enhances and protects your document, map, or print is an aesthetic as well as a technical undertaking. The critical measurements involve the width of the "white space" (i.e., between the image and the window) and the width of the border (i.e., between the window and the edge of the mat). The only rule of thumb is that the bottom border be larger than the top and the sides. This is particularly true if the object is going to be hung at eye level. (See Figure 6.10e.)

Begin by measuring the space between the image and the window. Place four strips of board around the image and gradually move them away until you are satisfied with the amount of "white space." Then determine how much border you want surrounding the "white space." Try different proportions. Cut a piece of board that accommodates the width of your border plus the width of the "white space." Cut another piece of board exactly the same size. These two pieces will be your window and back boards. The grain of these boards must be parallel to the longer sides.

Cutting the Window

On the back side of the window mat, draw intersecting lines that establish the boundaries of the window (see Figure 6.10f). Using a hand-held or board-mounted mat cutter, cut the window the appropriate size. For most objects, use the bevel cut, although for documents such as letters the straight cut is to be preferred. Make the cuts from the back side of the board (where the lines are). Always cut toward the outside edge and rotate the board 90 degrees each time you make a cut. After the window cutout has been removed, run your bone folder lightly over the sharp edges of the cuts on the back side of the mat. This step helps prevent any damage that the sharp edges may cause to the object, particularly if these mats are at any time going to be stacked for flat storage.

Standard Window Mat

Procedure

Making the tabs

1. Determine the number of tabs you need to support your object. One should be placed near each corner (no further away than ½ inch), and then spaced evenly between these two, if necessary. A good general size for the hinge tab is 1½ inches by ½ inch; for the crosspiece 2 inches by 1 inch. A medium-weight Japanese paper is generally suitable for hinging, although very fragile objects may require a lighter-weight paper for the hinge tabs themselves. (See Figure 6.11a.)

2. The hinge tabs must be torn, not cut. For methods of tearing Japanese paper, see Chapter 1. The crosspieces may be cut, since they are attached only to the board, not to the object itself. Tear two (or more) hinge tabs, and cut the same number of crosspieces.

Attaching a T-hinge

1. Only about one-third of the short dimension of the hinge tab is actually to be attached to the object. The rest of the tab is affixed to the board by the crosspiece. Place the hinge tabs between two pieces of wax paper, with the edge to be pasted out exposed (see Figure 6.11b). Paste out from the wax paper onto the hinge tab. The paste should be smooth and a little thin, although too much water in the paste will cause both the paper object and the hinge to cockle as they dry.

2. With a pair of tweezers, attach the pasted-out portion of the tabs to the back of the object at its top edge (see Figure 6.11c). Put a piece of spun polyester over the tabs, then a piece of blotting paper, and rub gently with a bone folder (see Figure 6.11d). The blotting paper will absorb the excess moisture. Put a weight on it and let dry. This should take only a few minutes.

3. Paste out a strip of wax paper and lay the crosspieces in the paste. Smooth them down with a bone folder. Allow these pieces time to absorb the paste (they will change color and become more transparent). Just before using them, lightly brush a thin layer of paste over them (see Figure 6.11e).

Figure 6.11. Making a Standard (T-hinge) Window Mat

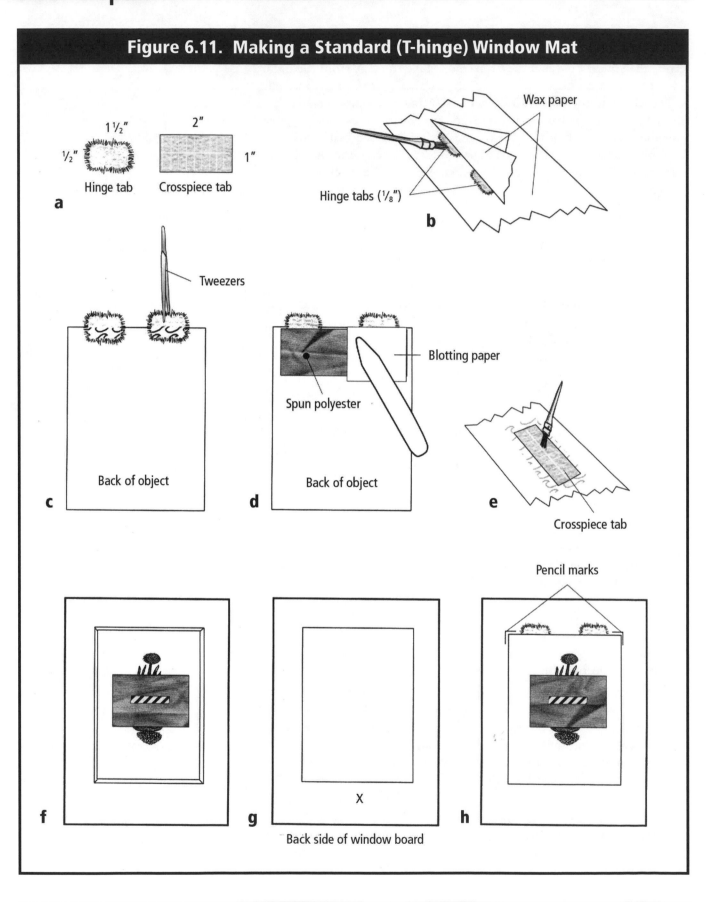

1½" ½" **Hinge tab**   2" 1" **Crosspiece tab**

a

Wax paper

Hinge tabs (⅛")

b

Tweezers

Back of object

c

Blotting paper

Spun polyester

Back of object

d

Crosspiece tab

e

f

X

Back side of window board

g

Pencil marks

h

4. Place the object face up on the back board and then the window board over it. Position the object as you want it, and place a piece of spun polyester and a weight on top (see Figure 6.11f). Remove the window board, and make a penciled "X" on the back side at the bottom border (see Figure 6.11g). On the back board, make two *light* pencil marks slightly above the top edge and beyond the side edges of the object (see Figure 6.11h).

5. With a pair of tweezers, place the crosspieces over the exposed hinge tabs, with the bottom edges being even with the horizontal pencil marks (see Figure 6.12a). There must be enough space between the top of the object and the crosspieces that the object may be lifted up without binding.

6. Put a piece of spun polyester over the crosspieces, then a piece of blotting paper, and rub gently with a bone folder (see Figure 6.12b). The blotting paper will absorb the excess moisture. Put a weight on it and let dry. This should take only a few minutes. Erase the pencil marks.

7. Place the window board up against the back board, making certain that the border with the "X" is at the bottom.

8. Cut a strip of linen hinging tape slightly shorter than the boards and adhere it evenly across the two boards. Rub with a bone folder. Erase the "X." (See Figure 6.12c.)

9. Close the window board over the back board. Your image should now show through the window in its correct position. The hinges should not be visible. (See Figure 6.12d.)

Floating Window Mat

Procedure

Follow the steps above for "Measuring," "Cutting the Window," and "Making the Tabs." Remember, however, that the "white space" now includes the *edges* of the object, since part of the image would be obscured otherwise.

Attaching a V-hinge

1. Place the object on the back board and the window board over it. Position the object in the window and place a piece of spun polyester and a weight on top of it. On the back board, make two *light* pencil marks slightly above the top edge and beyond the side edges of the object. These are your corner marks. (See Figure 6.13a.)

2. Remove the spun polyester and weight and flip the object vertically, with the top of the object resting on the horizontal lines you have just made. Place a piece of spun polyester and a weight on the upturned object.

3. Only about one-third of the short dimension of the hinge tab is actually to be attached to the object. The rest of the tab is affixed to the board by the crosspiece. Place the hinge tabs

Figure 6.12. Making a Standard (T-hinge) Window Mat, Continued

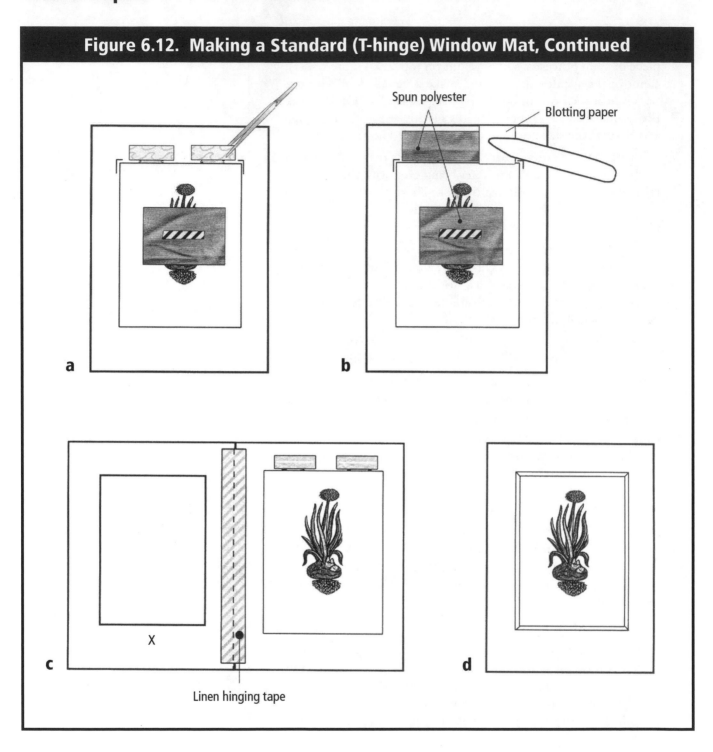

Spun polyester

Blotting paper

a

b

c

X

Linen hinging tape

d

between two pieces of wax paper, with the edge to be pasted out exposed (see Figure 6.11b). Paste out from the wax paper onto the hinge tab. The paste should be smooth and a little thin, although too much water in the paste will cause both the paper object and the hinge to cockle as they dry.

4. With a pair of tweezers, attach the pasted-out portion of the tabs to the back of the object about 1/16 inch in from its top

edge (see Figure 6.13b). Put a piece of spun polyester over the tabs, then a piece of blotting paper, and rub gently with a bone folder (see Figure 6.13c). The blotting paper will absorb the excess moisture. Put a weight on it and let dry. This should take only a few minutes. Make a crease in each tab at the paste line.

5. Paste out a strip of wax paper and lay the crosspieces in the paste. Smooth them down with a bone folder. Allow these pieces time to absorb the paste (they will change color and become more transparent). Just before using them, lightly brush a thin layer of paste over them. (See Figure 6.11e.)

6. With a pair of tweezers, place the crosspieces into the creases of the hinge tabs (see Figure 6.13d).

7. Place a piece of spun polyester and blotting paper on the wet crosspieces and rub with a bone folder (see Figure 6.13e). Let dry with a weight (see Figure 6.13f).

8. Remove the spun polyester and weight from the object and the board. Turn the object over and erase the corner marks. (See Figure 6.13g.)

9. Place the window board up against the back board, making certain that the border with the "X" is at the bottom.

10. Cut a strip of linen hinging tape slightly shorter than the boards and adhere it evenly across the two boards. Rub with a bone folder. Erase the "X." (See Figure 6.13h.)

11. Close the window board over the back board. Your object should now show through the window in its correct position. The hinges should be hidden behind the object. (See Figure 6.13i.)

Optional Mat Formats

Inner Window with Polyester Sheet

With a standard window mat or with a floating mat, it is often advisable to have a sheet of polyester film protecting the image. Because of the problems with static electricity, however, the polyester film should not touch the surface of any object that it might harm (see discussion under "Encapsulation"). A piece of 2-ply board is thus inserted between the window board and the back board, and the sheet of polyester film attached to it (see Figure 6.14a).

Procedure

1. The inner window board is inserted before the window board is attached to the back board. Cut a piece of 2-ply conservation board the exact size of the window and back boards. The grain must run parallel to the long side.

2. Using the *back side* of the window mat, draw a line around the inside of the window onto this new piece of board. Cut this window out with a *straight* cut rather than a beveled one.

3. Attach the inner mat to the back board with a strip of linen hinging tape.

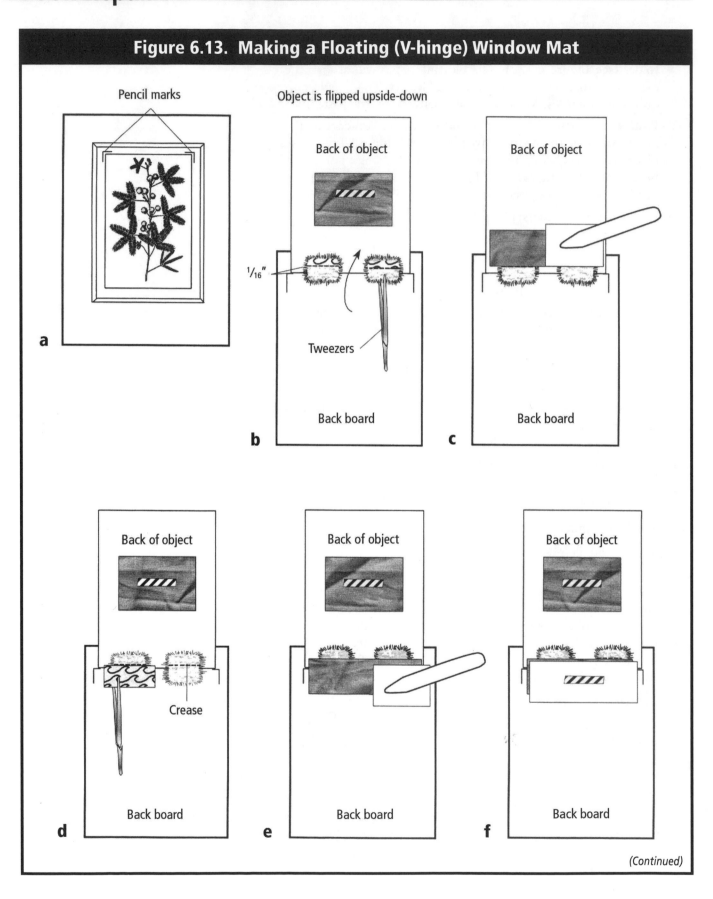

Figure 6.13. Making a Floating (V-hinge) Window Mat

(Continued)

Figure 6.13. Making a Floating (V-hinge) Window Mat *(Continued)*

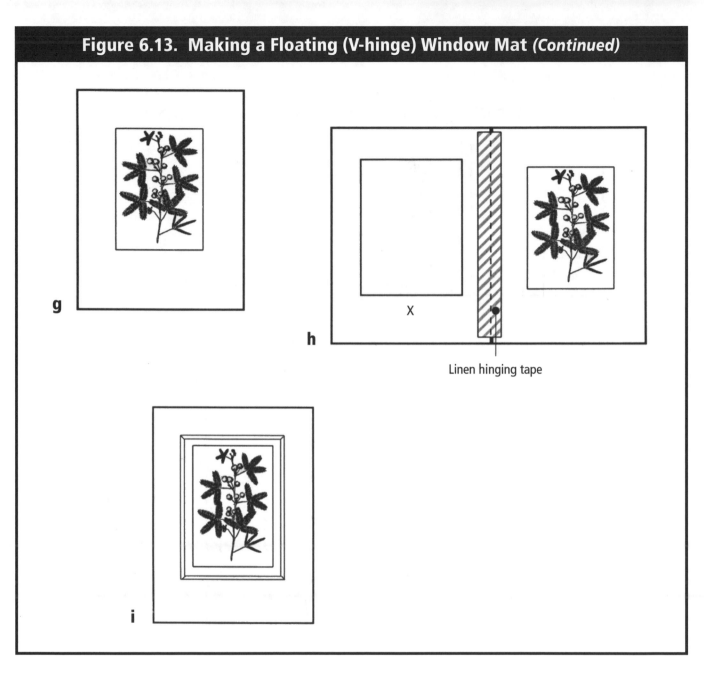

Linen hinging tape

4. Cut a piece of polyester film at least ½ inch larger on all sides than the window opening. Attach this to the top border of the inner mat with double-sided tape. If desired, this sheet of polyester film may be secured on additional edges with tape or on all corners with polyester corner mounts.

5. Attach the front window board to this inner board with linen hinging tape. Rub down with a bone folder.

Window Mat with Solid Front Board

Window mats can be an important storage medium, but they need further strength and support. This is particularly true if they are going to be

Figure 6.14. Optional Mat Formats

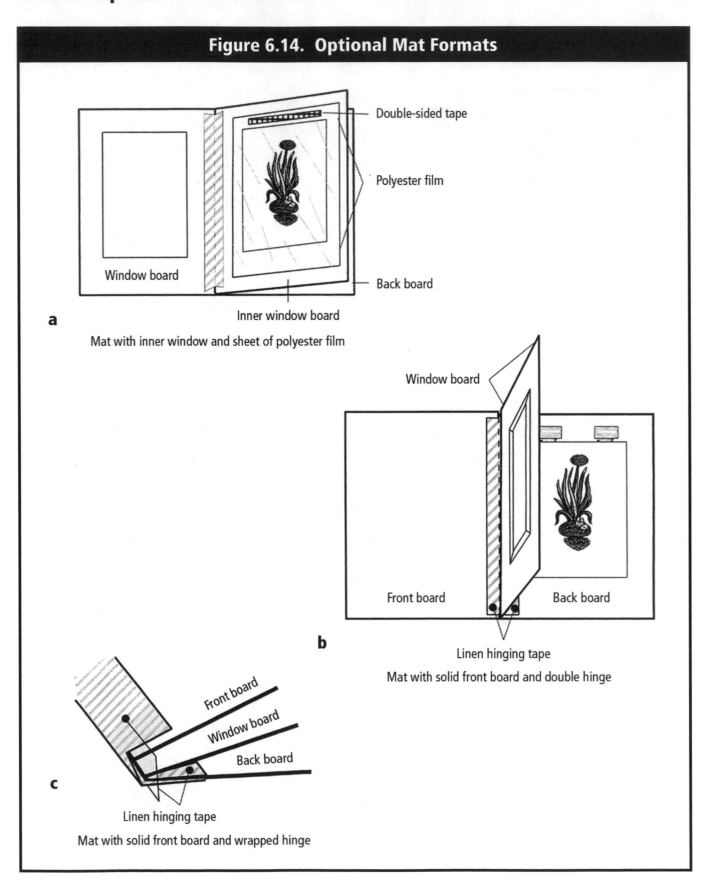

a

Double-sided tape

Polyester film

Window board

Back board

Inner window board

Mat with inner window and sheet of polyester film

b

Window board

Front board

Back board

Linen hinging tape

Mat with solid front board and double hinge

c

Front board

Window board

Back board

Linen hinging tape

Mat with solid front board and wrapped hinge

stored in flat stacks. The addition of a solid front board provides the necessary strength and support for the object. This format is used by many museums to house matted works of art on paper that are in storage and that are going to receive frequent consultation.

Procedure

1. Make a standard window mat or a floating window mat.

2. Cut another piece of board exactly to the size of the mat you have already made. The grain must run parallel to the long side.

3. There are two methods of attaching the solid front board to the finished mat:
   a. Cut a strip of linen hinging tape the same length as the inner hinging strip between the back board and the window board. Attach the solid front board to the window board with this strip of tape. Rub down with a bone folder. (See Figure 6.14b.)
   b. Cut a strip of linen hinging tape the same length as the inner hinging strip between the back board and the window board. Holding it closed, place the mat you have made in the middle of this second strip of linen hinging tape. With a bone folder, bring up the bottom flap and adhere it to the backside of the back board. Lay the mat flat and attach the top flap of the tape to the front of the solid front board. Rub down with a bone folder.

4. When the wrap is opened, the front and back boards will be attached to each other, and the window board and the back board will be attached to each other (see Figure 6.14c).

Enclosures for Three-Dimensional Objects

The difference between alternative enclosures is usually in the degree of protection offered by each enclosure. For example, a book with loose boards might be given a polyester book wrap, which would offer a thin, flexible layer of protection. This will be adequate if the book is seldom used or will soon be replaced or repaired. The same book might be given a phase box if it circulates more frequently and will receive no further treatment.

In all enclosures for three-dimensional objects, it is important to understand the terminology for dimensions. Three measurements must be taken for three-dimensional objects—the height of the book, the width of the book, and the depth of the book. The height of the book is measured from the top edge of the cover to the bottom edge of the cover. The width of the book is measured from the spine of the cover to the fore-edge of the cover. The depth of the book is measured from the front cover to the back cover. (See Figure 6.15.) It is important to take each measurement in at least two places and to use the larger of these measurements. This accommodates any irregularities of the book.

Figure 6.15. Book Measurements

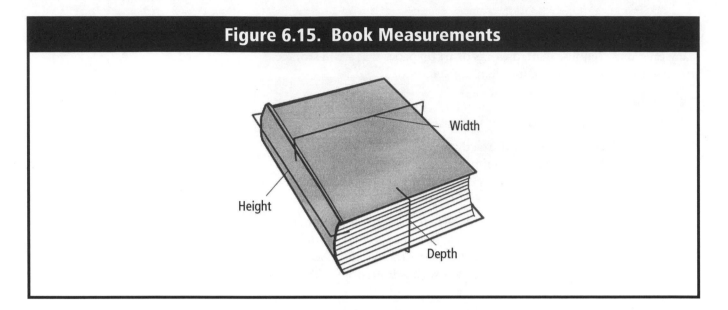

Polyester Film Book Wraps

Book wraps can be made of polyester film (Melinex) or polyethylene, the latter being recommended when the binding is particularly brittle or is made of deteriorated leather. Book wraps are most often used on books that have loose or separated boards and are seldom used. Many libraries have a number of books held together with rubber bands or strings. If these books are used infrequently, they are perfect candidates for book wraps. Polyethylene book wraps should be used if pieces of the cover or of the paper itself are fragile enough that the static electricity or sharp edges of Melinex will hasten the deterioration of the book. Otherwise, Melinex will be acceptable for the book wrap.

Supplies

Polyethylene or polyester film
Double-sided tape (¼-inch 3M Scotch Brand 415)
Bone folder

Procedure

1. Cut a piece of polyethylene or Melinex as wide as the book is tall and long enough to wrap around the book with about two inches of overlap (see Figure 6.16a).

2. Lay the book in the center of the film, being careful to line up the top and bottom edges of the book with the top and bottom edges of the film. Then wrap the right flap around the fore-edge of the book onto the front of the book. It is important that this flap be facing toward the spine of the book. (See Figure 6.16b.)

3. Cut a piece of double-sided tape approximately 1 inch shorter than the book, and place it on the top of the right or inner flap about ¼ inch from the edge. Rub down with a bone folder. (See Figure 6.16c.)

Figure 6.16. Making a Polyester Film Wrap

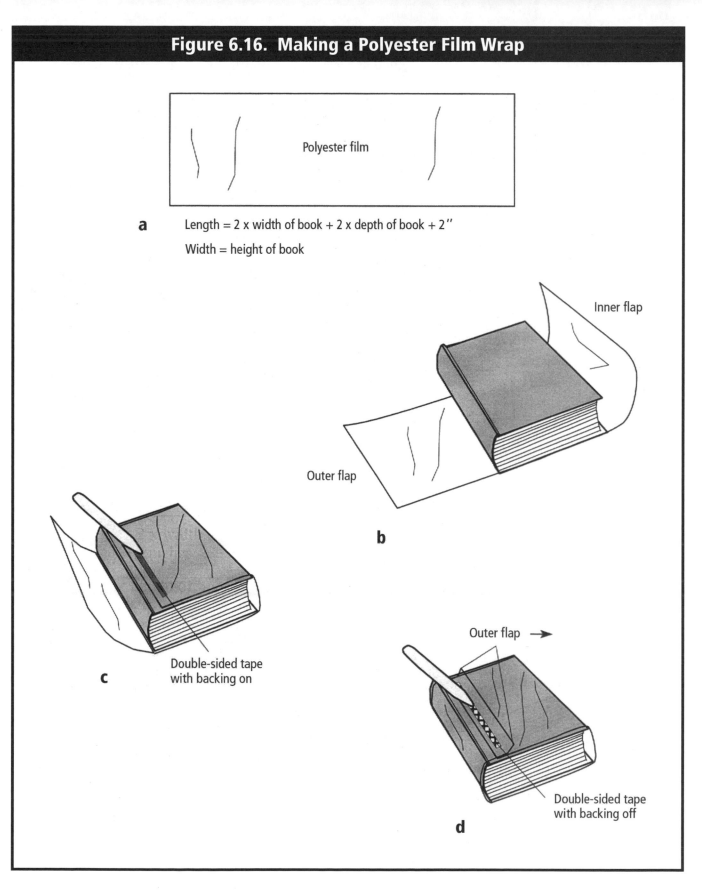

Polyester film

a Length = 2 x width of book + 2 x depth of book + 2''

Width = height of book

Inner flap

Outer flap

b

Double-sided tape with backing on

c

Outer flap →

Double-sided tape with backing off

d

4. Peel off the backing of the tape and wrap the left or outer flap around the front of the book, letting it fall on top of the double-sided tape. Smooth down with a bone folder. (See Figure 6.16d.) It is important that the outer flap be facing the fore-edge of the book so that it does not cut or scratch the book next to it when it is pulled off the shelf.

Polyester Film Book Jackets

Book jackets made of polyester film are used primarily on books that are somewhat deteriorated but still have attached boards, or on books with special bindings or covers (including paper dust wrappers) that need extra protection. There are several commercially available book jackets and book jacket systems. Many of these do utilize polyester film, but usually it is a lighter weight (1.5–2-mil) than that recommended here. However, if you intend to make a large number of book jackets, it may be more feasible to use one of these commercially available systems. Be aware, however, that adhesives used by some systems to attach the Melinex jackets to the books may eventually cause harm to those books.

Because polyester film clings to the book through static electricity, there is the possibility of moisture being trapped in humid conditions. This has been noted particularly with heavily dressed leather bindings, in which the wax has precipitated to the surface causing a milky white residue to appear. The leather may be lightly cleaned with ethanol and dried; then the book may be fitted with an acid-free and buffered paper jacket. Additionally, the static electricity will attract any pigment or particle lying on the surface of the binding.

Supplies

Polyester film (3-mil)
Bone folder
Cutting device (large paper cutter, or a ruler and X-Acto or Olfa knife or scalpel)
Pair of dividers or dissecting needle (optional)

Procedure

1. Cut a piece of polyester film as wide as the book is tall and five times longer than the book's width. If the book has a paper book jacket, leave it on while you measure and create the polyester jacket. It is very important that this piece of polyester film be cut exactly square. Because of this, you might want to cut the piece a little larger than needed, and then square it up and cut it to the exact size. (See Figure 6.17a.)

2. Measuring along one of the long sides of the polyester film, the first fold will be at a distance equal to the inside of the front cover, from gutter to fore-edge (or to the edge of the paper jacket if there is one). Because polyester film is sharp, however, it is best to leave a ¼-inch gap between the hinge of the book and the edge of the film. (See Figure 6.17b.) Pinch the Melinex at this

Figure 6.17. Making a Polyester Film Jacket

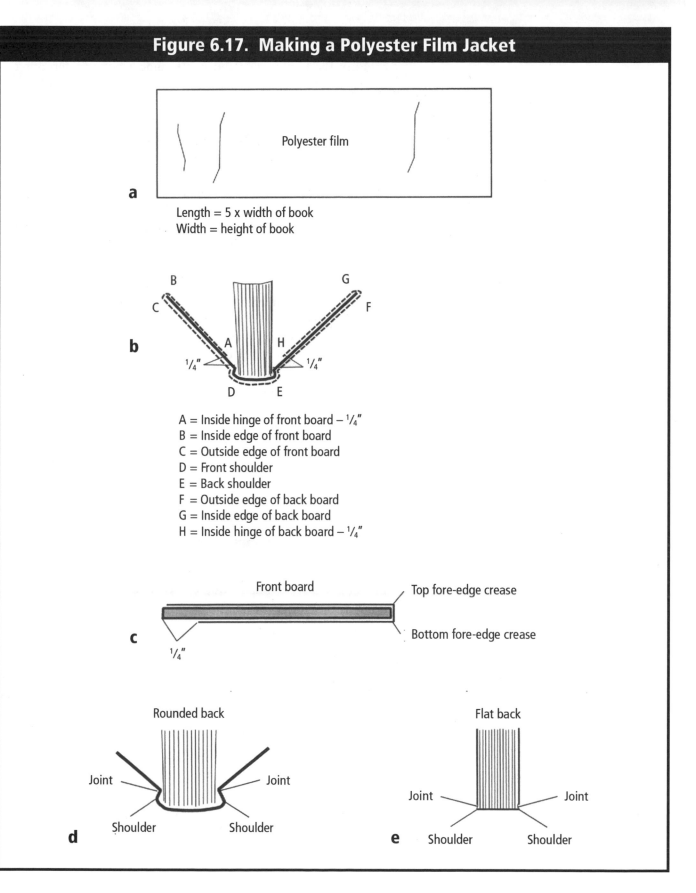

a

Polyester film

Length = 5 x width of book
Width = height of book

b

B   G
C   F
A   H
¼″   ¼″
D   E

A = Inside hinge of front board – ¼″
B = Inside edge of front board
C = Outside edge of front board
D = Front shoulder
E = Back shoulder
F = Outside edge of back board
G = Inside edge of back board
H = Inside hinge of back board – ¼″

c

Front board   Top fore-edge crease

Bottom fore-edge crease

¼″

d

Rounded back

Joint   Joint

Shoulder   Shoulder

e

Flat back

Joint   Joint

Shoulder   Shoulder

point to mark it; alternatively, make the mark with a dissecting needle or the point of a pair of dividers. Fold it over, holding the edges of the film parallel and gently slide a bone folder along the newly formed crease. Go over the crease more firmly with the bone folder one or two more times. If you have difficulty creasing the Melinex, score the underside first with a bone folder.

3. The next crease will be only ⅛ inch to ³⁄₁₆ inch from the first. This distance is determined by the thickness of the boards of the book (or by the paper jacket). It will be easier to make this second crease if the first has been flattened a little with your thumb. Again, mark the film with a pinch or measure and mark with a pair of dividers. Make this measurement at the top and bottom of the board, and use the larger dimension if necessary. (See Figure 6.17c.)

4. After the second crease is made, the two can be formed back into a square. From this point on, work with the book closed as much as possible, making sure that it stays taut against these folds. This will ensure that your book jacket will fit snugly. Again, if there is a paper dust wrapper on the book, you will need to allow for this in your measurements.

5. The next crease will be at a distance equal to the outside width of the board, from fore-edge to shoulder. It is important that this crease be made exactly at the point of the shoulder (see Figure 6.17d). Mark the place with a pinch or a scratch and make the crease. Allow the film to curve around the spine if the spine is curved or around the dust jacket if there is one.

6. Mark and make the crease at the other shoulder, then at the edges of the back board. Last, cut the film so that its end reaches to ¼ inch from the gutter inside the back board (see Figure 6.17b). The book jacket should be snug enough so that it does not spring off the boards when the book is open, but it should not be so tight that the boards of the book open by themselves.

Polyester Film Pamphlet Holder

Pamphlet holders made of polyester film are inexpensive and easy to make. They give good protection for thin or medium-thick pamphlets, although for heavily used items a holder made from heavier stock may be preferable. Also, you may add a piece of acid-free board between the inner and outer wraps if the polyester holder has difficulty standing up on your shelves.

Supplies

Polyester film (3-mil)
Double-sided tape (¼-inch 3M Scotch Brand 415)
Bone folder
X-Acto or Olfa knife or scalpel
Straightedge

Procedure

Inner Holder

1. Cut a piece of polyester film that can accommodate both the inner and the outer holder, or cut two separate pieces (see Figure 6.18a–b). If the pamphlet is thick, you will need to make two folds and include this depth in your measurement (see Figure 6.19a). The inner wrap should be wide enough that the spine or fore-edge of the pamphlet is not damaged when it is pulled out of or put back into the holder. Too wide a wrap, however, allows the pamphlet to flop around, which is damaging to its side and bottom edges.

2. Place the pamphlet on the polyester film strip, fold the strip over it, and lift the strip by its two ends. If the pamphlet is thick enough that it "binds" at the bottom, you will need to make two folds to accommodate it. When in doubt, particularly with fragile pamphlets, make two folds even though they are very close together.

3. Make a crease with a bone folder where the bottom of the pamphlet will rest. Either pinch the film where you want the crease, or mark it with the end of a pair of dividers. Make the crease with a bone folder, being sure that the sides of the polyester film strip are parallel. If the pamphlet is thick, measure the depth with a ruler or the dividers and make the second crease. Pamphlets often tend to be thicker at the spine, so it is good to measure at both the spine and fore-edge, taking the larger dimension. (See Figure 6.19b.)

   Insert the pamphlet, making sure it fits snugly but does not bind in the crease or creases you have made. Cut the corners of the inner holder diagonally, starting from the top edge of the pamphlet. (See Figure 6.19c.)

Outer Holder

1. In making the measurements for the outer holder, always use the inner holder with the pamphlet inside it.

2. Bring together the top and bottom edges of the film piece and place the inner holder in it. The two edges of the outer holder should come up to the top of the pamphlet, *not* to the top of the inner holder. This will allow the inner holder to be pulled out easily by the angled flaps.

3. With the inner holder held firmly in place, make Fold 1 by creasing the polyester film. Make Fold 2 the same way, if a second crease is necessary to accommodate the depth of the inner holder. (See Figure 6.19d.) Fold down the bottom flap of the outer holder (see Figure 6.19e).

4. Position the inner holder on the Fold 1, allowing for a 1-inch overlap of Flap A when the pamphlet holder is closed (see Figure 6.19f).

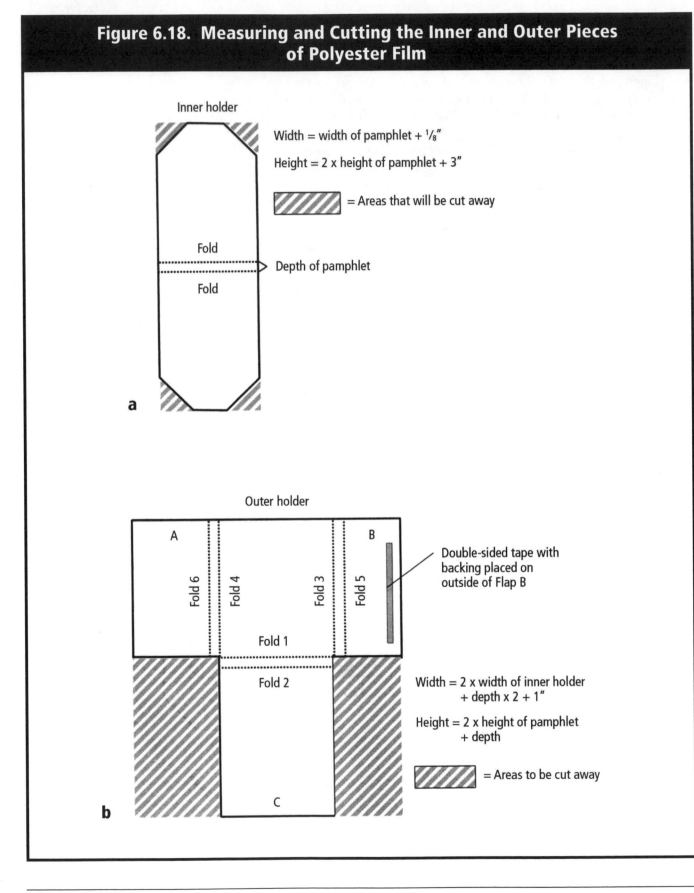

Figure 6.18. Measuring and Cutting the Inner and Outer Pieces of Polyester Film

Inner holder

Width = width of pamphlet + $\frac{1}{8}$″

Height = 2 x height of pamphlet + 3″

= Areas that will be cut away

Fold

Depth of pamphlet

Fold

a

Outer holder

A

B

Fold 6

Fold 4

Fold 3

Fold 5

Fold 1

Double-sided tape with backing placed on outside of Flap B

Fold 2

Width = 2 x width of inner holder + depth x 2 + 1″

Height = 2 x height of pamphlet + depth

= Areas to be cut away

C

b

Figure 6.19. Positioning the Inner Holder in the Outer Holder

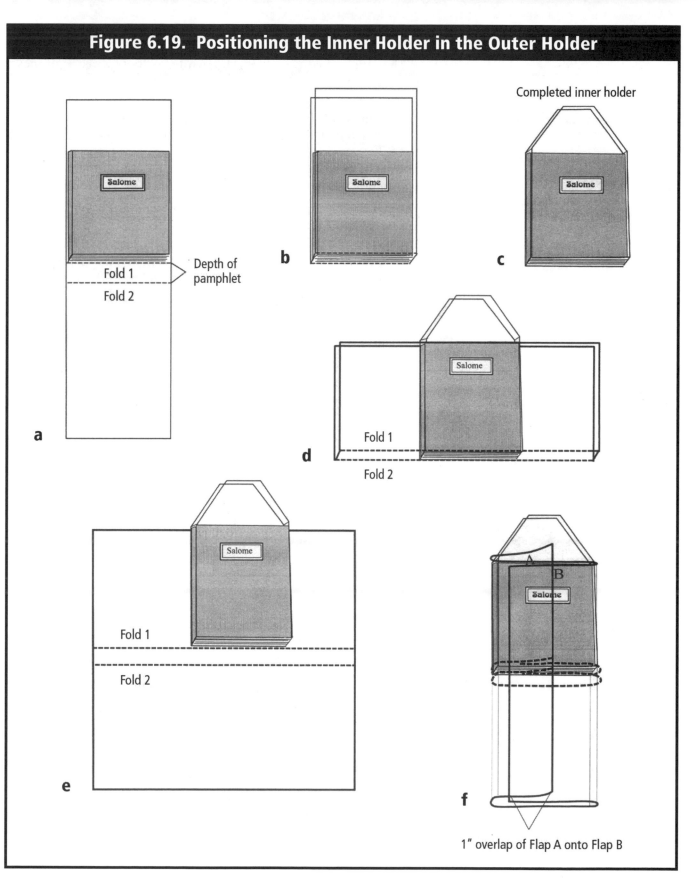

a Fold 1 — Depth of pamphlet — Fold 2

b

c — Completed inner holder

d — Fold 1 — Fold 2

e — Fold 1 — Fold 2

f — 1" overlap of Flap A onto Flap B

Salome

Keeping the inner holder with the pamphlet firmly in place, make a cut at the fore-edge of the inner holder from the *first* horizontal fold (i.e., Fold 1) down to the bottom edge of the outer holder (see Figure 6.20a).

Make a horizontal cut to the right edge of the outer holder beginning at the same place (see Figure 6.20b).

Repeat for the spine edge of the inner holder (see Figure 6.20c).

The outer holder has now the shape of a "T" with the vertical bar offset to the right. This now forms Flap C. (See Figure 6.20d.)

5. Make the bottom folds for the fore-edge and the spine of the outer holder (i.e., Folds 3 and 4). Remove the inner holder with its pamphlet. Fold Flap B in until there is a straight line from the right side of Flap C to the top of the polyester film strip. Crease Fold 3 with a bone folder. (See Figure 6.21a–b.)

6. Repeat step 5 to make Fold 4. Open Flaps A and B.

7. Measure the depth of the inner holder with its pamphlet (see Figure 6.21c). Mark this measurement to the right of Fold 3 and the left of Fold 4. Make and crease Folds 5 and 6. (See Figure 6.21d.)

8. Replace the inner holder and fold up Flap C (see Figure 6.22a). Fold over Flap B (see Figure 6.22b). It is important that Flap B be folded over first so that Flap A, which is facing away from the spine, is on top. Because polyester film has sharp edges, it can cause damage to adjacent books if it catches on them when the pamphlet holder is pulled off the shelf. Having Flap A on top prevents this from happening.

9. Cut a piece of double-sided tape 1 inch shorter than the height of the outer holder. Place this ¼ inch away from the edge of Flap B and rub down with a bone folder. Remove the paper backing. (See Figure 6.22c.)

10. Fold Flap A over Flap B and smooth over the tape with a bone folder (see Figure 6.22d).

11. Because polyester film holds through static electricity, it is likely that the inner holder will stick somewhat when you try to pull it out. If this happens, insert a bone folder between the front of the inner holder and the front of the outer holder, then again on the back side. This separation of the film should be enough to allow the inner holder to be pulled out smoothly.

Phase Boxes

Phase boxes are made out of two pieces of acid-free board that are glued together to form a protective housing, usually for a frequently used book that is losing its boards or even some of its pages.

Phase boxes are perhaps the most versatile of protective enclosures, as they can be adapted to all types of materials, from AV materials to photo

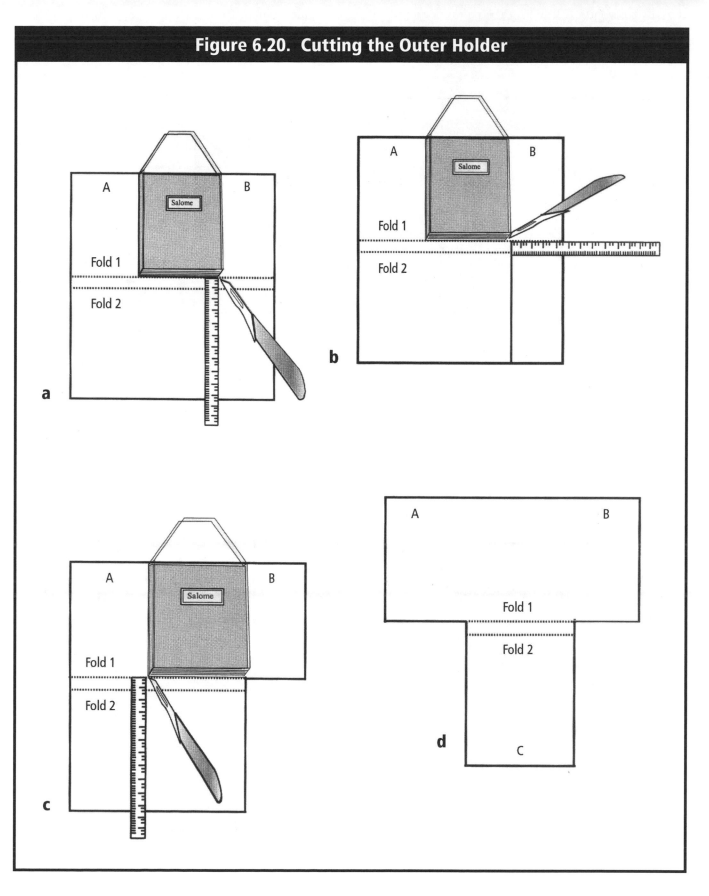

Figure 6.20. Cutting the Outer Holder

Figure 6.21. Folding the Outer Holder

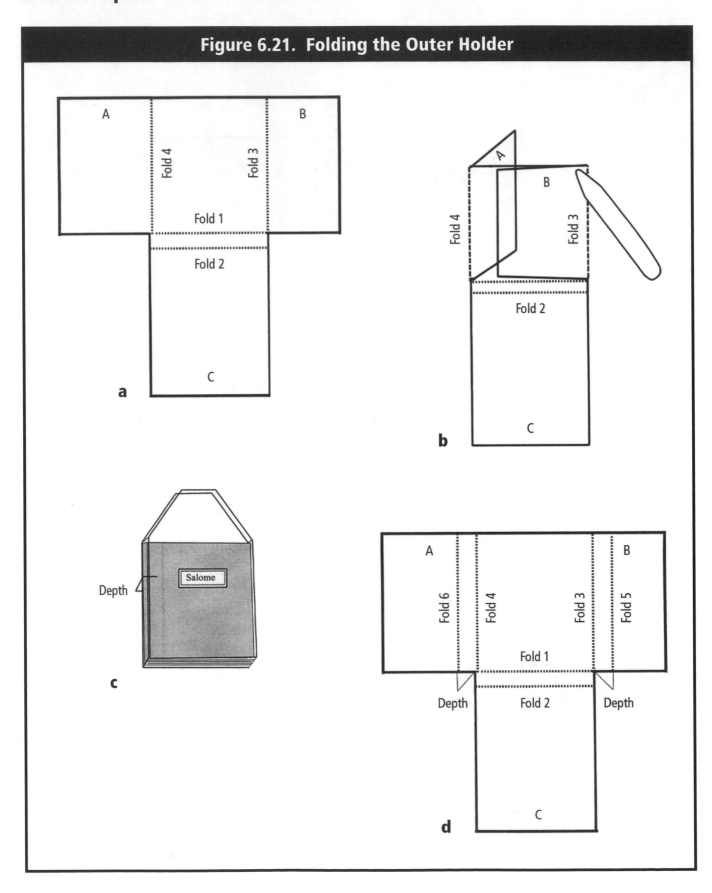

Figure 6.22. Folding the Outer Holder, Continued

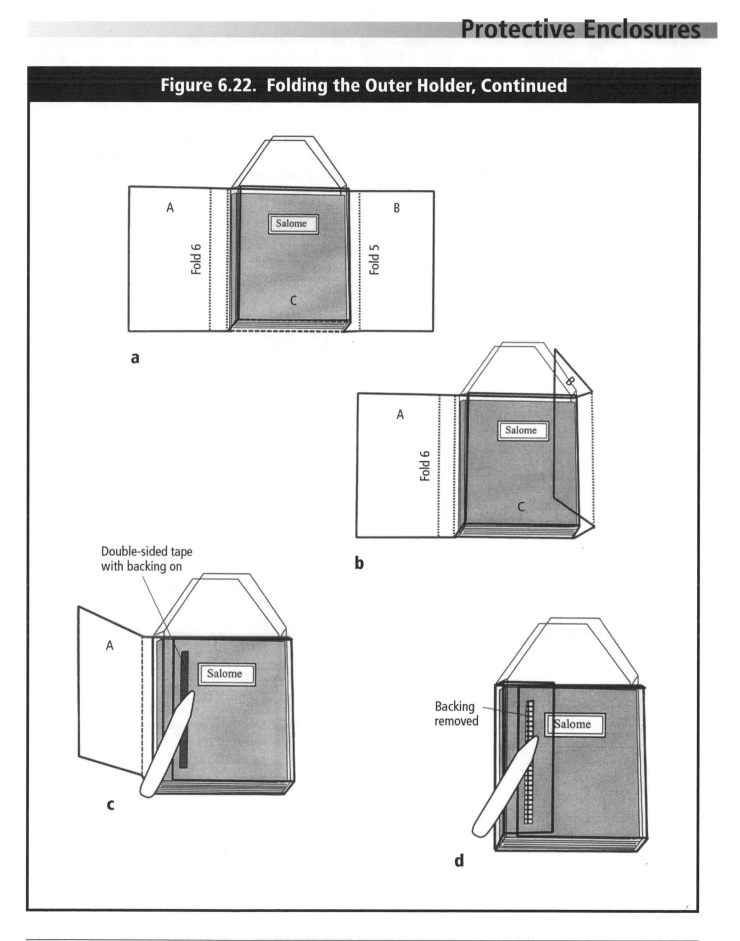

albums to realia. They are excellent for holding together groups of items, such as back issues of a magazine that are too brittle to bind or filmstrips and their accompanying audiocassettes. There are also commercial phase box kits available at a fairly reasonable cost. Although they are made of a somewhat lighter board and are less sturdy than a hand-made box, they are simple to use and can be very useful when only light protection is needed or when a phase box is needed on the spur of the moment. In addition, several companies offer ready-made phase boxes or "micro-climate" enclosures, which may be an economical alternative when time and personnel are considered.

Supplies

Acid-free barrier or phase box board (approximately 0.060 inch)
Glue
Glue brush
Ruler
Small Velcro fasteners (Velcoins or 1-inch square pieces of Velcro tape)
Utility knife and straightedge or metal ruler
X-Acto or Olfa knife or scalpel
Bone folder

Optional Supplies

Board shear
Board crimper
Corner rounder

Measuring

Use the book or other item to measure the inner box, and use the inner box to measure the outer box. If the book is uneven, make two marks and use the larger measurement. Since various thicknesses of board can be used for phase boxes, the actual board's width is important in measuring the amount of space that needs to be accounted for in the turn-under of the bottom flap. In addition, if you are using only a bone folder and scalpel, the space at the inner corners may be further reduced. The following measurements are for ⅛-inch board using a board crimper.

Inner Box

1. Cut a long piece of board to the width of the book. The grain should be parallel to the width of the book. The length of the board should be 3 times the height of the book, plus 2 times its depth, plus the width of one board. (See Figure 6.23a–e for steps 1–4.)

2. Lay the book flat in one corner of the board. Make a mark (Mark A) on the board at the end of the book.

3. Turn the book up on its end and make another mark (Mark B). Lay the book flat again, and place the book against this mark. Make a mark on the board ⅛ inch away from the end of the book (Mark C).

Figure 6.23. Measuring the Inner Board

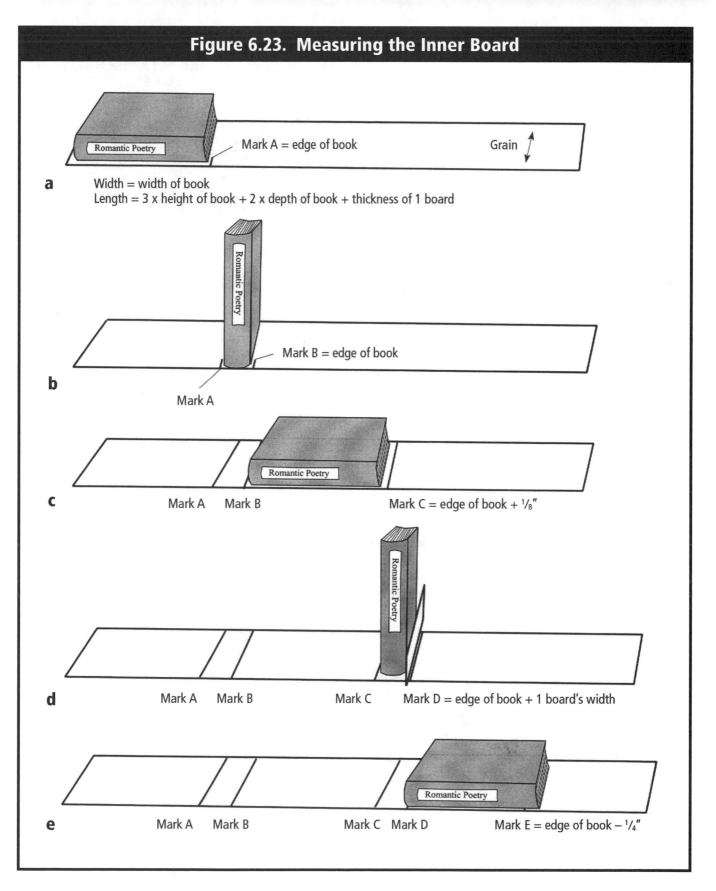

a
Width = width of book
Length = 3 x height of book + 2 x depth of book + thickness of 1 board

Mark A = edge of book   Grain

b
Mark B = edge of book
Mark A

c
Mark A   Mark B   Mark C = edge of book + ⅛″

d
Mark A   Mark B   Mark C   Mark D = edge of book + 1 board's width

e
Mark A   Mark B   Mark C   Mark D   Mark E = edge of book − ¼″

4. Turn the book up on its end and place against this mark. Place a piece of your board next to the book, and make a mark (Mark D). Lay the book flat against this mark, and cut the board off at the length of the book, minus ¼ inch (Mark E).

5. Use a board crimper, or make the creases in the following manner with a bone folder and scalpel. Crease the inner side of the board at each mark with a bone folder. If the board is heavy, this may need to be done more than once for each crease. Turn the board over, and score the outside layer of board with a scalpel on the back side of each crease you have made. Be sure not to cut all the way through the board, only through the outer layer.

6. Fold the inner board around the book, taking care that the book rests between Marks A and B with the spine to your left. Fold the rest of the board over the book. The width of Marks D–E will accommodate both the width of the book *and* the width of the board turn-in. (See Figure 6.24a–d.)

Outer Box

1. Cut a long piece of board the height of the inner box. Grain should be parallel to the spine of the book. (See Figure 6.25a.)

2. Place the box flat in one corner of the board. Make a mark on the board (Mark A).

3. Turn the box up on its edge and make a mark on the board (Mark B). Be sure that you measure this mark using all three pieces of board that are folded around the book (see Figure 6.25b).

4. Place the box flat against this mark. Make a mark ⅛ inch away from the edge of the box (Mark C).

5. Turn the box up on its edge, place a piece of board next to it, and make a mark (Mark D).

6. Lay the box flat against this mark, and cut the board off at the width of the box, minus ¼ inch (Mark E).

7. In making and folding the creases, follow the same steps you used for the inner box (see Figure 6.25c). Unfold the boxes and remove the book.

8. (Optional) Round the corners of the boards with a table-model or hand-held corner rounder (see Figure 6.26a).

Gluing the Inner and Outer Boxes

1. Glue out the middle section of the outer board (see Figure 6.26b).

2. Position the middle section of the inner board on the glued panel and rub down with a bond folder (see Figure 6.26c).

3. Press with weights for several hours (see Figure 6.26d).

Figure 6.24. Folding the Inner Box

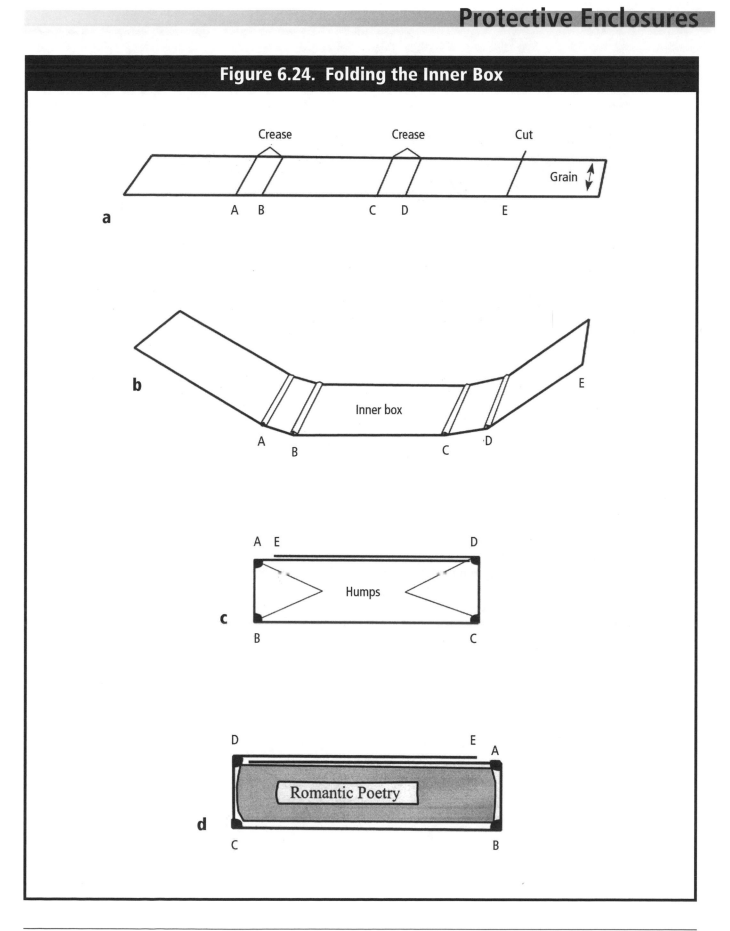

Figure 6.25. Measuring and Folding the Outer Box

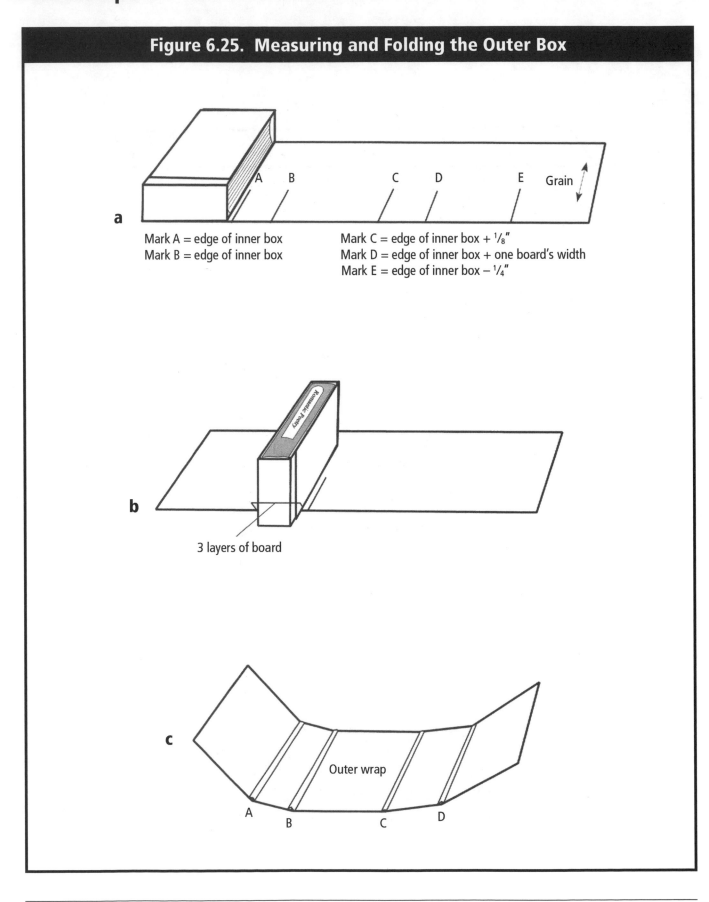

a

Mark A = edge of inner box
Mark B = edge of inner box

Mark C = edge of inner box + ⅛"
Mark D = edge of inner box + one board's width
Mark E = edge of inner box − ¼"

Grain

b

3 layers of board

Romantic Poetry

c

Outer wrap

A   B   C   D

Figure 6.26. Gluing and Completing the Phase Box

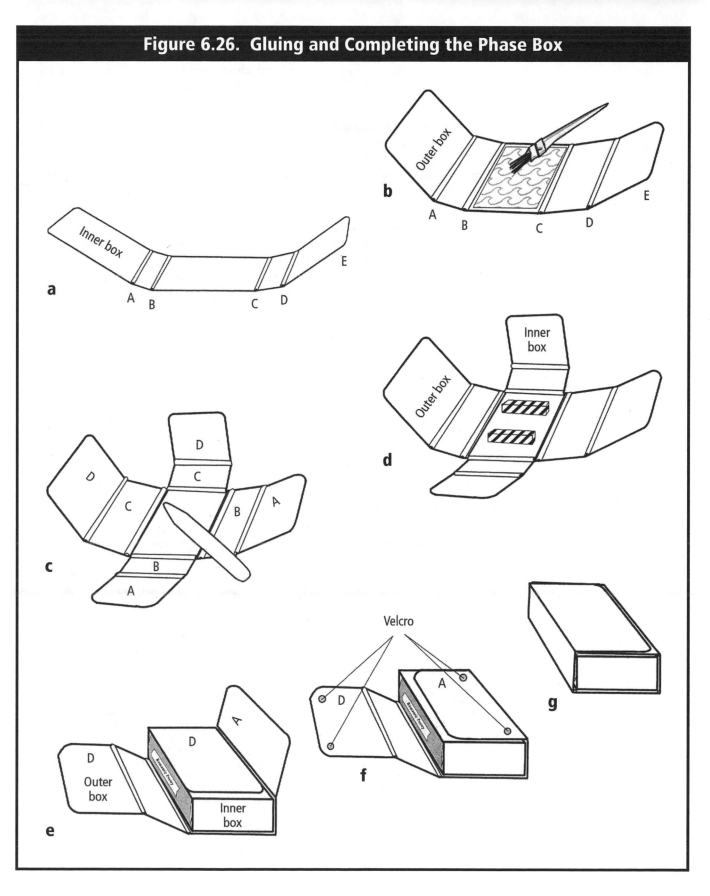

4. Place book in the center of the inner box; bring Flap A up onto the book, and then Flap D on top of Flap A (see Figure 6.26e).

5. Attach Velcro coins and close box firmly, rubbing over the corners where the Velcro has been attached (see Figure 6.26f–g).

The Clamshell Box

The clamshell or rare book box provides an enclosure that is individually made to give the best protection to a rare or fragile book. It is made of heavy binder's board, covered in fine book cloth, and lined with felt or paper. Even though these materials are not acid-free, the box does provide good protection against damage, warping, and environmental pollution. It may also be designed to fit many different sizes of books as well as to accommodate a book and a portfolio of materials. Specialist companies and many commercial binders also offer custom-made clamshell boxes. They are expensive but may be a practical alternative when time and personnel are considered.

Supplies

Binder's board (0.060–0.100 inch)
Bone folder
Bookcloth (e.g., cotlin, buckram, linen)
Brush
Felt or endsheet paper
X-Acto or Olfa knife or scalpel
Scissors
Straightedge or triangle
PVA

Part I: General Instructions

The standard clamshell box has a base shell, a lid shell, and a case-cover. It is made from binder's board covered with book cloth. The shells each have three walls, which are of single-board construction. (See Figure 6.27a–b.) There are also variations on this basic pattern, such as four walls with double-wall construction and T-joint corners (excellent for large heavy books), or a box with a pull-out tray to house portfolio materials.

Grain

The boards, cover materials, and lining materials used in making a clamshell box have a grain, which is created by the alignment of the fibers during the manufacturing process. The material flexes much more easily along the grain than across it. Thus, the grain of almost all the pieces should run parallel to the spine. The two exceptions are the head and tail walls and the material covering the walls, in which the grain should run lengthwise. (See Figure 6.27c.)

It is always a good idea to determine the grain of the piece of material you are cutting and then to mark the direction of the grain in several places. In this way, you will always know the grain direction of any small piece cut from the larger one.

Figure 6.27. Basic Elements of the Clamshell Box

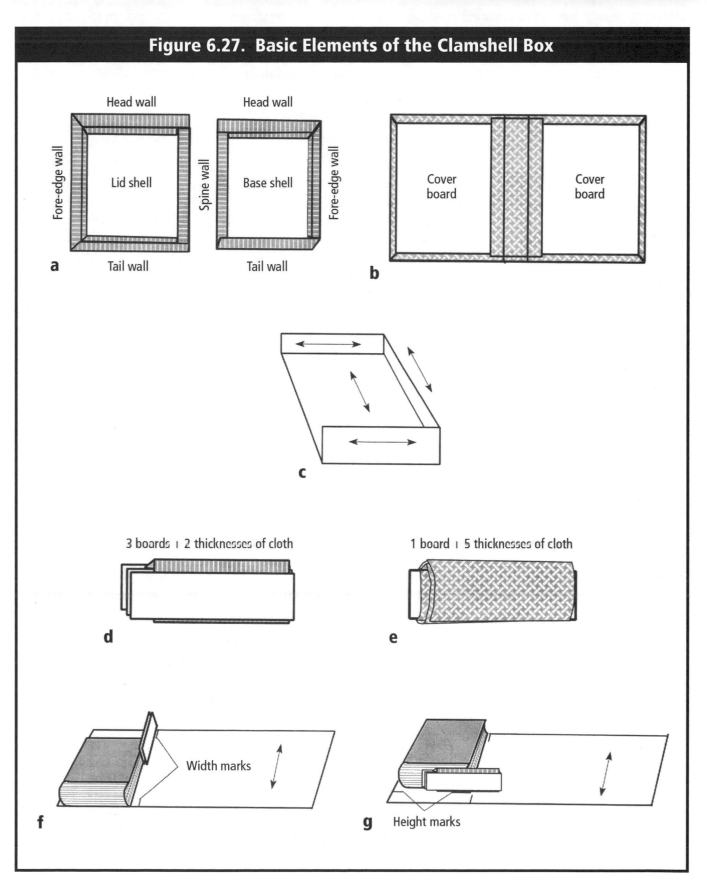

Head wall

Fore-edge wall

Lid shell

Tail wall

a

Head wall

Spine wall

Base shell

Fore-edge wall

Tail wall

Cover board

Cover board

b

c

3 boards ı 2 thicknesses of cloth

d

1 board ı 5 thicknesses of cloth

e

Width marks

f

Height marks

g

Measuring

Measuring is a critical aspect of making a clamshell box. The terms used in these instructions are as follows:

Shell	**Cover**
Height = head to tail	Height = top to bottom
Width = spine to fore-edge	Width = end to end
Depth = base to top of wall	

It is both more accurate and easier to use the materials themselves than to measure with a ruler. Thus, one uses the book itself to measure the base shell, the base shell to measure the lid shell, and the lid shell to measure the cover. If a book is not perfectly square, as is frequently the case, the largest dimension must always be used as the final measurement.

An easy method of measuring using board and cloth is to wrap a piece of cloth around a board the requisite number of times. This technique is used in determining the height of the boards and the width of the hinges. For the first, put a folded piece of cloth with 2 boards on the outside and 1 in the middle (see Figure 6.27d). For the second, wrap a piece of cloth around a board so that there will be 2 layers on one side and 3 layers on the other (see Figure 6.27e).

Throughout this discussion, it is assumed that the width of the binder's board or book board is $\frac{1}{8}$ inch. This is generally the thickness of most boards. Therefore, the measurement of "one board's width" has been translated to $\frac{1}{8}$ inch. If the board you are using is significantly different, however, use its width as your measuring unit.

Part II: The Base Shell

Measuring and Cutting the Boards

1. Make certain the board is square. Place the book in the corner, being careful not to let any part of the spine protrude. The grain of the board must be parallel to the spine.

2. To measure the width of the base board, place two thicknesses of binder's board next to the tail of the book. Make a mark at this point. Repeat for the head of the book. Choose the larger dimension for the final measurement of the width of the base. The two boards allow for the thickness of the fore-edge wall and a little extra space. (See Figure 6.27f.)

3. The base shell of the box has a wall at both the head and the tail. To measure the height of the base, place three pieces of board and two thicknesses of book cloth (see Figure 6.27d) up against the spine and make a mark at this point. Repeat for the fore-edge of the book. If the dimensions differ, use the larger one. (See Figure 6.27g.)

4. Cut the width and then the height to form the bottom of the base shell.

5. The depth of the base shell walls equals the depth of the book at its thickest point plus one piece of felt and one of board. Select

a piece of board that is wider than the depth of the book and longer than the height of the base shell plus twice its width (see Figure 6.28a).

6. Stand this piece of board on its edge and place it *on top* of the base shell board at one of the long edges. Bring the spine of the book up against this board, place the felt and then the board on top of the book, and mark the depth on this board. Make the same mark at each end of the board so that you will be able to cut it straight. Repeat for the fore-edge of the book, and use the larger measurement to make the cut. (See Figure 6.28b.) This step is important because some books, particularly older ones, may be severely warped.

7. Cut the strip of board to the depth you have measured. You now have one piece of board from which to make the three walls.

8. Mark the height of the base shell board on the board strip; then turn the shell board and mark its width two times (see Figure 6.28c).

9. Cut the board at each of these marks, and discard any extra board. You will now have 1 board the height of the base shell board (i.e., the fore-edge wall) and 2 boards the width of the base shell board (i.e., the head and tail walls) (see Figure 6.28d).

10. Because the length of the fore-edge wall board is exactly the height of the base shell board, the head and tail walls must each be cut 1 board's width shorter to accommodate its thickness. Measure and cut these two boards (see Figure 6.28 e).

11. When correctly cut, the 3 walls should fit exactly on the base shell board without any gaps or overhang (see Figure 6.28f).

12. Glue out the fore-edge wall piece along its bottom edge. Adhere it to the base and hold until it stays in place. Make sure that the board is evenly placed on one long edge.

13. Glue the bottom edge and one short edge of the head wall. Place this wall on top of the base shell, making sure that the glued end forms the corner with the fore-edge wall. Adhere it to the base, making sure the corner is firmly attached. Repeat for the tail wall. (See Figure 6.28g.) The three pieces should be adhered to the base shell board by their bottom edges as well as the inner corners (see Figure 6.28h).

Covering the Shell

1. Cut a piece of bookcloth that is long enough to go around the three sides, with 1½ inches overlap at each end. The width of the strip is equal to twice the depth of the base shell plus 2 inches. This allows for turn-ins on the bottom and the inside of the shell. The piece of cloth should be cut parallel to the selvage to ensure that its grain (warp) goes along the walls, not across them.

Figure 6.28. Making the Base Shell

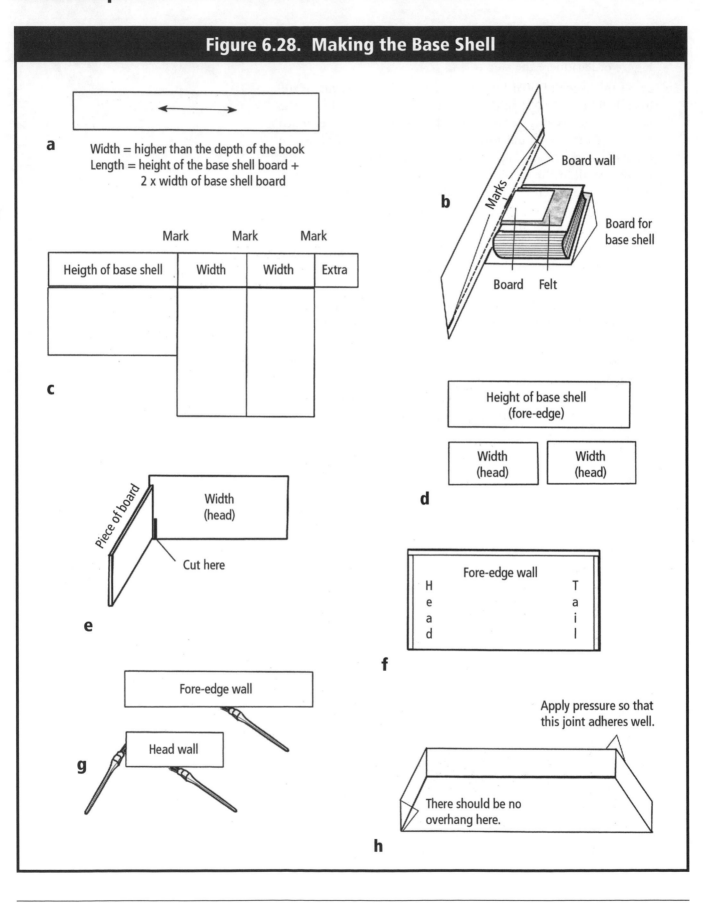

a
Width = higher than the depth of the book
Length = height of the base shell board +
2 x width of base shell board

b
Board wall
Board for base shell
Marks
Board   Felt

c

	Mark	Mark	Mark
Heigth of base shell	Width	Width	Extra

d
Height of base shell (fore-edge)

Width (head)   Width (head)

e
Piece of board
Width (head)
Cut here

f
Fore-edge wall
Head   Tail

g
Fore-edge wall
Head wall

h
Apply pressure so that this joint adheres well.
There should be no overhang here.

2. Draw a line across the back side of the strip of cloth that is 1 inch from its bottom edge. This will guide you as you turn the shell over to adhere the side boards to the cloth. In gluing the shell to the cloth, it is crucial that the open side be to your left and the bottom of the shell facing you; otherwise, there will not be enough cloth to make the turn-ins for the inside of the shell. (See Figure 6.29a.)

3. Glue out the head wall and place it against the line you have drawn and 1½ inches from the left end of the strip of cloth. Rub down the inside of this wall with your bone folder.

4. Glue out the long side of the shell, being careful not to let the glue "puddle up" where the wall rests on the cloth. Turn the shell down onto its long side, being careful to stay against the line. Press with your thumbs against the end of the fore-edge wall board (but *not* on the tail wall). This will help form a tight corner with the fore-edge and head walls. (See Figure 6.29b.) Rub down the inside of the long wall with your bone folder.

5. Turn the shell again and repeat for the tail wall (see Figure 6.29c).

6. Grasp the shell by the open edge, with the bottom up, and rest the inside of the shell on wooden blocks or covered bricks so that the edge of the cloth is not touching the surface of your work area (see Figure 6.29d).

7. Your objective is to cut off the two corners of book cloth so that the three flaps may be turned in and glued flat. Rest an open pair of scissors on one corner, and, keeping them parallel to the surface, raise the back of the scissors about ⅛ inch above the corner of the shell. Make the cut. Repeat for the other corner. Glue the three flaps down with PVA and smooth with a bone folder. (See Figure 6.29e–f.)

8. Place the shell on its bottom with the open side facing you (see Figure 6.29g). You are now ready to make the cuts that will give the book cloth smooth turn-ins, particularly at the corners of the shell.

Making the Cuts for the Shell Cover

1. To make the front short tabs, place a ruler level with the inside corner of the shell. Make a cut with a scalpel all the way from the edge of the board. (See Figure 6.30a.)

2. Turn shell on the tail wall. You will now make a series of cuts that will create a tab to cover the corner of the board. Place the end of the ruler against the edge of the tail wall and level with the top edge of the wall. Make a cut with a scalpel starting ⅛ inch from the edge of the board to the edge of the bookcloth. (See Figure 6.30b.)

3. Turn the shell, place the end of the ruler against the top edge of the tail wall, and move the ruler ⅛ inch to the right. Make a

Figure 6.29. Measuring and Cutting the Cloth for the Base Shell

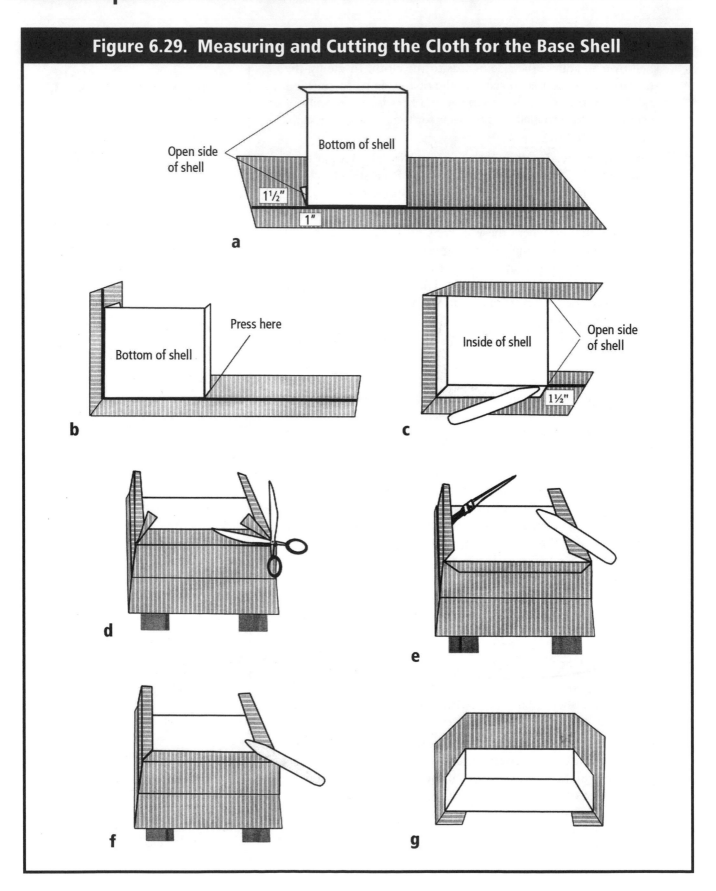

Figure 6.30. Measuring and Cutting the Cloth for the Base Shell, Continued

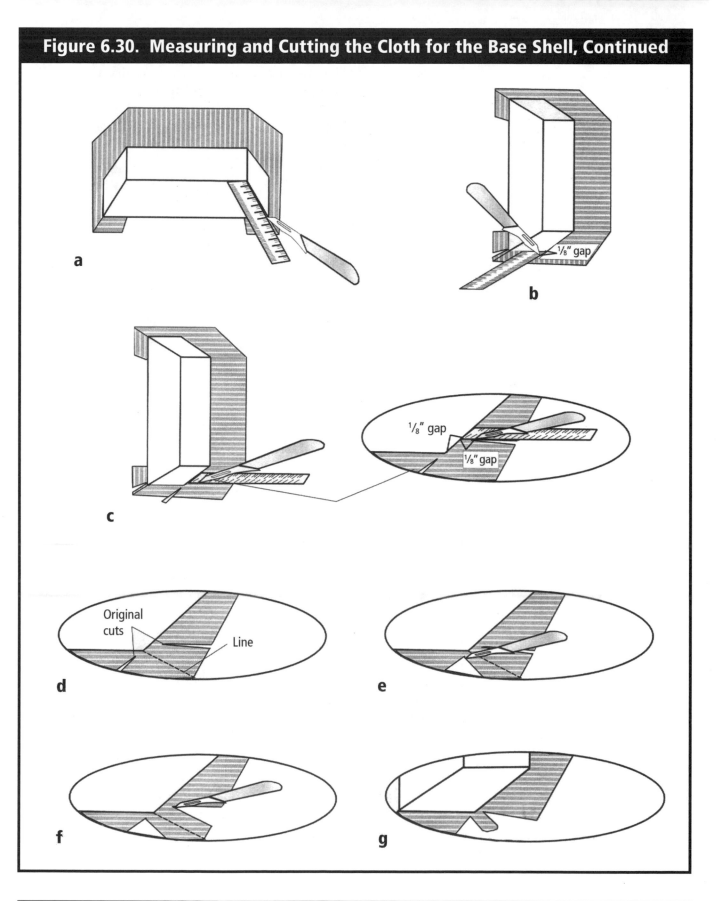

cut with a scalpel starting ⅛ inch from the edge of the board to the edge of the book cloth. (See Figure 6.30c.)

4. Using the illustrations as a guide, create a tab that is about ¾ inch long and about ½ wide. This will be large enough to cover the corner of the boards.

5. Draw a line from the corner of the box to the corner of the cloth (see Figure 6.30d).

6. Place your scalpel at the beginning of the cut that you made in step 2. Make a cut to the edge of the cloth halfway between the original cut and line you have drawn. Remove this piece. (See Figure 6.30e.)

7. Repeat for the cut made in step 3 (see Figure 6.30f). This will create a tab large enough to cover the corner of the board. If it is too large or is misshapen, you may trim it and round off the end. (See Figure 6.30g.)

8. Repeat steps 1–7 to cut the tabs for the tail wall (see Figure 6.30a–g).

You are now ready to make the cuts that will form the turn-ins for the three walls.

1. Place the shell upright on the fore-edge wall. Place a ruler next to the inside of the left corner. Make a cut starting ⅛ inch away from the edge to the board to the edge of the cloth. Repeat for the right corner. (See Figure 6.31a.)

2. Turn the fore-edge flap down into the shell and crease it where the wall meets the bottom of the shell (see Figure 6.31b).

3. Make 45-degree angle cuts from this crease to the edge of the cloth.

4. Turn the shell onto the tail wall and make a mark level with the angle cut on the fore-edge flap (see Figure 6.31c).

5. Place a ruler up against the bottom of the box and inside the corner. Cut from the mark you have made (*not* from the shell itself) to the edge of the cloth. Cut off this tab where you have made the mark. (See Figure 6.31d.) Mark and cut the flap for the head wall.

Gluing the Tabs and Turn-Ins

1. The front tabs and the wall flaps that you have just made now need to be glued, turned in, and smoothed down. The tabs are done first. They are glued in the order shown in the illustration (see Figure 6.32a).

2. Glue out Tab 1 of the tail wall and pull it down over the corner and smooth into place (see Figure 6.32b).

3. Immediately take your bone folder and press down the two "ears" of cloth until they adhere to the edge of the boards (see Figure 6.32c–d).

Figure 6.31. Measuring and Cutting the Cloth for the Base Shell, Continued

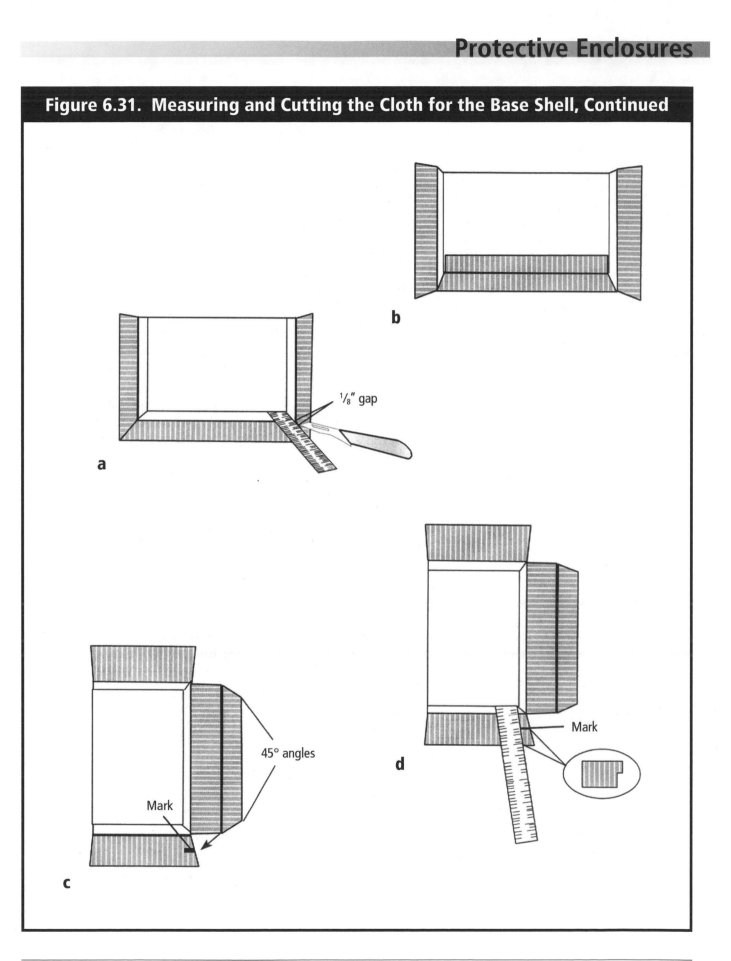

4. Glue out Tab 2 and pull it over the board tightly, keeping the top edge of the tab even with the top edge of the wall. Smooth down on both the edge and the side of the board. Be sure that the cloth fits snugly into the groove where the wall and base board meet. (See Figure 6.32e.)

5. Glue out Tab 3 and pull it tightly onto the board and into the corner. Use your bone folder to make sure that the fit is snug. Smooth down on both the edge and the side of the board. (See Figure 6.32f.)

6. Repeat steps 2–5 for the head wall of the base shell.

7. The wall flaps are turned in the following order: tail, head, fore-edge. It is most important that the fore-edge wall flap be the last that is turned in, since it will cover the tabs that you made for the head and tail wall flaps. (See Figure 6.33a.)

8. Glue out the tail wall flap and turn it into the shell, being careful to firmly adhere it to the edge and side of the wall board. Use your bone folder to press the cloth into the corner and to smooth it down on the board. (See Figure 6.33b.) Repeat for the head wall.

9. Glue out the fore-edge flap, being careful to firmly adhere it to the edge and side of the board. Extra caution is needed as you pull the flap down so that its glue does not get onto the head and tail wall flaps (see Figure 6.33c). Smooth down with your bone folder (see Figure 6.33d).

Making the Spine Edge Piece

1. The final step in making the base shell is to cover the spine edge of the base board with a strip of book cloth.

2. Cut a strip of book cloth the length of the inside of the base shell and 2 inches wide. Glue out. (See Figure 6.33e.)

3. Place this strip on the spine edge of the base shell so that one-half of the cloth strip is on the top and one-half on the bottom. Smooth down with your bone folder. The base shell is now completed. (See Figure 6.33f.)

Part III: The Lid Shell

In making the lid shell, you will use the base shell for measuring, just as you used the book in making measurements for the base shell. Repeat the steps in "Measuring and Cutting the Boards," "Covering the Shell," "Making the Cuts for the Shell Cover," "Gluing the Tabs and Turn-Ins," and "Making the Spine Edge Piece."

Exception: When measuring the depth of the wall boards, delete the additional piece of board (see Figure 6.28b, p. 220). Use only the addition of a piece of felt.

Part IV: The Cover

The cover of a clamshell box is a case made up of three pieces of board covered with book cloth. The base and lid shells will be glued to the two larger boards; the third board forms the spine piece.

Figure 6.32. Gluing the Cloth for the Base Shell

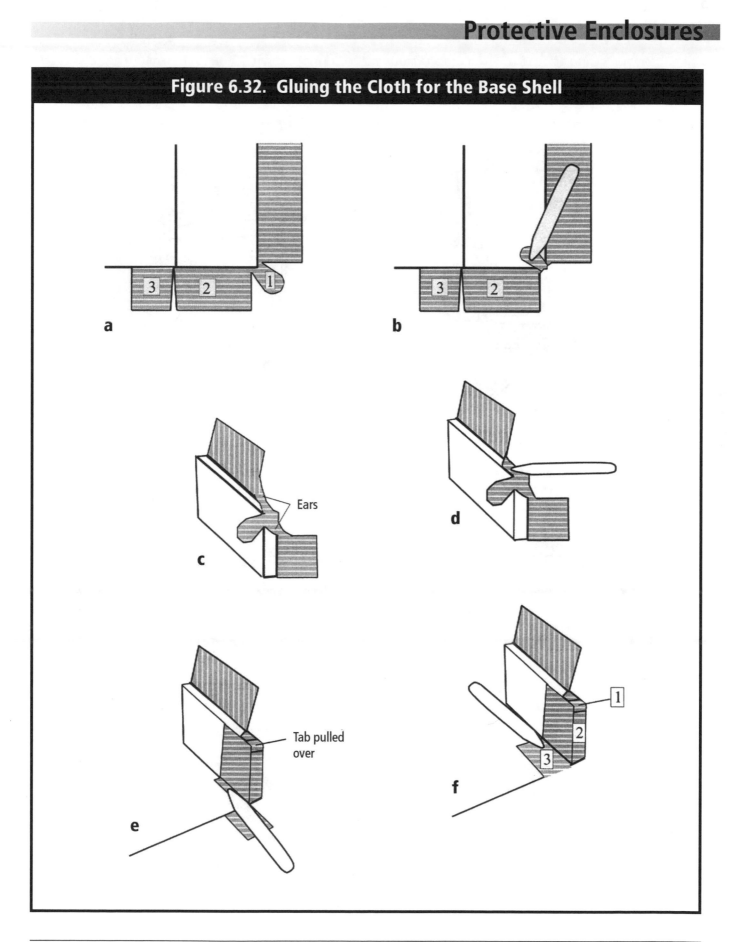

Figure 6.33. Gluing the Cloth for the Base Shell, Continued

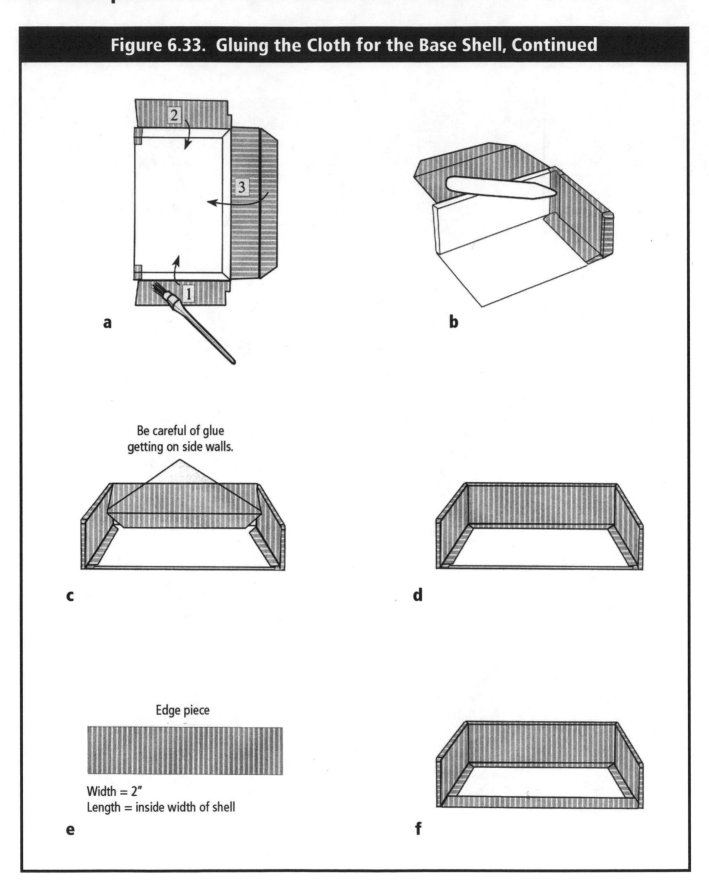

Be careful of glue getting on side walls.

Edge piece

Width = 2"
Length = inside width of shell

1. The two cover boards are each the height and width of the finished lid shell, with the addition of ⅛ inch in both directions. The spine piece is equal to the height of the finished lid shell plus ⅛ inch and the outside depth of the finished lid shell. The grain of the board should be parallel to the spine.

2. Cut one piece of binder's board larger than needed for the three pieces. Mark the height and cut the board. Measure the spine piece width and cut it off. Measure one cover board width and cut it off. Repeat for the second cover board. You now have three pieces of the same height. (See Figure 6.34a.)

3. Cut a piece of book cloth that is 3 inches taller than the height of the boards and 3 inches wider than the three boards laid side by side. In judging the width, you will also need to add the space of two board's widths plus ten layers of cloth. (See Figure 6.34b.) The measuring device pictured in the "Measuring" section (see Figure 6.27e, p. 217) will help you do this easily. The grain (warp) of the cloth should be parallel to the height of the boards.

4. With the piece of cloth outside-down on your work surface, make a line across the cloth that is 1½ inches from the bottom. Make another line 1½ inches from the left-hand side of the cloth. Glue out one of the large pieces of board and place at the juncture of these two lines, making sure that the "nicked" corners of the board are facing outward and that the bottom of the board is straight on your guide-line. (See Figure 6.34c.)

5. Glue out one of the large pieces of board and place against your mark at the left end of the piece of cloth. Be sure that the nicked corners are facing outward and that the bottom of the board is correctly aligned with your marks. Smooth down with your bone folder.

6. The distance between the spine board and each of the shell boards is a critical space because it will form each of the hinges of the clamshell box. If the hinges are too tight, the box will not close. If they are too loose, the box will bulge at the spine. The best measurement is one board's width plus five layers of book cloth. (See Figure 6.27e, p. 217.)

7. Place your measuring tool against the glued board and make a mark at the bottom and top of this board. Glue out the spine piece and place against these marks. Make sure that distance between the shell and spine boards is the same at both top and bottom. Smooth down the spine board with your bone folder. Repeat these steps for the second shell board, again making sure that the nicked corners are facing outward. (See Figure 6.34d.)

8. Turn over the cover to smooth out any wrinkles or bubbles that have occurred.

9. With the cover outside-down again, cut each corner of the cloth diagonally, leaving about ¼ inch of cloth to turn in (see Figure 6.34e).

10. Glue out the top exposed strip of cloth and turn over onto the boards. Immediately press the cloth into the hinge grooves with your bone folder. This must be done while the cloth is still pliable. Smooth down the turn-in over the rest of the board area. (See Figure 6.34f.) Press down the "ears" of cloth at the corners with your bone folder onto the edge of the board (see Figure 6.34g). Repeat for the bottom edge of the cloth.

11. Turn in the two ends of the cloth, again smoothing the cloth with bone folder and pressing down the "ears" of the corners (see Figure 6.34h).

12. Cut a piece of book cloth ¼ inch shorter than the height of the cover and wide enough to extend at least 1 inch onto each of the shell boards (see Figure 6.34i).

13. Glue out and center onto the spine area of the cover. Smooth down the spine area *first* with your bone folder. Firmly press the cloth down into the hinge grooves. Then smooth out the extensions onto the boards. (See Figure 6.34j.)

14. Fold over the cover boards to make certain that the cloth has adhered to them and that the hinges are the correct width (see Figure 6.34k).

15. Glue out the bottom of the *lid shell* and place on the left-hand board equidistant from the top and bottom edges and up against the hinge edge of the board (see Figure 6.35a–b).

16. Fold the cover up to the shell to make certain that the walls meet at right angles and that there are no gaps (see Figure 6.35c). Open and press on the base board with your bone folder. The shell should now be securely adhered to the cover board.

17. Glue out the bottom of the *base shell* and place on the right-hand board up against the hinge edge of the board and centered between the walls of the lid shell. Fold the box over to make certain that it will shut properly. Open and press on the base board with your bone folder.

18. Press the open box in a book press or place weights in the shells to make them adhere to the boards (see Figure 6.35d). Leave for several hours or overnight.

19. Cut 2 pieces of felt and 2 pieces of paper, making both of them larger than you need for the base shell. Glue out each paper smoothly and press the felt onto it. (See Figure 6.35e.) After the pieces have dried, trim them to fit exactly into the bottom of the base shell.

20. Glue out the paper backing of one piece and adhere to the inside of the base shell. Smooth down with your bone folder. Glue out the paper backing of the other piece and position on the front edge of the lid shell, centered between the head and tail walls, so that there is space around the felt for the walls of

Figure 6.34. Making the Cover

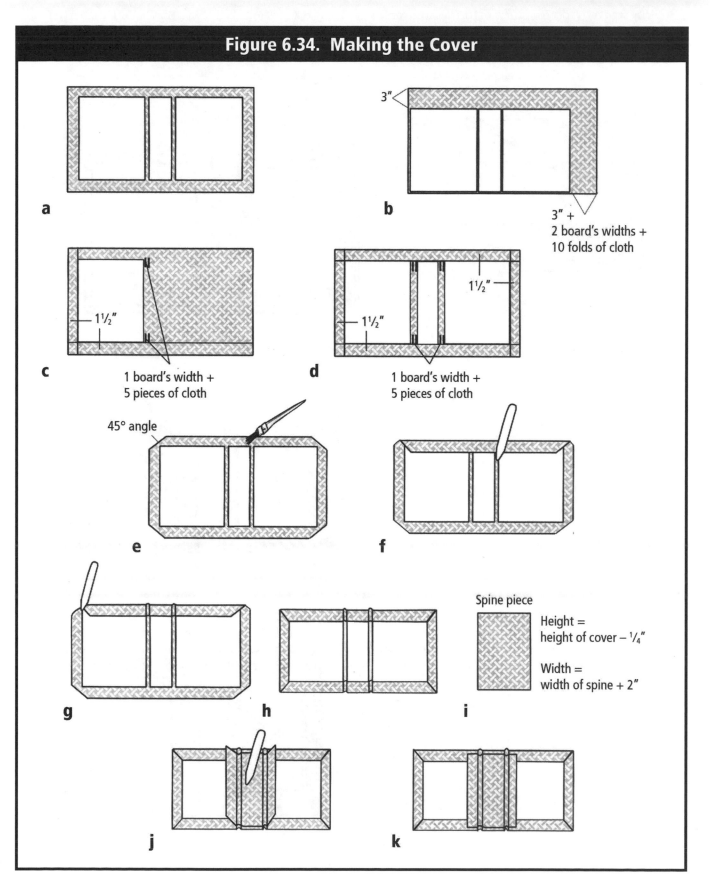

a

b

3"

3" +
2 board's widths +
10 folds of cloth

c

1½"

1 board's width +
5 pieces of cloth

d

1½"

1½"

1 board's width +
5 pieces of cloth

45° angle

e

f

g

h

i

Spine piece

Height =
height of cover − ¼"

Width =
width of spine + 2"

j

k

Figure 6.35. Completing the Clamshell Box

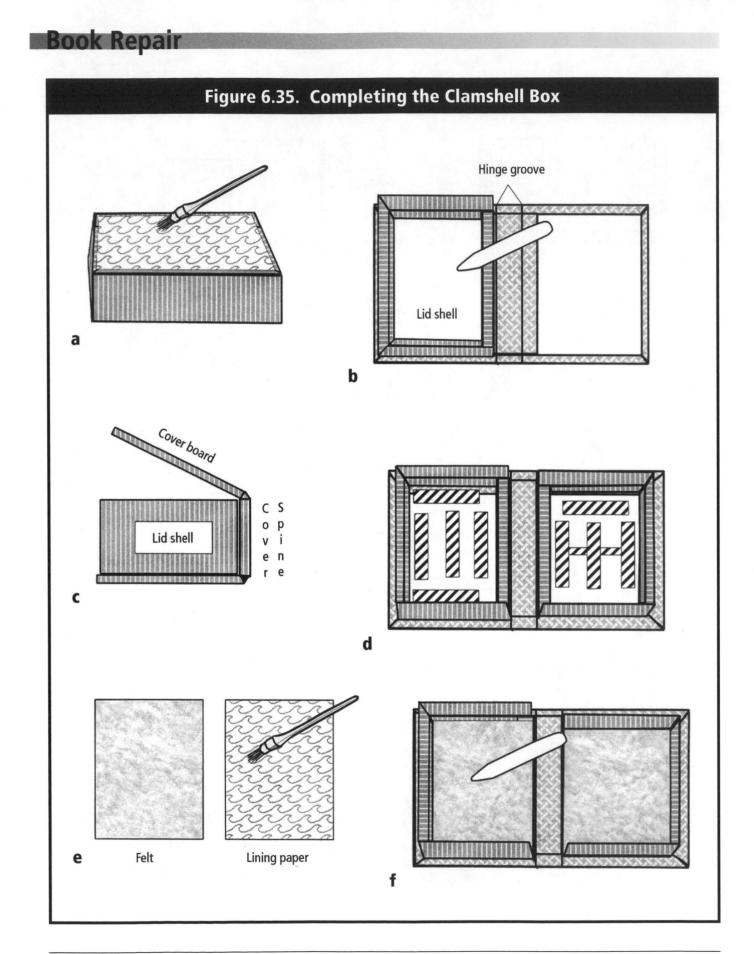

a

Hinge groove

Lid shell

b

Cover board

Lid shell

Cover   Spine

c

d

Felt   Lining paper

e

f

the base shell when the box is closed. Smooth down with your bone folder and allow to dry. (See Figure 6.35f.)

Resources

Two-Dimensional Objects

Folders

Ritzenthaler, Mary Lynn. *Preserving Archives and Manuscripts*. Chicago: Society of American Archivists, 1993. See pp. 195–198.

Encapsulation

Greenfield, Jane. *Books: Their Care and Repair*. New York: H.W. Wilson, 1983. See pp. 83–89.

Morrow, Carolyn, and Carole Dyal. *Conservation Treatment Procedures: A Manual of Step-by-Step Procedures for the Maintenance and Repair of Library Materials*. 2nd ed. Littleton, CO: Libraries Unlimited, 1986. See pp. 117–122 and 164–176.

Ritzenthaler, Mary Lynn. *Preserving Archives and Manuscripts*. Chicago: Society of American Archivists, 1993. See pp. 189–193.

Mats

American Institute for Conservation of Historic and Artistic Works. *Matting and Hinging of Works of Art on Paper*. Washington, DC: AIC, 1994.

Clapp, Anne F. *Curatorial Care of Works of Art on Paper*. 2nd ed. rev. Oberlin, OH: The Intermuseum Laboratory, 1974. See pp. 58–62.

Ellis, Margaret H. *The Care of Prints and Drawings*. Nashville: AASLH Press, 1987. See pp. 109–144.

Glaser, Mary Todd. "How to Do Your Own Matting and Hinging." *NEDCC Technical Leaflet*, Section 6, Leaflet 6. Andover, MA: Northeast Document Conservation Center, 1999.

Smith, Merrily A., and Margaret R. Brown. *Matting and Hinging Works of Art on Paper*. Washington, DC: Library of Congress, 1981.

Three-Dimensional Objects

Polyester Jackets

Greenfield, Jane. *The Care of Fine Books*. New York: Nick Lyons Books, 1988. See pp. 115–119.

Phase Boxes

Brown, Margaret R., comp. *Boxes for the Protection of Rare Books: Their Design and Construction*. Washington, DC: Library of Congress Preservation Office, 1982. See pp. 1–38.

Greenfield, Jane. *Books: Their Care and Repair*. New York: H.W. Wilson, 1983. See pp. 159–170.

Kyle, Hedi. *Library Materials Preservation Manual*. New York: Nicholas T. Smith, 1983. See pp. 95–99.

Morrow, Carolyn, and Carole Dyal. *Conservation Treatment Procedures: A Manual of Step-by-Step Procedures for the Maintenance and Repair of Library*

Materials. 2nd ed. Littleton, CO: Libraries Unlimited, 1986. See pp. 132–141.

Clamshell Boxes

Brown, Margaret R., comp. *Boxes for the Protection of Rare Books: Their Design and Construction.* Washington, DC: Library of Congress Preservation Office, 1982. See pp. 247–289.

Morrow, Carolyn, and Carole Dyal. *Conservation Treatment Procedures: A Manual of Step-by-Step Procedures for the Maintenance and Repair of Library Materials.* 2nd ed. Littleton, CO: Libraries Unlimited, 1986. See pp. 142–163.

Webberley, Marilyn, and JoAn Forsyth. *Books, Boxes & Wraps: Binding and Building Step-by-Step.* Kirkland, WA: Bifocal Publishing, 1998. See pp. 203–208.

Zeier, Franz. *Books, Boxes, and Portfolios.* New York: Design Press, 1990. See pp. 158–163.

A Disposable Box of Paper or Polyester Film

Appendix A

This useful box is commonly made by printers to mix their inks in. For this purpose it is made of heavy coated paper, but with a little practice it can be also be made of polyester film. Although the box is not waterproof, it will hold viscous liquids such as PVA, dyes, and paste mixtures.

Although the actual measurements of the box may be adjusted as needed, a rectangle with a ratio of 1:1.4 (e.g., 5 by 7) is a good size to work with.

Supplies

Heavy paper or polyester film (3-mil)
Bone folder

Procedure

1. Cut a rectangle and fold it into three sections; Section 2 will be on the bottom, Section 3 in the middle, and Section 1 on the top (see Figure A.1a).

2. Fold Section 1 in half, making a "valley" (i.e., V) fold; repeat for Section 3 (see Figure A.1b).

3. Bring these two folds together; Section 2 lies on the bottom, and Sections 1 and 3 are folded on top (see Figure A.1c).

4. Fold the left two corners of Sections 1 and 2 up under Section 1; fold the right two corners of Sections 3 and 2 up under Section 3 (see Figure A.1d–e). Crease sharply with a bone folder.

5. Spread Sections 1 and 3 apart with your thumbs while straightening the two sides with your fingers (see Figure A.1f).

6. The two pairs of corners (Sections 1 and 3, front and back) must come down to meet each other to form the ends of the box (see Figure A.1g).

7. Make creases at the corners of the box (a); make creases for the bottom edges of the box (b) (see Figure A.1h).

Figure A.1. Making a Disposable Box

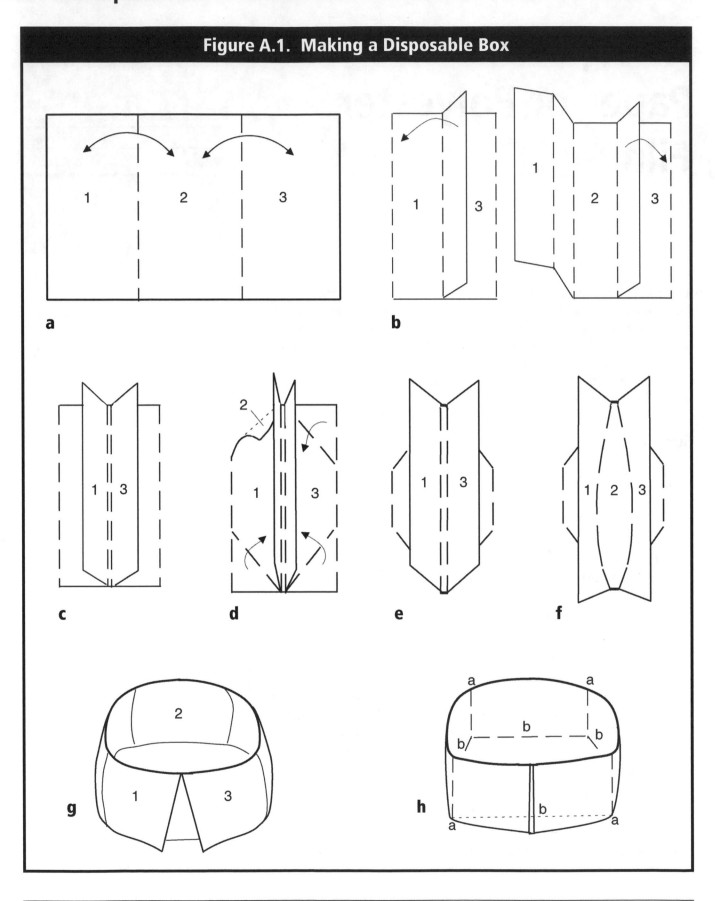

Supplies

Appendix B

Art Supplies (General)

Daniel Smith, Dick Blick, Reuel's, Utrecht

Binders (Folders)

Archival Methods, Archivart, Brodart, Dick Blick, Gaylord, Hollinger, Library Binding Service, Light Impressions, University Products

Board

Barrier (Phase Box)

Conservation Resources, Gaylord, Hollander's, Hollinger, Talas, University Products, Library Binding Service

Binders (Davey)

Archivart, BookMakers, Colophon, Conservation Resources, Dick Blick, Hiromi, Hollander's, Lineco, Talas, University Products

Bristol

BookMakers, Dick Blick, Reuel's, Talas, University Products, Utrecht

Folder Stock

Conservation Resources, Gaylord, Library Binding Service, Talas

Mat (Museum Mounting)

Archival Methods, Conservation Resources, Gaylord, Hollinger, Light Impressions, Talas, University Products

Bone Folders

Archival Methods, BookMakers, Brodart, Colophon, Daniel Smith, Dick Blick, Gaylord, Hiromi, Hollander's, Lineco, Reuel's, Talas, University Products

Book Cradles

Hollinger, Benchmark

Boxes

Archival Storage

Archival Methods, Brodart, Conservation Resources, Dick Blick, Gaylord, Hollinger, Library Binding Service, Light Impressions, Museum Services, Talas, University Products, Utrecht

Clamshell (Rare Book)

Conservation Resources, Gaylord, Hollinger

Phase (Ready-Made or Custom-Made)

Conservation Resources, Gaylord, Hollinger, University Products

Brushes

BookMakers, Colophon, Conservation Resources, Daniel Smith, Dick Blick, Gaylord, Hollander's, Hollinger, Lineco, Reuel's, Talas, University Products, Utrecht

Hake

Daniel Smith, Dick Blick, Hiromi, Reuel's, Talas, University Products, Utrecht

Cleaners

Absorene

Brodart, Gaylord, Hollinger, Talas, University Products

Crepe (Rubber Cement) Pickup Square

Dick Blick, Hollinger, Talas, Utrecht

Document Cleaning Pad

Brodart, Gaylord, Hollinger, Lineco, SicPress, Reuel's, Talas, University Products, Utrecht

Dry Cleaning Sponge

Brodart, Gaylord, University Products

Cloth

Book

BookMakers, Daniel Smith, Hiromi, Hollander's, Library Binding Services, Lineco, Reuel's, Talas, University Products, Utrecht

Jaconette

BookMakers, Hollander's

Super (Cotton, Linen)

BookMakers, Gaylord, Hiromi, Hollander's, Hollinger, Lineco, Talas, University Products

Cutters

Board Shear (Chopper)

BookMakers, Gaylord, Talas

Corner Rounder

Conservation Resources, Gaylord, University Products

Dissecting Needle

Daniel Smith, Lineco, Reuel's, Science Fair, Utrecht

Encapsulation Kits

University Products

Erasers

Compound

Daniel Smith, University Products, Utrecht

Gum

Brodart, Daniel Smith, Dick Blick, Gaylord, Hollinger, Reuel's, SicPress, University Products

Kneaded Rubber

Daniel Smith, Dick Blick, University Products, Utrecht

Plastic/Vinyl

Brodart, Daniel Smith, Gaylord, Hollinger, Reuel's, SicPress

Glue

Polyvinyl Acetate, Acid-Free (PVA)

BookMakers, Brodart, Daniel Smith, Dick Blick, Conservation Resources, Gaylord, Hollander's, Lineco, Museum Services, SicPress, Talas, University Products

Heating (Tacking) Iron

Large

BookMakers, Brodart, Gaylord, Light Impressions, Talas, University Products

Small

BookMakers, Conservation Resources, Dick Blick, University Products

Heat-Set Tissue

BookMakers, Conservation Resources, Gaylord, Talas, University Products

Knives and Scalpels

Olfa (Breakaway)

Dick Blick, Hollanders, Talas, University Products

X-Acto

Daniel Smith, Dick Blick, Conservation Resources, Gaylord, Hollander's, Hollinger, Reuel's, University Products

Scalpels and Blades

BookMakers, Conservation Resources, Conservator's Emporium, Gaylord, Museum Services, SicPress, University Products

Paper

Blotting

Archivart, BookMakers, Dick Blick, Gaylord, Hollander's, Light Impressions, University Products

Endsheets

BookMakers, Daniel Smith, Colophon, Conservation Resources, Gaylord, Hollander's, Hollinger, Light Impressions, Talas, University Products

Japanese

Archivart, BookMakers, Daniel Smith, Gaylord, Hiromi, Hollander's, Talas, University Products

Marbled

BookMakers, Colophon, Daniel Smith, Dick Blick, Gaylord, Hollander's, Reuel's, Skycraft, University Products

Release (Silicone)

BookMakers, Brodart, Conservation Resources, Dick Blick, Gaylord, Reuel's, Talas, University Products

Tissue

Archivart, Archival Methods, Conservation Resources, Dick Blick, Gaylord, Hollander's, Hiromi, Light Impressions, Talas, University Products

Paste

Methyl Cellulose

BookMakers, Conservation Resources, Dick Blick, Gaylord, Reuel's, SicPress, Talas, University Products

Rice

Dick Blick, Hollander's, Lineco, Talas, University Products

Wheat

Archivart, BookMakers, Conservation Resources, Daniel Smith, Gaylord, Hiromi, Hollander's, Lineco, SicPress, Talas, University Products

Polyester Film

Envelopes

Archival Methods, Conservation Resources, Gaylord, Library Binding Services, Light Impressions, Talas, University Products

Rolls

Brodart, Conservation Resources, Gaylord, Light Impressions, Talas, University Products

Sheets

Conservation Resources, Gaylord, Light Impressions, Talas, University Products

Polyester (Nonwoven, Spun)

BookMakers, Daniel Smith, Gaylord, Talas, University Products

Ruling Pen

Reuel's, Utrecht

Scissors

Binder's Shears

BookMakers, Conservation Resources, Dick Blick, Hollander's, Reuel's, Talas, University Products

Embroidery (Surgical)

BookMakers, Conservator's Emporium, Talas

Spatulas

BookMakers, Conservation Resources, Dick Blick, Gaylord, Hollander's, Hollinger, SicPress, Talas, University Products, Utrecht

Tape

Archival (Document) Repair

Brodart, Dick Blick, Gaylord, Hollinger, Light Impressions, SicPress, Talas, University Products

Double-Sided (3M Scotch 415)

Brodart, Conservation Resources, Gaylord, Hollinger, Light Impressions, Talas, University Products

Linen Hinging

Brodart, Daniel Smith, Dick Blick, Conservation Resources, Gaylord, Hiromi, Hollinger, Light Impressions, Lineco, University Products, Utrecht

Thread (Binder's)

BookMakers, Brodart, Colophon, Daniel Smith, Dick Blick, Gaylord, Hiromi, Hollander's, Hollinger, Lineco, Talas, University Products, Utrecht

Vacuums

Brodart, Conservation Resources, Gaylord, Talas, University Products

Suppliers

Appendix C

Several online sites list book repair or book conservation businesses. Check these sites for the most current information:

The Book Arts Web: http://www.philobiblon.com/suppliers.shtml

Northeast Document Conservation Center: http://www.nedcc.org/ resources/suppliers.php

Amigos Library Services: http://www.amigos.org/search/node/Preservation/Conservation %20Suppliers

Archival Methods
235 Middle Road
Henrietta, NY 14467
(866) 877-7050 or (585) 334-7050
Fax: (585) 334-7067
mail@archivalmethods.com
http://www.archivalmethods.com

Archivart
40 Eisenhower Drive
Paramus, NJ 07652
(800) 804-8428
Fax: (888) 273-4824
http://www.archivart.com

Benchmark
P.O. Box 214
Rosemont NJ 08556
(609) 397-1131
Fax: (609) 397-1159
ask@benchmarkcatalog.com
http://www.benchmarkcatalog.com

BookMakers, Inc.
8601 Rhode Island Ave.
College Park, MD 20740
(301) 345-7979

Fax: (310) 345-7373
bookmakers@earthlink.net
http://www.bookmakerscatalog.com

Brodart Co.
1609 Memorial Ave.
Williamsport, PA 17705
(888) 820-4377
Fax: 800-283-6087
http://www.shopbrodart.com

Colophon Book Arts
3611 Ryan Street SE
Lacey, WA 98503
(360) 459-2949
Fax: (360) 459-2945
colophon@earthlink.net
http://www.colophonbookarts.com

Conservation Resources International
5532 Port Royal Road
Springfield, VA 22151
(800) 634-6932 or (703) 321-7730
Fax: (703) 321-0629
sales@conservationresources.com
http://www.conservationresources.com

Daniel Smith, Inc.
P.O. Box 84268
Seattle, WA 98124-5568
(800) 426-7023
Fax: (206)224-0404
customer.service@danielsmith.com
http://www.danielsmith.com/

Dick Blick
P.O. Box 1267
Galesburg, IL 61402-1267
(800) 723-2787
Fax: (800) 621-8293
info@dickblick.com
http://www.dickblick.com

Gaylord Brothers Archival Solutions
Box 4901
Syracuse, NY 13221-4901
(800) 962-9580
Fax: (800) 272-3412
http://www.gaylord.com/archivalsolutions.asp

Hiromi Paper International, Inc.
Bergamot Station
2525 Michigan Avenue, Unit G-9
Santa Monica, CA 90404

(866) 479-2744 or (310) 998-0098
Fax: (310) 998-0028
washi@hiromipaper.com
http://hiromipaper.com

Hollander's
410 N. Fourth Avenue
Ann Arbor, MI 48104
(734) 741-7531
Fax: (734) 741-7580
info@hollander.com
http://www.hollanders.com

Hollinger Metal Edge
9401 Northeast Dr.
Fredericksburg, VA 22404
(800) 634-0491
Fax: (800) 947-8814
info@hollingermetaledge.com
http://www.hollingercorp.com

Library Binding Service (LBS) Archival Products
1801 Thompson, P.O. Box 1413
Des Moines, IA 50306-1413
(800) 526-5640 or (515) 262-3191
Fax: (888) 220-2397
info@archival.com
http://www.archival.com

Light Impressions Corp.
P.O. Box 2100
Santa Fe Springs, CA 90670
(800) 828-6216
Fax: (800) 828-5539
http://www.lightimpressionsdirect.com

Lineco Inc.
P.O. Box 2604
Holyoke MA 01041-2604
(800) 322-7775
Fax: (800) 298-7815
info@lineco.com
http://www.lineco.com

MuseuM Services Corporation
385 Bridgepoint Way
South Saint Paul, MN 55075
(651) 450-8954
Fax: (651) 554-9217
info@museumservicescorporation.com
http://www.museumservicescorporation.com

Reuel's Art & Frame
370 South West Temple

Salt Lake City, Utah 84101
(888) 355-1713
Fax: (877) 232-4567 or (801) 328-2818
info@reuels.com
http://www.reuels.com

The Science Fair, Inc.
P.O. Box 934
St. Augustine, FL 32085
(904) 824-9323
Fax: (904) 823-8883
thesciencefair@bellsouth.net
http://www.thesciencefair.com

Sic Press
Joyce Godsey
14 Pleasant St.
Methuem, MA 01844
(978) 376-5619
Fax: (866) 416-6101
http://sicpress.com

Skycraft Marbled Paper
26395 South Morgan Road
Estacada, OR 97023
(503) 578-5708
info@skycraft.com
http://www.skycraft.com

Talas
330 Morgan Avenue
Brooklyn, NY 11211
(212) 219-0770
Fax: (212) 219-0735
info@talasonline.com
http://www.talas-nyc.com

University Products
517 Main Street, P.O. Box 101
Holyoke, MA 01041
(800) 628-1912
Fax: (800) 532-9281
custserv@universityproducts.com
http://www.universityproducts.com

Utrecht Art Supplies
6 Corporate Drive
Cranbury, NJ 08512
(800) 223-9132
Fax: (800) 382-1979
http://www.utrechtart.com

Bibliography of Print and Electronic Resources

The basic principles of book conservation do not change over time and well-tested materials and techniques never grow obsolete. Unlike informational resources in other areas, you don't need to be deterred by older copyright dates—but, always search out the best methods to learn.

When searching the Internet, keep in mind that not all sources and not every piece of information are reputable. Some sites may suggest potentially damaging repair procedures. University or established library sites are a good place to start but, when in doubt, check several sources for consensus before proceeding.

General Conservation

Print Sources

Association of Research Libraries, Office of Management Studies. *Collection Conservation Treatment: A Resource Manual for Program Development and Conservation Technician Training.* Washington, DC: Association of Research Libraries, Office of Management Studies, 1993.

Balloffet, Nelly, and Jenny Hille. *Preservation and Conservation for Libraries and Archives.* Chicago: American Library Association, 2005.

Banks, Paul N., and Roberta Pilette, ed. *Preservation: Issues and Planning.* Chicago and London: American Library Association, 2000.

Carrabba, Sheryl. "Guidelines for Testing." In *Conservation of Archival Materials*, 73–79. Austin, TX: Harry Ransom Humanities Research Center, Conservation Department, 1985.

Depew, John N. *A Library, Media, and Archival Preservation Handbook.* Santa Barbara, CA: ABC-CLIO, 1991.

Higginbotham, Barbara Buckner, and Judith Wild. *Preservation Program Blueprint.* Chicago, IL: American Library Association, 2001.

Jones, Maralyn, comp. *Collection Conservation Treatment: A Resource Manual for Program Development and Conservation Technician Training.* Washington, DC: Association of Research Libraries, Office of Management Studies, 1994.

Milevski, Robert J., and Linda Nainis. "Implementing a Book Repair and Treatment Program." *Library Resources & Technical Services* 31 (April/June 1987): 159–176.

Morrow, Carolyn Clark, with Gay Walker. *The Preservation Challenge: A Guide to Conserving Library Materials*. White Plains, NY: Macmillan, 1983.

Ritzenthaler, Mary Lynn. *Archives & Manuscripts: Conservation. SAA Basic Manual Series*. 1st ed.; 2nd ed. Chicago: Society of American Archivists, 1983; 1993.

Ritzenthaler, Mary Lynn. *Preserving Archives and Manuscripts*. Chicago: Society of American Archivists, 1993.

Electronic Sources

Book Arts Web. Links to a large selection of book arts–related Internet sites. http://www.philobiblon.com.

Canadian Bookbinders and Book Artists Guild. http://www.cbbag.ca/home.html.

Canadian Conservation Institute. http://www.cci-icc.gc.ca/.

Conservation Center for Art and Historic Artifacts. http://www.ccaha.org/.

CoOL (Conservation OnLine). Links to organizations and publications with searchable full-text articles. http://cool.conservation-us.org/.

DeCandido, Robert, ed. *Collections Conservation*. Washington, DC: Association of Research Libraries, 1993. Available online at Google books.

Guild of Bookworkers. http://guildofbookworkers.org/.

Library of Congress. "Preservation (Library of Congress)." http://www.loc.gov/preservation/.

National Archives and Records Administration (NARA). "Preservation and Archives Professionals." http://www.archives.gov/preservation/index.html.

The National Committee to Save America's Cultural Collections. "Caring for Your Collections/American Art." http://americanart.si.edu/research/tools/art/care.

National Park Service. "Conserve O Grams" (numerous topics). http://www.cr.nps.gov/museum/publications/conserveogram/conserv.html.

Northeast Document Conservation Center. "Preservation 101: An Online Instructor-Led Introduction to Preservation" (webinar). http://www.nedcc.org/education/preservation101/preservation101.php.

Northern States Conservation Center. "Museum Collection Care" (website with full-text articles, searchable by type of material). http://www.collectioncare.org/.

Ogden, Sherelyn. 1999. *Preservation of Library and Archival Materials: A Manual*. 3rd ed. Andover, MA: Northeast Document Conservation Center http://www.nedcc.org/resources/pubs.php.

Patkus, Beth. *Assessing Preservation Needs: A Self-Survey Guide*. Andover, MA: Northeast Document Conservation Center, 2003. http://www.nedcc.org/resources/downloads/apnssg.pdf.

University of California, San Diego. "Preservation Education and Awareness for Library Users." http://libraries.ucsd.edu/preseduc.

Book Repair and Book Binding

Print Sources

Abbott, Kathy. *Bookbinding: A Step-by-Step Guide*. Wiltshire, UK: The Crowood Press, 2010.

Greenfield, Jane. *Books and Their Care*. New York: H.W. Wilson, 1983.

Greenfield, Jane. *The Care and Repair of Fine Books*. New York: Nick Lyons Books, 1988.

Horton, Carolyn. *Cleaning and Preserving Bindings and Related Materials.* 2nd ed. Chicago: American Library Association, 1969.

Illinois Cooperative Conservation Program. *A Simple Workstation for the Conservation of Library Materials.* Carbondale, IL: Illinois Cooperative Conservation Program, 1984.

Johnson, Arthur W. *The Practical Guide to Book Repair and Conservation.* New York: Thames and Hudson, 1988.

Johnson, Arthur W. *The Thames and Hudson Manual of Book Binding.* London: Thames and Hudson, 1978.

Kyle, Hedi. *Library Materials Preservation Manual.* New York: Nicholas T. Smith, 1983.

Lindsay, Jen. *Fine Bookbinding: A Technical Guide.* New Castle, DE: Oak Knoll Press, 2009.

Middleton, Bernard C. *The Restoration of Leather Bindings.* 3rd ed. New Castle, DE: Oak Knoll Press, 1998.

Milevski, Robert J. *Book Repair Manual.* Carbondale, IL: Illinois Cooperative Conservation Program, 1984.

Morrow, Carolyn Clark, and Carole Dyal. *Conservation Treatment Procedures: A Manual of Step-by-Step Procedures for the Maintenance and Repair of Library Materials.* 2nd ed. Littleton, CO: Libraries Unlimited, 1986.

Ogden, Sherelyn, ed. *Preservation of Library and Archival Materials: A Manual.* 3rd rev. ed. Andover, MA: Northeast Document Conservation Center, 1999.

Roberts, Matt T., and Don Etherington. *Bookbinding and the Conservation of Books: A Dictionary of Descriptive Technology.* Washington, DC: Library of Congress, 1982.

Schechter, Abraham. *Basic Book Repair Methods.* Littleton, CO: Libraries Unlimited, 1999.

Swartzburg, Susan. *Preserving Library Materials: A Manual.* 2nd ed. Metuchen, NJ: The Scarecrow Press, 1995.

Webberley, Marilyn, and JoAn Forsyth. *Books, Boxes and Wraps: Binding and Building Step-by-Step.* Kirkland, WA: Bifocal Publishing, 1998.

Young, Laura G. *Bookbinding and Conservation by Hand.* New Castle, DE: Oak Knoll Press, 1995.

Electronic Sources

BonaDea, Artemis. *Conservation Book Repair: A Training Manual.* Alaska State Library. http://www.library.state.ak.us/hist/conman.html.

Bonefolder. Online journal for bookbinders and book artists. http://www.philobiblon.com/bonefolder/.

BookArts-L. Features links to book arts–related sites, tutorials, and reference materials. http://www.philobiblon.com/.

Bookbinders Workshop. "Instructional DVDs." http://www.bookbindersworkshop.com/dvd.htm.

Canadian Bookbinders and Book Artists Guild. "Home Study Programme." http://www.cbbag.ca/HomeStudy.htm.

Coelacanth Books. "Book Repair Links." http://coelacanthbooks.pbworks.com/w/page/16057781/Book-Repair-Links.

Cool Conservation OnLine (CoOL). Full-text library of conservation information. http://cool.conservation-us.org/.

Dartmouth College Library. *A Simple Book Repair Manual.* Hanover, NH: Dartmouth College, 2000. http://www.dartmouth.edu/~library/preservation/repair/index.html.

Dyal, Carole, and Pete Merrill-Oldham. *Three Basic Book Repair Procedures.* Book Arts Web: http://www.philobiblon.com/bkrepair/BookRepair.html; Michigan State University Libraries: http://www.lib.msu.edu/preservation/hinge1.jsp.

Harrison, Garry. *Repair and Enclosure Treatments Manual.* Indiana University Libraries. http://www.indiana.edu/~libpres/manual/mantoc.html.

Harry Ransom Center, Conservation Department. "Articles Written by Harry Ransom Center Conservation Department Staff Since 1980." http://www.hrc.utexas.edu/conservation/resources/articles/.

Jones, Douglas W. *Bookbinding: A Tutorial.* University of Iowa Department of Computer Science and Center for the Book. http://www.cs.uiowa.edu/~jones/book/.

Kosar, Heather Marie. "Understanding Book Repair Terminology: Basic Preservationally Sound Conservation Treatments and Techniques." Suite101, August 10, 2009. http://www.suite101.com/content/understanding-book-repair-terminology-a137389#ixzz1ApuFc3qz.

Library of Congress. *Library Preservation: Fundamental Techniques.* Washington, DC: Library of Congress, 1986. 6 VHS color videotapes.

Northeast Document Conservation Center. http://www.nedcc.org/.

Smith, Margit J. "Repairing Books and Preserving the General Collection." *Archival Products News* 10, no. 2: 1–5. http://www.archival.com/newsletters/apnewsvol10no2.pdf.

University Library. *Procedures and Treatments Used for Book Repair and Pamphlet Binding.* University of Illinois at Urbana-Champaign. http://www.library.illinois.edu/prescons/preserve/procedures.html.

University of Michigan. *Introduction to Book Repair.* University of Michigan handout. http://michigan.gov/documents/hal/book_repair_handouts_251280_7.doc.

Visual Education, prod. *Basic Book Repair with Jane Greenfield.* Written and directed by Mark Schaeffer. Bronx, NY: H.W. Wilson Company, 1988. Video.

Protective Boxes

Brown, Margaret R., comp. *Boxes for the Protection of Rare Books: Their Design and Construction.* Washington, DC: Library of Congress Preservation Office, 1982.

Hollander, Tom, and Cindy Hollander. *Constructing and Covering Boxes: A Beginner's Guide.* Atglen, PA: Schiffer Publications, 2009.

Zeier, Franz. *Books, Boxes, and Portfolios.* New York: Design Press, 1990.

Conservation of Works of Art on Paper

American Institute for Conservation of Historic and Artistic Works. *Matting and Hinging of Works of Art on Paper.* Washington, DC: American Institute for Conservation of Historic and Artistic Works, 1994.

Clapp, Anne F. *Curatorial Care of Works of Art on Paper.* 2nd ed. rev. Oberlin, OH: The Intermuseum Laboratory, 1974.

Ellis, Margaret H. *The Care of Prints and Drawings.* Nashville: AASLH (American Association for State and Local History) Press, 1987.

Glaser, Mary Todd. "How to Do Your Own Matting and Hinging." *NEDCC Technical Leaflet*, Section 6, Leaflet 6. Andover, MA: Northeast Document Conservation Center, 1999.

Smith, Merrily A., and Margaret R. Brown. *Matting and Hinging Works of Art on Paper*. Washington, DC: Library of Congress, 1981.

Disaster Response and Water Damage

Print Sources

Dion, Kathleen B. "These Leaves Were Not Made to Be Wet, Or... Help, My Books Have Water on Them!" *The New Library Scene* (September 1997): 24–26.

Fortson, Judith. *Disaster Planning and Recovery: A How-To-Do-It Manual for Librarians and Archivists*. New York: Neal-Schuman, 1992.

Kahn, Miriam. *Disaster Response and Planning for Libraries*. Chicago: American Library Association, 1998.

Electronic Sources

Bishop Museum, Honolulu. *Disaster Preparedness and Recovery for Works of Art on Paper*. Bishop Museum Art Conservation Handout. http://www.bishop museum.org/research/pdfs/cnsv-disaster.pdf.

Buchanan, Sally. "Emergency Salvage of Wet Books and Records." *NEDCC Technical Leaflet*, Section 3, Leaflet 7. Andover, MA: Northeast Document Conservation Center, 1999. http://www.nedcc.org/tleaf37.html.

Conservation Center for Art and Historic Artifacts. Technical bulletins on salvaging wet art on paper, photographs, and books. http://www.ccaha.org/publications/technical-bulletins.

Frellsen, Ann V. "Thawing Frozen Books." *Conservation DistList*, January 26, 1995.

Kaplan, Hilary A. "Mold: A Follow-Up." Cool Conservation OnLine, February 1998. http://cool.conservation-us.org/byauth/kaplan/moldfu.html.

Library of Congress. "Emergency Drying Procedures for Water Damaged Collections—Collections Care." Preservation, Library of Congress. http://www.loc.gov/preservation/care/dry.html.

McCrady, Ellen. "Mold: The Whole Picture, Parts 1–4." *The Abbey Newsletter*, 23 (1999). http://cool.conservation-us.org/bytopic/mold/.

Michigan Alliance for the Conservation of Cultural Heritage. "Conservation and Disaster Resources." http://www.macch.org/.

Michigan State University Libraries. "Preservation—Wet Books." Michigan State University. http://www.lib.msu.edu/preservation/wetbooks.jsp.

National Library of Australia. "Water Damage at Home—You Can Recover: Parts 1 and 2." National Library of Australia. http://www.nla.gov.au/pres/conver/041095.html (Part 1); http://www.nla.gov.au/pres/conver/181095.html (Part 2).

Northeast Document Conservation Center. Technical and preservation leaflets. http://www.nedcc.org/.

Nyberg, Sandra. "Invasion of the Giant Spore." *SOLINET Preservation Program Leaflet* No. 5. Atlanta, GA: SOLINET, 1987. http://www-sul.stanford.edu/tools/tutorials/html2.0/spore.html. Updated version: http://cool.conservation-us.org/byauth/nyberg/spore.html.

Patkus, Beth Lindblom. "Emergency Salvage of Moldy Books and Paper." *NEDCC Technical Leaflet*, Section 3, Leaflet 9. Andover, MA: Northeast Document Conservation Center, 1999. http://www.nedcc.org/resources/leaflets/3Emergency_Management/08SalvageMoldyBooks.php.

Price, Lois Olcott. "Managing a Mold Invasion: Guidelines for Disaster Response." *CCAHA Technical Series* No. 1. Philadelphia: Conservation Center for Art and Historic Artifacts, 1996.

The Restoration Resource. "Wet Books and Documents: Find Out Ways to Dry Them at Home." The Restoration Resource. http://therestorationresource .com/Wet_Books_and_Documents_Find_Out_Ways_to_Dry_Them_at_Home .html.

University Library, Preservation Division. "How to Salvage Wet Books." University of Michigan. www.lib.umich.edu/files/services/preservation/ wetbooks-1.pdf.

University of Delaware Library. "How to Dry a Wet Book." University of Delaware Library. http://www2.lib.udel.edu/Preservation/wet_books.htm.

Waters, Peter. *Procedures for Salvage of Water-Damaged Materials*. Washington, DC: Library of Congress, 1993. http://cool.conservation-us.org/bytopic/ disasters/primer/waters.html.

Glossary

Small capital letters within definitions indicate the term is defined elsewhere in the glossary.

You can find additional or more complete definitions in Bookbinding and the Conservation of Books: A Dictionary of Descriptive Terminology, *compiled by Matt T. Roberts and Don Etherington. It is available electronically at http://cool.conservation-us.org/don/don.html.*

acid-free: Materials that contain no free acid and have a pH value of 7.0 or greater. These materials are said to be ARCHIVAL.

adhesive: A general term for any of several substances capable of bonding materials to each other that may be activated by water, pressure, or heat. Adhesives used in bookbinding need to remain flexible when dry and not damage the book or paper over time. *See also* DOUBLE FAN ADHESIVE BINDING; PERFECT BINDING.

adhesive binding: *See* DOUBLE FAN ADHESIVE BINDING.

against the grain: Paper that has been cut or folded at right angles to the paper grain; the direction the paper fibers tend to lie. Paper and book board will not fold or bend as well against the grain. *See also* GRAIN.

animal glue: An adhesive derived from an animal product, usually hide, connective tissue, or bone. Animal glue has been supplanted by PVA adhesive. *See also* ADHESIVE.

archival: Materials that are considered safe and PERMANENT and should not cause damage due to an acidic content. *See also* ACID-FREE.

archival mending tape: Repair material made of archival paper and a relatively safe pressure-sensitive adhesive.

awl: A pointed tool used to pierce holes in paper for sewing.

backing: After ROUNDING the TEXTBLOCK, the process of shaping the outermost signatures on both sides of the sewn textblock to form a shoulder. The depth of the shoulder is scaled to match the thickness of the book board. Also is used to indicate the lining of a paper object with another material, such as Japanese paper or heat-set tissue.

barrier paper: Material that is resistant or impervious to water, such as wax paper.

beeswax: An animal wax obtained from bees used to lubricate the sewing thread in books.

bind: The process of attaching pages to one another to form a TEXTBLOCK, or creating a finished book.

blotting paper: An unsized sheet of thick paper used to absorb excess moisture from wet repairs.

board: *See* BOOK BOARD.

board shear: A lever type of cutter mounted on a flat bed used for cutting paper or book board; sometimes also called a board chopper.

bone folder: *See* FOLDER.

book: A collection of paper pages bound together and enclosed in a protective cover. *See also* CODEX.

book board: A special paper board commonly used to create the front and back covers of a hardback book, also called binder's board.

book cloth: Fabrics used to cover books, usually woven fabric and sometimes filled with sizing, backed with paper or embossed with a pattern.

book conservation: The process of maintaining or repairing all aspects of a book, including binding techniques, RESTORATION, paper chemistry, and other material technology. Also the knowledge pertinent to the preservation of archival resources.

book jacket: A detachable outer cover for a bound book, designed to protect the binding.

book press: A simple machine that applies pressure evenly over the surface of a piece of paper or book.

case binding: A style of bookbinding in which the sewn or glued textblock is made in one operation and the case or covers of the book is made in a separate operation. The two parts are brought together when the textblock is attached to the covers in a procedure called CASING-IN.

casing-in: The process of joining the textblock to the finished case in a CASE BINDING style book.

cloth: *See* BOOK CLOTH.

coated paper: Paper filled with starch or a finely pulverized clay to provide a heavier stock and slick surface for printing. Coated papers are not strong and are easily damaged by water.

codex: The common form of the Western-style book. The codex form is based on groups of pages attached to one another at the back of the book, than placed between two covers.

collate: To put pages in their correct order and to determine that no material is missing.

cords: Thick linen twine used as a sewing support in some styles of book binding.

corner: The juncture of the two edges of a book cover at the FORE-EDGE and HEAD and TAIL.

cover: The outer covering placed around a TEXTBLOCK to protect it during use or storage; often consists of a front cover board, a SPINE, and a back cover board.

crash: *See* SUPER.

dissecting needle: A thin, pointed tool used to pierce holes in paper for sewing.

document repair tape: *See* ARCHIVAL MENDING TAPE.

dog eared: A page of a BOOK with one or more CORNERS folded or damaged or the damaged corners of a book cover.

double fan adhesive binding: A binding style in which the SPINE edges of individual pages are fanned in both directions; ADHESIVE is applied on the fanned edge of each piece of paper so that when the pages are returned to their original position, they adhere together to form a glued TEXTBLOCK.

edges: The three outer edges of the book cover or a page of the BOOK: the top, the bottom and the FORE-EDGE.

encapsulation: Protecting a piece of paper or page of a BOOK by enclosing it in clear, stable POLYESTER FILM.

endpaper: Two or more pieces of paper attached to the front and back of the TEXTBLOCK that protect the pages from damage and cover the SUPER where it attaches the textblock to the COVER BOARDS.

endsheet: *See* ENDPAPER.

fan binding: *See* DOUBLE FAN ADHESIVE BINDING.

finishing: The process of embellishing the SPINE with the title of the book or decorating. Finishing can also include decorating the edges of the TEXTBLOCK as well. *See also* FORWARDING.

flat back: A book with a TEXTBLOCK that has not been rounded or backed. *See also* ROUNDING and BACKING.

flyleaf: The part of the ENDPAPER that is attached only at the SPINE and is free to turn when the book is opened or closed. The second half of the ENDPAPER that is glued to the inside of the cover board is called the PASTEDOWN.

folder: A thin length of bone, plastic, wood or Teflon 5–7 inches long. Most folders are about ⅛ inch thick and have one rounded end and one pointed end, sometimes called a BONE FOLDER.

fore-edge: The front edge of the TEXTBLOCK that is opposite the SPINE.

forwarding: All the steps involved in binding a book up to titling or decorating of the cover. *See also* FINISHING.

gathering: *See* SIGNATURE.

glue: *See* ADHESIVE.

gluing-up: The process of applying ADHESIVE to the SPINE of a TEXTBLOCK after the SIGNATURES have been sewn together.

gold foil: A plastic film with a deposit of gold or other metal, backed by a pressure-sensitive adhesive. The metallic foil is used to stamp book titles on the book spine with the assistance of a heated tool.

gold leaf: A sheet of gold 3¼ inches square of an even thickness of 1/200,000 to 1/250,000 inch, used to apply hand lettering and decorate book bindings with specially heated tools.

grain: The direction most of the fibers lay when paper, cloth, or BOARD are made. Most materials fold or bend easier along the GRAIN than AGAINST THE GRAIN.

grain long: A term used to indicate that the paper GRAIN is parallel to the longer dimension of a piece of paper.

grain short: A term used to indicate that the paper GRAIN is parallel to the shorter dimension of the piece of paper.

guard: A strip of cloth or paper pasted around the fold of a page or SIGNATURE to reinforce the paper for sewing.

hand sewing: The process of sewing a book without using a machine.

head: The top of the spine of a book or TEXTBLOCK, opposite the TAIL.

headband: A sewn or woven band at the HEAD and TAIL of a TEXTBLOCK. Historically, headbands served a structural purpose, but modern headbands are mostly decorative.

headcap: The leather covering at the SPINE HEAD and TAIL, formed by turning the leather on the spine and shaping.

heat-set tissue: A thin tissue prepared with a heat-activated adhesive used for strengthening or mending torn paper. Heat-set tissue is especially useful for repairing COATED PAPER.

height: The overall dimension of a bound volume from HEAD to TAIL, including the SQUARES.

hinge: The interior juncture of the cover board and the TEXTBLOCK; the outer juncture is usually referred to as the JOINT. Also a piece of folded repair paper attached to a separated page to reattach it to the TEXTBLOCK.

hinging-in: The act of attaching a loose page into a TEXTBLOCK by pasting a JAPANESE REPAIR TISSUE hinge to the page and then attaching that HINGE into the TEXTBLOCK. *See also* TIPPING-IN.

hollow back: A style of bookbinding with a space between the SPINE of the TEXTBLOCK and the spine of the cover. The cover is attached to the textblock at the JOINTS at the front and back cover.

humidify: The process of relaxing damaged or curled paper by allowing it to safely absorb moisture and then drying it flat under weight.

inner margin: The part of the page adjacent to the binding edge of the textblock. It is the left-hand margin of the recto and the right-hand margin on the VERSO.

interleaving: The process of placing barrier sheets or blotter paper between sheets of paper to protect them or facilitate their drying. Interleaving can also be used to dry book pages bound into a book.

Japanese paper: *See* JAPANESE REPAIR TISSUE.

Japanese repair tissue: A generic term for various handmade papers that have very long, strong fibers. These papers are applied to paper tears with wheat or rice paste. This kind of paper is sometimes generically called rice paper but it has nothing to do with rice.

joint: The exterior juncture of the cover board and the textblock. The inner juncture is usually referred to as the HINGE.

kettle stitch: A stitch made closest to the HEAD and TAIL of a sewn book, which holds the sections together.

leaf: The smallest physical unit of a book, comprising a front side (recto) and a back side (verso). Thus, there are two pages to any one leaf.

leather: The outer covering of an animal, tanned so as to be rendered flexible and usable. Several types of animal leather are generally used in bookbinding.

library corner: A style of a book CORNER in which the covering material, instead of being cut and abutted, has the excess taken up in two diagonal folds, one under each turn-in.

linen thread: *See* THREAD.

marbled paper: Paper that has been decorated in one of several traditional patterns using a particular decorating method. Marbling began in the Middle East and was introduced into Europe in the early 1600s.

Melinex: *See* POLYESTER FILM.

mending: Minor repair of a book with no replacement of any material or dismantling of the TEXTBLOCK or COVER.

micro-spatula: A thin double-bladed metal tool, about 10 inches long, used in a variety of repair techniques.

mold: A growth caused by micro-organisms that derive their food from the materials of a book. Also called mildew, molds often lead to staining that is difficult to remove.

mull: *See* SUPER.

nonsupported sewing: A sewing structure that has no tapes or cords to provide support. Each SIGNATURE is sewn to the signatures on either side.

oversewn: A binding style in which the individual pages are whip stitched together at the INNER MARGIN. Oversewing is very strong, but it is not very flexible, and over time the pages often break along the sewing line.

paper: Matted or felted sheets of fiber formed into various thicknesses. The finished product can be coated or uncoated. *See also* COATED PAPER.

paste: A soft ADHESIVE created by heating a mixture (usually wheat or rice) of starch and water.

pastedown: The part of the ENDPAPER attached to the inside of the front and back cover. The second half of the endpaper that is attached only at the spine and is free to open and close is called the FLYLEAF.

perfect binding: A binding style in which a hot, fast melting ADHESIVE is laid onto the back of the TEXTBLOCK. The adhesive is generally not very flexible and the book operates poorly. Perfect bindings are commonly used in paperback books.

permanent: Materials that have a neutral pH and will remain stable over time.

pH: A measurement of acidity or alkalinity as expressed metrically on a continuum. Materials with a measurement of greater than 7.0 are said to be alkaline, while materials that measure less than 7.0 are said to be acidic.

polyester film: A clear plastic film that is waterproof and stable; it will not become brittle or turn yellow.

polyvinyl acetate: *See* PVA.

press: *See* BOOK PRESS.

press board: A piece of plywood or Plexiglass placed on either side of a book before it is placed in a BOOK PRESS. The press board helps distribute the press pressure evenly and protects the finished book. Glass can be used to apply pressure on a repair outside the book press.

PVA: Polyvinyl acetate (PVA) is a water-white resin adhesive that is easily diluted with water. PVA dries flexible and is considered relatively harmless for bookbinding. PVA has supplanted the use of ANIMAL GLUE in bookbinding.

reback: The process of replacing the original SPINE on a damaged book with a new spine. Whenever possible, the original spine is mounted over the new spine.

rebind: To re-create an already bound book by RESEWING the SIGNATURES together and recasing the TEXTBLOCK into the original or a new cover. *See also* RECASE.

recase: To reattach the TEXTBLOCK into its original COVER.

recto: The right-hand page of an open book.

repair tissue: Long-fibered handmade paper used to repair damaged pages or book covers. This tissue comes in a variety of weights and is also called Japanese repair tissue, Japanese paper, or rice paper.

resewing: Repairing a previously sewn TEXTBLOCK by sewing it back together in the same sewing structure as the original textblock.

restoration: The process of returning a book as nearly as possible to its original condition.

rice paper: *See* JAPANESE REPAIR TISSUE.

rounding: The process of gently molding the TEXTBLOCK SPINE into an arc approximately one-third of a circle. Rounding is accomplished after the textblock is sewn together.

score: To crease a piece of paper, BOOK CLOTH, or BOOK BOARD prior to bending or folding it.

section: *See* SIGNATURE.

selvage: The edges of a piece of BOOK CLOTH that show the weaving pattern or rough edges that are usually cut off and discarded. The GRAIN of the cloth usually runs parallel to the selvage.

sewing: The process of attaching pages together with THREAD using one of a variety of sewing techniques.

sewing cords: *See* CORDS.

sewing thread: *See* THREAD.

shoulder: The edges of the TEXTBLOCK SPINE where the SIGNATURES or leaves are attached to one another. In the BACKING process these shoulders are gently bent over to form the shoulder at right angles to the textblock to accommodate the cover board.

side sewing: A style of sewing leaves together in which holes are punched through the INNER MARGIN of each page and then all the leaves are sewn together with LINEN THREAD. Side-sewn books can be very strong, but the pages do not open easily or lie flat.

signature: A group of sheets folded in half, usually joined by sewing through the fold. Recently made books can be manufactured with signatures that are glued together.

spine: The back of the TEXTBLOCK where the SIGNATURES or leaves are sewn or glued together or the part of the book cover between the front and back cover. The spine can be flat or rounded.

spine lining: The cloth material that is glued onto the spine of a TEXTBLOCK to consolidate and support the sewn glued SIGNATURES.

square: The part of the BOOK CLOTH TURN-IN that shows around the perimeter of the PASTEDOWN part of the ENDPAPER.

stub: The remnant of a torn-out page still attached to the TEXTBLOCK or a very narrow strip of paper sewn into a book for the purpose of attaching another page to it or creating space for a thicker item.

super: An open-weave, starched cloth used to line the SPINE of the TEXTBLOCK to consolidate the SIGNATURES or leaves into a cohesive whole. The edges of the super usually extend past the HINGE area and are glued to the inside of the book covers, then covered with the PASTEDOWN part of the ENDPAPERS. Also called CRASH or MULL.

supported sewing: The process of sewing each SIGNATURE to TAPES or CORDS that support the entire TEXTBLOCK.

swell: The additional thickness in the SPINE of a TEXTBLOCK caused by the thickness of the sewing THREAD.

tacking iron: A small heated iron used with HEAT-SET TISSUE or to dry a moist repair.

tail: The bottom edge of the SPINE of a book or TEXTBLOCK, opposite the HEAD.

tapes: Strips of materials, often woven linen, to which the SIGNATURES of a book are sewn.

textblock: A gathering of SIGNATURES or individual leaves sewn or glued together.

thread: Thin string used to sew SIGNATURES or leaves together to form a TEXTBLOCK. Linen is the best thread to use in bookbinding.

tipping-in: The act of attaching a loose leaf into a TEXTBLOCK by gluing it in place. *See also* HINGING-IN.

trim: To cut a very thin amount of paper off the edge of a leaf or TEXTBLOCK.

turn-in: The excess BOOK CLOTH that is turned over and glued to the inside of the front and back COVER BOARD. The turn-in is covered by the PASTEDOWN part of the ENDPAPER.

uncoated paper: *See* PAPER.

unsupported sewing: The process of sewing each SIGNATURE to one another without TAPES or CORDS to support the TEXTBLOCK. *See also* SUPPORTED SEWING.

verso: The left-hand page of an open book.

weights: Any type of protective weight used to hold material in place as repairs dry.

wheat paste: Also called wheat starch. *See also* PASTE or ADHESIVE.

whipstitching: The process of sewing single sheets into groups or sections, the thickness of the sections depending on the thickness of the paper. The sections are then sewn onto TAPES or CORDS.

Index

Page numbers followed by the letter "f" indicate figures.